"Too often, churches abandon all aspects of tradition in favor of a stripped-down, watered-down worship experience that eventually leaves us let down and wishing for something . . . anything . . . that connects us to a story bigger than ourselves and our little slice of history. In *RetroChristianity*, Michael Svigel has argued well for redeeming and rediscovering a historical and substantive Christianity that can and will stand the test of time, while being nimble enough to incarnate Christ to the culture around us. This book is a well-researched and well written call to engage with historical Christianity both personally and corporately."

Philip Taylor, Executive Pastor, Mosaic Church, Orlando, Florida

"Many evangelicals are recovering their pre-Reformation roots in the early apostolic church and patristic studies. Michael Svigel has shown how pastors and churches can begin to implement this recovery and how to think about it. This is a wise and helpful book that will be exceptionally valuable to those who engage in this revitalization."

Thomas C. Oden, Professor Emeritus, Drew University; author,
Classic Christianity; general editor, Ancient Christian Commentary on Scripture

"Reading Michael Svigel's *RetroChristianity* is like a visit to your physician for an annual exam. It's uncomfortable. It's embarrassing. It's necessary. And, if you follow his instructions, it's healing. His diagnosis of contemporary evangelicalism is tough to swallow, but if we take the medicine prescribed by Dr. Svigel, evangelicalism can be revived."

D. Jeffrey Bingham, Department Chair and Professor of Theological Studies,
Dallas Theological Seminary

"When story is removed from history, it may be factual—but it's *really* boring. *Retro-Christianity* combines the history of evangelicalism with the pen of an engaging writer. The result is a much-needed and levelheaded analysis of the snags in the evangelical church as well as some practical solutions to get us back to our forgotten faith. If I want to read history with story in it—history that makes me laugh as well as think— I want to read Michael Svigel."

Wayne Stiles, author, *Waiting on God*

"Michael Svigel's *RetroChristianity* is hard to classify. It is at the same time a book on the doctrine of the church, a study in church history, and a contemporary analysis and critique of modern evangelicalism. Svigel begins by analyzing why so many evangelicals have wandered away from their nests, and ultimately challenges evangelicals to rethink how they understand the church and return to a more authentic expression of the faith—one that is rooted in the great doctrines and traditions of the church and yet continues to hold to the core tenets of evangelicalism. Svigel's book succeeds in this and will challenge your thinking! I am requiring it for my master's students studying ecclesiology, but the book would also be very helpful for pastors, church leaders, and educated laymen to help reformulate and recast their vision for the local church."

David C. Hard, Professor, Philadelphia Biblical University

"Rarely does one find a book so rich in content communicated so well. *RetroChristianity* is anything but retrenchment. Instead, Michael Svigel advances an agenda to move the church forward without losing the moorings of sound theology grounded in a history of biblical conviction. His words say it best: 'It's not rewinding to a more favorable era, but reclaiming the forgotten faith for the future.' This is a most worthy read!"

Mark L. Bailey, President, Dallas Theological Seminary

"We live in an age when looking like Buddy Holly, practicing the 'domestic arts,' and being a throwback artisan is *en vogue*. To be current in the present is to be conversant with the past. This trend has influenced evangelical churches in numerous ways. Michael Svigel's fun and rich book helps us rediscover our vibrant Christian heritage even as he steers us clear of many common evangelical pitfalls. Full of expertly explained church history, cultural connections, and more clever phrasing than there were hairs in Athanasius's beard, *RetroChristianity* is an excellent guide for those who justly wish to allow the story and theology of God's historic church to breathe fresh life into modern faith."

Owen Strachan, Assistant Professor of Christian Theology and Church History, Boyce College; coauthor, *Essential Edwards Collection*

"I absorb Michael Svigel's work only to slow down and ask brutal questions about the ministry to which I apply myself—whether or not we are the faithful expression of a rich ecclesial history, or just one more autonomous assembly aroused by size and success and hungrily searching for the comfortable pathway. His is an unsettling read, but timely and, frankly, necessary."

Matthew R. St. John, Teaching Pastor, Bethel Church, Fargo, North Dakota

"*RetroChristianity* is exactly what the evangelical church needs today. We often lament the issues of shallowness and novelty about the church, but rarely do we offer solid biblical answers beyond these complaints. This book makes the case that we need to get over our 'chronological snobbery' by rediscovering our roots. It is winsome and incredibly fun to read. Michael Svigel does not complain about evangelicalism as a teenagers complain about their parents after they have run away. He loves evangelicalism, is committed to it, and seeks to offer hope from within. I love this book."

C. Michael Patton, Founder, President, and fellow, The Credo House, Edmond, Oklahoma

Retro-
Christianity

Retro-Christianity*

Reclaiming the Forgotten Faith

MICHAEL J. SVIGEL

∷ CROSSWAY®

WHEATON, ILLINOIS

Cover design: Samm Hodges
Interior design and typesetting: Lakeside Design Plus
First printing 2012
Printed in the United States of America

Trade Paperback ISBN: 978-1-4335-2848-4
PDF ISBN: 978-1-4335-2849-1
Mobipocket ISBN: 978-1-4335-2850-7
ePub ISBN: 978-1-4335-2851-4

Library of Congress Cataloging-in-Publication Data

Svigel, Michael J., 1973–
    RetroChristianity : reclaiming the forgotten faith / Michael J. Svigel.
        p. cm.
    Includes bibliographical references and index.
    ISBN 978-1-4335-2848-4 (trade pbk.)—ISBN 978-1-4335-2849-1 (PDF)—ISBN 978-1-4335-2850-7 (mobipocket)—ISBN 978-1-4335-2851-4 (ePub) 1. Evangelicalism. 2. Choice of church.
    3. Evangelicalism—United States. 4. Reformation. 5. Reformed Church—Doctrines. I. Title. II. Title: Retro Christianity.

BR1641.A1S85 2012
277.3'083—dc23
                                 2011043828

Crossway is a publishing ministry of Good News Publishers.

If the Church Fathers or Reformers Showed Up at Your Church,
Would They Worship . . . *or Run?*

Contents

CHURCH HISTORY TIME LINE

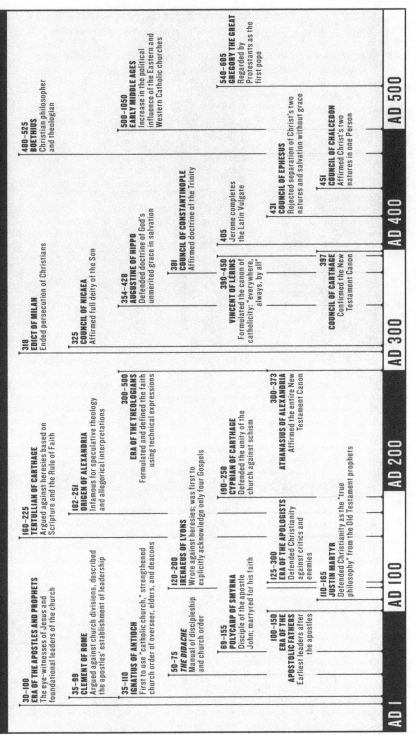

30–100
ERA OF THE APOSTLES AND PROPHETS
The eye-witnesses of Jesus and foundational leaders of the church

35–99
CLEMENT OF ROME
Argued against church divisions, described the apostles' establishment of leadership

35–110
IGNATIUS OF ANTIOCH
First to use "catholic church," strengthened church order of overseer, elders, and deacons

50–75
THE DIDACHE
Manual of discipleship and church order

69–155
POLYCARP OF SMYRNA
Disciple of the apostle John; martyred for his faith

100–150
ERA OF THE APOSTOLIC FATHERS
Earliest leaders after the apostles

110–165
JUSTIN MARTYR
Defended Christianity as the "true philosophy" from the Old Testament prophets

120–200
IRENAEUS OF LYONS
Wrote against heresies; was first to explicitly acknowledge only four Gospels

125–300
ERA OF THE APOLOGISTS
Defended Christianity against critics and enemies

160–225
TERTULLIAN OF CARTHAGE
Argued against heresies based on Scripture and the Rule of Faith

182–251
ORIGEN OF ALEXANDRIA
Infamous for speculative theology and allegorical interpretations

190–258
CYPRIAN OF CARTHAGE
Defended the unity of the church against schism

300–500
ERA OF THE THEOLOGIANS
Formulated and defined the faith using technical expressions

300–373
ATHANASIUS OF ALEXANDRIA
Affirmed the entire New Testament Canon

310
EDICT OF MILAN
Ended persecution of Christians

325
COUNCIL OF NICAEA
Affirmed full deity of the Son

354–428
AUGUSTINE OF HIPPO
Defended doctrine of God's unmerited grace in salvation

381
COUNCIL OF CONSTANTINOPLE
Affirmed doctrine of the Trinity

390–450
VINCENT OF LERINS
Formulated the canon of catholicity: "everywhere, always, by all"

397
COUNCIL OF CARTHAGE
Confirmed the New Testament Canon

405
Jerome completes the Latin Vulgate

431
COUNCIL OF EPHESUS
Rejected separation of Christ's two natures and salvation without grace

451
COUNCIL OF CHALCEDON
Affirmed Christ's two natures in one Person

480–525
BOETHIUS
Christian philosopher and theologian

500–1050
EARLY MIDDLE AGES
Increase in the political influence of the Eastern and Western Catholic churches

540–605
GREGORY THE GREAT
Regarded by Protestants as the first pope

| AD I | AD 100 | AD 200 | AD 300 | AD 400 | AD 500 |

CHURCH HISTORY TIME LINE (CONT.)

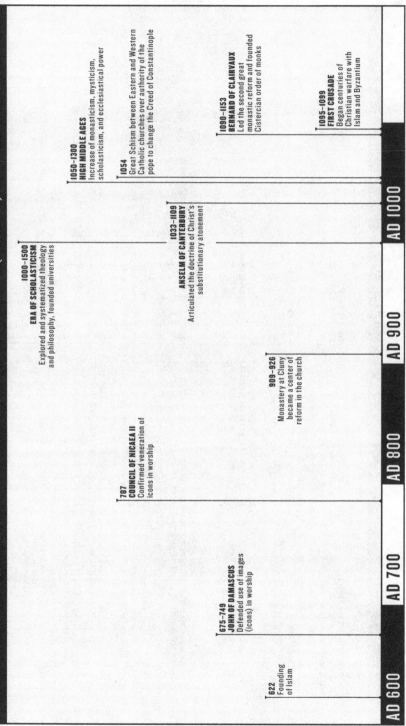

AD 600

622
Founding of Islam

675–749
JOHN OF DAMASCUS
Defended use of images (icons) in worship

AD 700

AD 800

787
COUNCIL OF NICAEA II
Confirmed veneration of icons in worship

909–926
Monastery at Cluny became a center of reform in the church

AD 900

ANSELM OF CANTERBURY
1033–1109
Articulated the doctrine of Christ's substitutionary atonement

1000–1500
ERA OF SCHOLASTICISM
Explored and systematized theology and philosophy, founded universities

AD 1000

1050–1300
HIGH MIDDLE AGES
Increase of monasticism, mysticism, scholasticism, and ecclesiastical power

1054
Great Schism between Eastern and Western Catholic churches over authority of the pope to change the Creed of Constantinople

1090–1153
BERNARD OF CLAIRVAUX
Led the second great monastic reform and founded Cistercian order of monks

1095–1099
FIRST CRUSADE
Began centuries of Christian warfare with Islam and Byzantium

CHURCH HISTORY TIME LINE (CONT.)

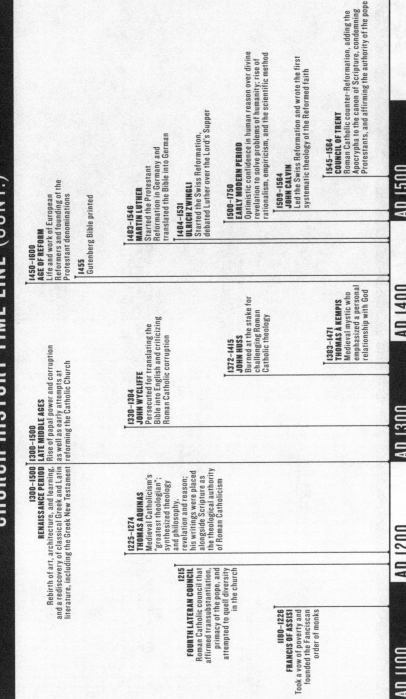

AD 1100

1180–1226
FRANCIS OF ASSISI
Took a vow of poverty and founded the Franciscan order of monks

1215
FOURTH LATERAN COUNCIL
Roman Catholic council that affirmed transubstantiation, primacy of the pope, and attempted to quell diversity in the church

AD 1200

1225–1274
THOMAS AQUINAS
Medieval Catholicism's "greatest theologian"; synthesized theology and philosophy, revelation and reason; his writings were placed alongside Scripture as the theological authority of Roman Catholicism

AD 1300

1300–1500
RENAISSANCE PERIOD
Rebirth of art, architecture, and learning, and a rediscovery of classical Greek and Latin literature, including the Greek New Testament

1300–1500
LATE MIDDLE AGES
Rise of papal power and corruption as well as early attempts at reforming the Catholic Church

1330–1384
JOHN WYCLIFFE
Persecuted for translating the Bible into English and criticizing Roman Catholic corruption

1372–1415
JOHN HUSS
Burned at the stake for challenging Roman Catholic theology

AD 1400

1383–1471
THOMAS À KEMPIS
Medieval mystic who emphasized a personal relationship with God

1450–1600
AGE OF REFORM
Life and work of European Reformers and founding of the Protestant denominations

1455
Gutenberg Bible printed

1483–1546
MARTIN LUTHER
Started the Protestant Reformation in Germany and translated the Bible into German

1484–1531
ULRICH ZWINGLI
Started the Swiss Reformation, debated Luther over the Lord's Supper

1500–1750
EARLY MODERN PERIOD
Optimistic confidence in human reason over divine revelation to solve problems of humanity; rise of rationalism, empiricism, and the scientific method

1509–1564
JOHN CALVIN
Led the Swiss Reformation and wrote the first systematic theology of the Reformed faith

1545–1564
COUNCIL OF TRENT
Roman Catholic counter-Reformation, adding the Apocrypha to the canon of Scripture, condemning Protestants, and affirming the authority of the pope

AD 1500

CHURCH HISTORY TIME LINE (CONT.)

AD 1600

1611
King James Bible translated

1614–1691
BROTHER LAWRENCE
Christian mystic who emphasized the constant presence of God through prayer

AD 1700

1703–1758
JONATHAN EDWARDS
American theologian who emphasized God's sovereignty and holiness

1703–1791
JOHN WESLEY
Anglican revivalist preacher, founder of Methodism

1750–1900
LATE MODERN PERIOD
The "Enlightenment," characterized by destructive criticism of Scripture and rise of liberal theologies that sought to redefine Christianity according to modern science and philosophy

AD 1800

1875–1925
The modernist-fundamentalist controversy, division of Protestant denominations into liberal and conservative churches

1851–1921
B. B. WARFIELD
Conservative Presbyterian theologian during early years of the fundamentalist movement

AD 1900

1886–1968
KARL BARTH
Reacted against liberal theology, but denied inerrancy of Scripture, ushering in neo-orthodox and neo-liberal theologians

1920–Present
POSTMODERN PERIOD
Reacted against optimism of modern period, including confidence in human reason and the attainment of certainty in truth

1925–1950
Rise of evangelicalism, emphasizing orthodox theology, personal conversion, and the inerrancy of Scripture

AD 2000

Acknowledgments

Though I am personally responsible for the content of *Retro-Christianity*, several men and women have contributed to the completion of this project either directly or indirectly. These deserve not only my mention, but also my thanks:

My interns for the years 2010–2012, Caleb Ernst, Kymberli Allen, Coleman Ford, and Nathan Peets, for both contributing to this project and keeping my other projects afloat in the process of writing *RetroChristianity*.

My colleagues and peers whose critiques of my thinking and writing helped shape the concepts of *RetroChristianity*, even when they disagreed with some of its details: Dr. Glenn Kreider, Dr. D. Jeffrey Bingham, Dr. Bryan Litfin, Dr. Paul Hartog, Dr. John Adair, Dr. Wayne Stiles, and Dr. Jeffery VanGoethem.

Pastors, students, and friends who read and critiqued various parts of *RetroChristianity* in various stages of its development, providing helpful feedback: Kimber Burgess, Gene Burrows, Fair Colvin, Kevin Dodge, Hans Googer, Will Groben, Mark Howell, and Dean Zimmerman.

My agent, Steve Laube, and all the folks at Crossway for their assistance in the publishing process.

And most of all my wife, Stephanie, and my kids, Sophie, Lucas, and Nathan, for putting up with me as I wrote two books simultaneously during the 2010–2011 academic year. I'll never do that again! I dedicate this work to you.

Introduction

 ack in the 1990s, when I was a student at a conservative evangelical Bible College, one of my fellow students shocked many
in the student body (and alarmed several professors) when he
announced that he was becoming Greek Orthodox.

This confused me.

Weren't Orthodox Christians just Greek-speaking Catholics without
a pope? Didn't they pray to saints and worship Mary? And their worship! Didn't they kiss icons, sniff incense, sprinkle holy water, and rattle
off irrelevant prayers and creeds that had nothing to do with either the
Bible or real life? Why in the world would anybody convert to *that*?

Then I heard about a free church evangelical who became Anglican—
still Protestant, of course, but it made me wonder what would motivate
a person to make such a drastic change in doctrine, church order, and
worship style. Then I heard about a Baptist who converted to Roman
Catholicism, leaving Protestantism completely behind. Surely this had
to be some kind of sign of the end times!

However, before too long I learned that many Low Church or
free church Protestants had left what they regarded as evangelical
"wilderness wanderings" to follow the "Roman Road,"[1] the "Way to
Constantinople,"[2] or (for those who desired to remain within the
Protestant tradition while restoring a liturgical worship) the "Canterbury
Trail."[3] Those who couldn't take such radical steps into a High Church
community sometimes ended up in more traditional conservative
Protestant denominations like the Presbyterians or Lutherans. Over
and over again I kept running into more examples like these: men and

women leaving the open fields of free roaming evangelicalism for the gated gardens of a clearly defined denomination.

Naturally, I was curious about why anybody would go from Southern Baptist to Eastern Orthodox, from Lutheran to Roman Catholicism, or from an Evangelical Free church to an Episcopal church.[4] As a young believer who was perfectly happy in my evangelical subculture, these radical departures seemed inexplicable.

Through the years, though, I discovered that these conversions were not isolated cases. Rather, they represented a widespread movement, especially among younger evangelicals, away from free church and Low Church communities toward more traditional High Church denominations. In order to better understand this trend, I began to discuss these conversions with the converts themselves and to read books and articles on the phenomenon. As I did, I discovered that these converts tended to fall into one of three categories:

1. Aversion-Driven Converts
2. Attraction-Driven Converts
3. Preference-Driven Converts

The Three Trails toward Traditionalism

Let me briefly explain each of these motivations and then explain how this book helps address their concerns.

Aversion-Driven Converts

The *aversion-driven converts* are those who simply have had enough of Low Church, free church, or no-church evangelicalism.[5] Frustrated with the "anything goes" instability of their evangelical megachurches or megachurch wannabes, some just can't stomach the ever-shifting sands upon which their churches seem to be built. Or they have endured just too many church coups, splits, or hostile takeovers to continue appreciating the "who's in charge here anyway?" debates within their independent congregations. Or they've "had it up to here" with the stifling legalism and heartless dogmatism of their fundamentalist upbringing. In other words, their motivation to convert to a stable, well-defined, traditional denomination has more to do with what they're running *from* than what they're running *to*.

The problem with this kind of conversion, however, is simply this: reaction against something—even if that something is bad—is no way to make a wise choice *for* something. It's no wonder that many of these aversion-driven converts become dissatisfied with their destination tradition and end up reacting even to that! Lesson learned: if you don't know what you're looking for, you'll never find it.

Attraction-Driven Converts

The *attraction-driven converts* are completely different. They don't start with any particularly serious problem with their current evangelical churches. Instead, their entrée into the traditional, historical denominations comes more gradually.[6] The attraction-driven converts claim to arrive at "the Historic Christian Faith," or to discover "the One True Church," or to happen upon "the Holy Tradition" either by accident or by careful investigation. As they explore these churches more deeply, they become disillusioned with their historically shallow evangelical background while coming to believe that the traditional denomination has a greater continuity with ancient and historical orthodoxy. They conclude, then, that their Protestant evangelical tradition is really a Johnny-come-lately at best or a devilish usurper at worst. These converts then claim that they were compelled to forsake their evangelical tradition because of their study of church history.

The problem with this approach, however, is that those who claim to have found the one true church through the study of the ancient church often have no idea *how* to study church history.[7] Rather than engaging in a so-called objective exploration of the facts of church history, they are often unwittingly fed a particular *version* of church history that just so happens to favor a particular tradition.

Preference-Driven Converts

Finally, the preference-driven converts are motivated not by the ills of evangelicalism or the merits of classic Christian denominations, but by personal preferences regarding worship. I've heard numerous friends, colleagues, and students tell me they switched to a High Church or non-Protestant tradition because they "like the liturgy." They love traditional forms of worship such as lighting candles, offering incense, reciting creeds, partaking of weekly Eucharist, observing the Christian calendar, or some other element of worship completely missing in or outright rejected by many evangelical churches. Thus, their decision to convert to a liturgical church was more about adopting a worship style that felt more authentic, appealed to their sense of mystery, engaged their senses, or made them feel connected to a broader and deeper historical faith than their narrow and shallow evangelical churches. In the final analysis, they have nothing against Baptists and Bible churches, but those less formal ways of worship just aren't for them.

The problem with the preference-driven converts is that they make their decisions in an extremely me-centered, consumerist fashion. They're less concerned about *content* and more concerned with *contentment*. They're less interested in *fact* and more interested in *feeling*. Though they opt out of the typical external forms of the evangelical subculture, they do so in a very typical evangelical way—through *individualistic personal preference*!

The Path of RetroChristianity

While I sympathize with many of the concerns shared by those who have chosen to travel the trails toward traditionalism, it seems that many have abandoned their evangelical heritage far too hastily and unwisely, driven by emotion, ignorance, or unquestioned assumptions about Scripture, history, and theology. On the other hand, we need to understand *why* many evangelicals are driven away from their evangelical heritage or attracted to other traditions. I believe the answer is simple. Despite its strengths, there are severe problems with contemporary evangelicalism that are reaching a point of crisis.

Why does evangelicalism appear to be spinning out of control, losing appeal to younger generations, dwindling in numbers, or selling out to pop culture to muster a crowd? Where is evangelicalism headed? What can we do about it? This book will introduce concerned evangelicals to the historical theological branches of the Christian faith that have grown through the Patristic, medieval, Reformation, and modern eras. *RetroChristianity* seeks to challenge us to begin thinking both critically and constructively about history and how it informs our current beliefs, values, and practices as evangelicals. However, unlike many attempts to change the present by looking to the past, this book also begins exploring practical ways for both individuals and churches to apply its principles today. Arguing that the way forward is to draw on the wisdom of the *whole* Christian past, *RetroChristianity* not only points out the trailhead of the biblical, historical, and theological path, but it supplies provisions for the journey without forsaking the healthy developments that have benefited Christianity along the way.

RetroChristianity doesn't naively defend evangelicalism as if everything were just fine. By the end of chapter 1, you'll see that things are in bad shape and are likely to get worse. However, I don't believe the retreat into traditionalism is the necessary or most beneficial response—though it is certainly the easiest.

RetroChristianity fully acknowledges the frustrating and upsetting elements of evangelicalism. However, we can't afford to simply whine about the flaws of the evangelical movement. We need to provide directions for addressing these problems, resting firmly on biblical, theological, and historical foundations. This will help us respond appropriately to extremes within evangelicalism and contribute to its improvement rather than its destruction.

RetroChristianity also acknowledges the egocentric nature of many evangelicals' approaches to church and spirituality. We need to counter the preference-driven mentality rampant among so many churches, replacing it with a more biblical, historical, and theological framework through which we can make informed decisions regarding doctrine, practice, and worship. This will help us wisely balance the vital elements of church, worship, ministry, and spirituality, avoiding excesses, extremes, distractions, and distortions.

In short, I believe that careful biblical, theological, and historical reflection should make us *better* evangelicals, not *former* evangelicals.

Overview

Having framed the canvas, let me now sketch the four parts of this book, each of which contains three chapters.

Part 1, "The Case for RetroChristianity," explores how evangelicalism found itself in its present midlife crisis and makes the case that a more intentional historical perspective holds the key to addressing some of its more severe problems. In part 2, "RetroOrthodoxy: Preserving the Faith for the Future," we discuss the concepts of doctrinal unity and continuity of orthodoxy, the reality of doctrinal diversity, and the hopes of doctrinal development. This framework will enable us to begin to explore more practical matters in the second half of the book.

Part 3, "RetroClesiology: Beyond the Preference-Driven Church," begins by dispelling four common myths and spelling out four classic marks of the historical body of Christ. On this foundation, we build a biblically, historically, and theologically informed doctrine of the church by constructing the essential marks and works of authentic and healthy local congregations. Then part four, "RetroSpirituality: Living the Forgotten Faith Today," explores the concept of individual and corporate spiritual growth, concluding with several suggestions for both churches and individuals to move forward in reclaiming the forgotten faith for the future.

During the journey through *RetroChristianity*, we will occasionally pause to consider practical ideas about how to implement some of its core concepts. A feature called "Going Retro" suggests ways for individuals to personally embrace the deep and rich legacy of the historical Christian faith within their evangelical churches. Another feature, "Retrofitting," addresses those in church leadership who may have opportunities to make wise, prayerful, and timely course corrections in their ministries in conformity with biblical, theological, and historical guidelines. These two practical features provide suggestions for both individuals and churches to adjust their attitudes and actions in order to renew personal and corporate identity and to lead evangelicals along a time-tested path toward the future.

Part 1

The Case for RetroChristianity

Do not move the ancient landmark
  that your fathers have set. —Proverbs 22:28

Thus says the LORD:
"Stand by the roads, and look,
  and ask for the ancient paths,
where the good way is; and walk in it,
  and find rest for your souls." —Jeremiah 6:16

As a whole—and in many of its parts—evangelicalism today has lost its way. Having moved the ancient landmarks that had long pointed out the safe path (Prov. 22:28), evangelicals have wandered into a deep forest of forgetfulness. Though they are citizens of the Kingdom of God and heirs of the ancient faith, evangelicals stand at a fork in the road. One path leads home through seeking the

23

ancient paths of the good way (Jer. 6:16); the other leads deeper into
the forest toward an uncertain future.

Though many evangelical leaders realize that we stand at an important crossroads in our history, this book is less about evangelicalism's
problems and more about what each of us can do about them. This
is why the first three chapters of this book present "The Case for
RetroChristianity." We will begin by exploring the state of contemporary evangelicalism. Where did evangelicalism come from? What is
it? How did we end up in the predicament we're in? This is our evangelical family history or life story; we need to know where we came
from in order to understand where we are and to decide where to go.

Then I make the case for a more conscious, deeper historical perspective as a key to remind evangelicalism of its forsaken roots and its
neglected legacy. Evangelicalism must draw on wisdom and insight from
the church's past—retrieving the momentous markers and retracing
the historical paths without forsaking the vitality of the more recent
developments in the evangelical tradition.

Then we will sketch the contours of the specific approach I call
RetroChristianity, explaining what it is and what it isn't. Though the
details of this approach will be filled in over the course of the book,
an initial introduction to some key concepts is necessary to frame the
argument.

Excursus: What Is Evangelicalism?

Because of the ambiguities surrounding the term, I probably ought to
step back and describe what I mean by "evangelicalism."[1] This isn't an
easy task.[2] A recent definition, intended to represent a broad constituency of evangelicalism, describes evangelicals as "*Christians who define
themselves, their faith, and their lives according to the Good News of Jesus
of Nazareth.*"[3] The same document identifies evangelicalism as one
of the "great traditions in the Christian Church," sharing the creedal
core of orthodoxy while emphasizing certain evangelical distinctions.
These distinctions include the person and work of Christ, salvation
by grace alone through faith alone, the regenerating work of the Holy
Spirit, the inspiration and authority of Scripture, the future return of
Christ, and an emphasis on evangelism, missions, and discipleship.[4]
By implication, if you adhere to these doctrinal distinctions, you're
an "evangelical."

A common misconception is that "evangelical" refers only to independent, nondenominational churches, such as free churches, or to loosely associated denominations like Baptists. However, a great majority of evangelicals align themselves with the moderate to conservative branches of classic Protestant denominations such as Lutheran, Presbyterian, Episcopalian, Methodist, and the like. In fact, individual Christians can regard themselves as evangelicals without attending a typical evangelical church or denomination. Even the most liberal denominations can have a significant evangelical membership.

A general description of "evangelicalism" might be something like this: *Evangelicalism is an interdenominational Protestant movement that (1) emphasizes a personal relationship with God through faith in the person and work of Jesus Christ, (2) insists on the paramount place of inspired Scripture as the final authority in matters of faith and practice, (3) adheres to fundamental Protestant doctrines relative to God, Christ, and salvation, and (4) seeks to engage the world through evangelism and missions.*[5]

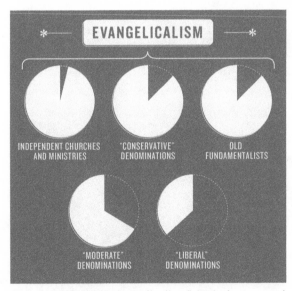

Broadly defined, "evangelicalism" includes several traditions to varying degrees: (1) Almost all independent churches and ministries; (2) The majority of "conservative" denominations; (3) Most old fundamentalists, though some think evangelicals are too "liberal"; (4) Many "moderate" denominations; and (5) Some members of "liberal" denominations.

How Did It Come to This?

*I*n order to find the way home, we must first admit we're lost. This first chapter describes in broad terms how I believe evangelicalism has lost its way. Before I tell this story, please know that I'm addressing evangelicalism as a loving brother who is confronting a misguided sibling. I write as an insider who fully embraces the strengths of evangelicalism and happily functions as one of its teachers. In fact, I believe that for much of its history and in most of its subgroups even today, the strengths of evangelicalism far outweigh its weaknesses. I also firmly believe the alternative nonevangelical Christian traditions were (and still are) less equipped to handle the coming challenges of our post-Christian world.

However, my desire is to see our evangelical tradition come to terms with its roots, retrieve its distinctly Christian identity, and then grow into the wise, mature adult I believe it can become. I'm keenly aware of some significant areas of immaturity evangelicalism must outgrow—and significant character flaws it must mend in order to emerge from the forest of forgetfulness. When it does, it can have a Christ-honoring global impact for generations to come. If it doesn't, ours may very well be the last generation of evangelicalism.[1]

So what's the problem with evangelicalism today? Where did evangelicalism come from? Where is it going? Let me answer these important questions with an analogy, a parable, and a metaphor. Though some of this background may be new to many readers, bear with me. An understanding of the crisis is necessary to appreciate the solution.

Peanut Butter Christianity: An Analogy

One day my wife sent me to the store to buy peanut butter—specifically, *natural* peanut butter. In other words, no fake stuff. This seemed simple enough . . . until I arrived in what looked like the peanut butter *department* of the grocery store. I suppose managing that aisle alone must be a full-time job. The options overwhelmed me—creamy, chunky, extra chunky, honey-flavored, jelly-filled, low fat, organic—and countless sizes, shapes, brands, and prices! My head spun.

There I stood, paralyzed with indecision, wanting nothing more than to snatch the cheapest jar of peanut butter and dash for the checkout. Instead, showing due diligence, I searched for "natural peanut butter" amidst the flashy brand names that virtually called out from the shelves like brochure pushers on the Vegas Strip: "Pick me! Pick me!" Don't you remember all those commercials you saw as a kid? All those smiling faces? Those cool special effects showing golden roasted peanuts magically spread into smooth, creamy peanut butter?

Lured by the flashy labels, my eyes landed on one popular brand paired with the keyword "Natural." How convenient!

I grabbed it from the shelf.

I felt rather victorious until I got home and took a closer look at the back label. I then discovered that "natural" peanut butter isn't necessarily a literal description. That particular brand of natural peanut butter *did* include roasted peanuts, of course. But it also contained sugar, palm oil, and salt. So that's what we mean by *natural*? Really? All those things naturally grow on a peanut plant? I guess from one perspective these ingredients are natural as opposed to, say, "supernatural." And at least I couldn't find any unpronounceable ingredients like monosodiumtriglyceraticidipropylol. And to be fair to that brand, if we were to compare its ingredients to that peanut butter–like substance found in the candy aisle of a grocery store, that jar of peanut butter looked like pure gold.

But is junk-food peanut butter really the standard? When I contrast that version of natural with a different, lesser-known brand's natural peanut butter, I'm a little less forgiving. The ingredients lists for several others simply say, "Peanuts." No salt, no oil, no emulsifier, no sweetener, no chemicals added to preserve freshness or enhance flavor. Just plain peanuts. Call me naïve, but to me, *that's* natural whether we like how it tastes or not. Shouldn't peanut butter made of just puréed peanuts serve as the standard for what constitutes natural peanut butter?

Over the next couple of weeks, as my mind periodically returned to the out-of-control peanut butter situation, something struck me. The failure of most peanut butters to actually live up to the natural standard reminds me of the out-of-control state of much of what is happening in contemporary evangelicalism. If I were to liken authentic, classic Christianity to the truly natural form of undiluted, unmixed, real peanut butter, then the multiple forms of evangelicalism that diverge more and more from this standard become, well, less and less authentic.

What I'm suggesting is this: over the last several decades, many of us evangelicals have become increasingly accustomed to a less "natural" form of Christianity. While still essentially Christian, many aspects of evangelicalism have become victims of "enrichment" by non-Christian ingredients that are meant to enhance the faith. This "enrichment" has been done to make the gospel more convenient, palatable, or marketable. Yet as these added ingredients take up more and more space, the essentials of the faith are necessarily displaced.

Take a stroll with me through the virtual aisles of our evangelical subculture—gift shops, radio stations, television programs, websites, even many of the new, trendy churches. We find ourselves surrounded by positive thinking, self-help, and behavior modification. We're lured in by self-esteem best sellers, do-it-yourself Christianity, and countless authors presenting the spiritual life as an ascending ladder: seven steps to this, three keys to that, the one prayer that will revolutionize your world, expand your influence, fulfill your desire for happiness. Let's just be honest. Much of the garbage stinking up the shelves of Christian bookstores is passed off as Christian Living, but it's mostly psychobabble or practical proverbs no better than what we find in the secular self-help or generic spirituality sections of our online booksellers.

Modern evangelical Christians who have become accustomed to this trendy, diluted form of Christianity have all but forgotten what the pure faith actually tastes like! In fact, many who are then exposed to a less adulterated faith—a form without all the unnecessary additives—find themselves actually disgusted by the original pure flavor of authentic Christianity, spitting it out and rejecting it as something foreign and inferior—or at least unpleasant to the palate.

The irony is that this purer form of Christianity is the authentic faith once for all delivered to the saints. The biblical gospel proclaimed, the sacraments rightly administered, discipline properly maintained, evangelism and discipleship emphasized, repentance and renewal preached—there is nothing really fancy about these things. In fact, they are so simple to identify and maintain that churches focusing on these fundamentals and freeing themselves from the frills appear to be washed-out has-beens or incompetent wannabes to most big-production glitz-and-glamour evangelicals.

Let's return to the peanut butter aisle once again. We have to admit that all those peanut butter products do contain peanuts, and so they can genuinely be called "peanut butter." Similarly, to varying degrees the marks of authentic Christianity are found in most of the products that fill the shelves of the evangelical church market. And to the degree that they retain those essential marks they are, in fact, Christian. Yet many forms of evangelical Christianity have been so colored with dyes, so mixed with artificial ingredients, or so drenched in candy coating that they are in danger of becoming cheap imitations that serve merely to distract from—not point to—the essential ingredients of the historical faith.[2]

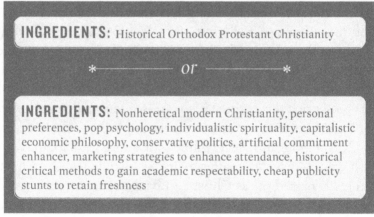

INGREDIENTS: Historical Orthodox Protestant Christianity

———— or ————

INGREDIENTS: Nonheretical modern Christianity, personal preferences, pop psychology, individualistic spirituality, capitalistic economic philosophy, conservative politics, artificial commitment enhancer, marketing strategies to enhance attendance, historical critical methods to gain academic respectability, cheap publicity stunts to retain freshness

"Christianity" Labels

Just like additive-rich peanut butters that appeal to flavor rather than to nutrition, far too many evangelicals shop for me-centered, feel-good church experiences rather than Christ-centered worship, discipleship, and authentic community. In fact, like sour-faced kids who reject all-natural peanut butter, many evangelicals turn their noses away from authentic expressions of church and spirituality. They would rather keep dabbling in the artificial than adjust their tastes to the real thing.

It seems we've reached a point in the evangelical church market where it's no longer enough to read just the front label. Now we have to focus on the fine print and see what place is given to the true marks of classic Christianity. The problem is, too few evangelicals are familiar enough with the original and enduring faith to sort the real from the fake.

So, how did it come to this?

The Current Evangelical Midlife Crisis: A Parable

Evangelicalism in the twenty-first century appears to be going through a midlife crisis. As we look back on its growth as a distinct Christian tradition, we can make several observations leading to this present crisis. I will employ a parable of evangelicalism's historical growth through five stages:

- infancy (1900–1915)
- toddler years (1915–1930)
- teenage phase (1930–1950)
- young adulthood (1950–1980)
- hasty marriage (1980–2000)
- midlife crisis (2000–present)[3]

Infancy (1900–1915). The baby version of what we know today as evangelicalism barely survived its infancy as a modern Christian movement. During that time, what had been a haphazard tangle of squabbling mainline denominations on one side and independent, nondenominational ministries and churches on the other side, forged an odd alliance against a common enemy—"theological liberalism." It's important to understand a little about twentieth-century liberalism to grasp the historical context in which evangelicalism was born and raised. Gary Dorrien writes, "The essential idea of liberal theology is that all claims to truth, in theology as in other disciplines, must be made on the basis of reason and experience, not by appeal to external authority."[4] Liberalism thus ousted such external authorities as tra-

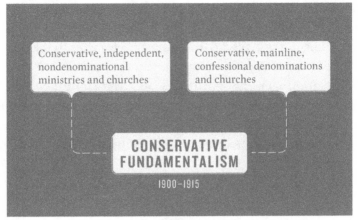

Conservative fundamentalism originated from both conservative mainline denominational leaders and conservative independent leaders.

dition, creeds, confessions, denominational structures, and inspired Scripture. Why would liberals do this?

Throughout the 1800s, liberalism had been attempting to update the classic Christian faith to fit the cultural and intellectual standards of the modern, scientific world. Eventually these revisions of Christianity resulted in a rejection of Christ's unique person and work and a denial of the Bible's authority. One theologian famously summarized nineteenth-century liberal theology this way: "A God without wrath brought men without sin into a kingdom without judgment through the ministrations of a Christ without a cross."[5] When liberalism sloughed off such doctrines, the authority structures that had long supported them also had to go. What replaced them? Human reason, emotion, and conscience became the chief guides in religion.

This is the theological neighborhood into which evangelicalism was born under its original name, "fundamentalism." As the old proverb goes, "Adversity makes strange bedfellows." The odd couple that gave birth to fundamentalism consisted of two types of conservative Christians: (1) those loyal to their denominational confessions, such as traditional Presbyterians with their Westminster Confession, and (2) nontraditional independent churches and ministries worried less about traditional confessional commitments and more about the authority of Scripture and the protection of evangelism and missions. That is, the mother and father of evangelicalism were those groups of

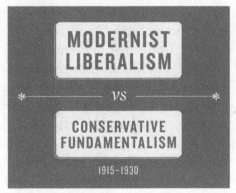

Conservative fundamentalism spent all of its political and social capital fighting a losing battle against modernist liberalism.

Christians who had the most to lose if liberals succeeded in destroying classic Protestant Christianity.

Thus, American fundamentalism was born.[6] As fundamentalists fled their increasingly liberal denominations, they either formed their own organizations or backed out of all denominations entirely.[7] As we shall see, if conservative denominationalism was the father and conservative independents the mother of fundamentalism, then mommy ended up playing a far greater influence on their petulant child than daddy, steering fundamentalism in a distinctively independent-minded direction.

Toddler Years (1915–1930). In its toddler years, fundamentalism experienced what can only be described as developmental problems. It constantly said inappropriate things, fussed over little things, and kept tripping over itself. As the fundamentalist movement grew, it was supposed to have either converted or driven off the children of its liberal neighbors. However, the younger liberals proved to be quite tenacious, heaping verbal and social abuse on the odd fundamentalist child. All the while the fundamentalist movement focused its youthful energies on fighting a losing battle against that same liberal establishment.[8] Fundamentalism's stand against liberalism, though, was a valiant effort . . . *the stuff of legend.* But in this "David and Goliath" story, David's sling proved ineffective.[9]

But in the midst of the conflict something truly tragic occurred—something ultimately more damaging than even the apparent victories of liberalism. Fundamentalism began to drift from the roots it had in the stable denominations. As long as fundamentalists listened to the fatherly guidance of their Protestant confessions, their identity would be formed by the historical Christian faith. Yet when the fundamentalists strayed from their denominational ties, they were left in the hands of their mother: the independent, noncreedal, non-denominational movement. This left fundamentalism with very few commitments to the classic Christian faith and the stable identity it provided.[10] Yes, mommy offered simple faith, heartfelt devotion, and a passion for souls, but in order for it to grow as a balanced Christian tradition, fundamentalism needed both depth and devotion, both history and heart. Unfortunately, fundamentalism would tend to take after its mother.

Awkward Adolescent to Troubled Teen (1930–1950). Though fundamentalism may have faded from the center of mainline church and mainstream political life, it took root in new places.[11] As fundamentalism began to make an awkward transition toward its more respectable form called "evangelicalism" between 1930 and 1950, it grew into its own identity with great pains.

In the 1930s and '40s, fundamentalism established radio ministries, mission organizations, breakaway denominations, Bible institutes, colleges, seminaries, and publishing companies.[12] Slowly these interwoven networks grew into regional, national, and ultimately international alliances. This new growth marked the transformation of fundamentalism into the more cultural-friendly "evangelicalism." This new made-over

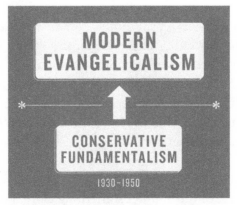

By the middle of the twentieth century, defeated fundamentalism made a comeback as modern evangelicalism, from which it was ready to grow in cultural, social, and political influence.

adolescent was now prepared to reengage science, academics, and culture with a renewed boldness.

But, not everything in these adolescent years was positive. The classic creeds and confessions of the faith had once connected the Protestant emphasis on scriptural authority to the ancient church's emphasis on Christ and orthodox theology. However, for the most part independent-minded evangelicalism exchanged the wisdom and learning of the ages for a naïve and historically inauthentic Bible-only Christianity that had little need for any other norm of doctrine than the so-called "plain reading of Scripture." In this entirely new approach to biblical theology, the individual student of Scripture—from the pulpit to the pew, from the lectern to the latrine—was now a self-ordained theologian. Not only did modern evangelicals hold to the sufficiency of Scripture, but they held more and more to the sufficiency of self—the competency of the individual Bible-reader to accurately handle Scripture without the input of anybody else.[13]

The result? In many sectors of the growing evangelical subculture, Christianity started all over with a blank slate, an open Bible, and a thousand personal opinions about what those black and red words *really* mean. By the 1950s, when evangelicalism entered its adolescent phase, its diverse proponents were like schoolyard boys fighting over a ball, each wanting to play their own game by their own rules. So, the Bible and its proper understanding were tossed to and fro in the fray with the faint hope that one day, through the proper application of modern rules of interpretation, the squabbling brats would finally find peace.

Young Adulthood (1950–1980). Nobody remains a teenager forever. In the sixties and seventies evangelicalism grew in leaps and bounds. As a direct heir of nineteenth-century revivalism of the tent and camp varieties, evangelicalism had always included elements of emotional conversions and moving evangelistic meetings. But by the 1950s, these evangelistic crusades grew to staggering proportions—filling stadiums instead of tents, and football fields instead of campgrounds. The crusade model of ministry quickly influenced typical evangelical Sunday morning worship, in which the service often climaxed with some kind of "altar call" or crisis decision for either conversion or recommitment. Large numbers of converts were added to the evangelical fold. As such, the pulpit, the sermon, and hence the preacher became the sole center

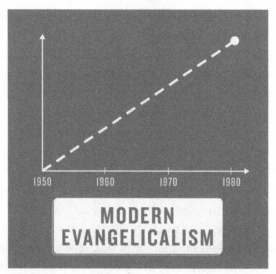

By the end of the twentieth century, evangelicalism had grown in size—but not necessarily in maturity.

of morning worship, around which everything else revolved and to which everything was directed.[14]

Soon even the mainline Protestant church (evangelicalism's long-forgotten father) found itself influenced by evangelicalism's successful methods and popular messages. Books, radio programs, schools, and churches popped up everywhere. Missionaries exported the sprouting evangelical faith worldwide. Liberals, who had already been severely censured by revolutions in European theology, now had to begin to take notice of the claims of these once-spurned upstarts. By the time evangelicalism neared the end of its young adult years in the 1970s, it had become a force to be reckoned with—socially, politically, and theologically.

Hasty Marriage to a Hapless Culture (1980–2000). Yet something happened between the 1980s and the turn of the century. Evangelicalism's physical growth far outpaced its theological maturity. It had the body of an adult, but the wisdom of a juvenile. Because it had neglected the historical and theological legacy that had given it life, as a movement evangelicalism had no clear sense of identity, no feeling of belonging to something bigger than itself, no concept of being an heir of an ancient treasure passed down for generations.

To assuage the feeling of identity drift, many evangelicals found themselves yoked in marriage to various aspects of a constantly

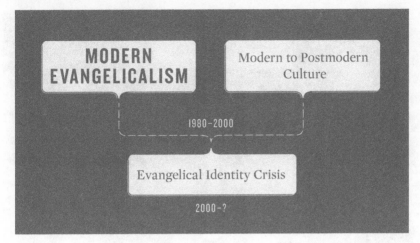

In the postmodern cultural shift, evangelicalism—born and raised in a modernist view of the world—experienced an identity crisis.

changing modern culture—media, entertainment, marketing, economics, politics, academia, and the like. As a result, evangelicals had numerical and social *breadth*, but they lacked historical and theological *depth*. What's worse, few evangelicals knew *why* they couldn't seem to get their act together. By the end of the century, the movement itself began to fragment into numerous "evangelicalisms."

The Current Midlife Crisis (2000–). This brings us to the modern day—the early decades of the twenty-first century. Today, evangelicalism as a loose association of very different movements is in the midst of a midlife crisis. It's like a forty-something husband and father who has spent the past twenty years hopping from job to job trying to find his "calling" . . . or running from wife to wife to find the perfect mate. More than ever before, evangelicalism is starving for an identity, a calling, a stabilizing force. And if it doesn't find one soon, I fear it will simply end its life in despair.

Some evangelicals are handling the current midlife crisis by actually (and mostly unknowingly) retracing the liberal steps of the nineteenth century that had originally given birth to the fundamentalist reaction. Many pastors, teachers, and young seminarians are exchanging biblical authority for what they regard as a more "intellectually honest" faith and "nuanced" view of the inspiration and inerrancy of Scripture. In the process, they downplay classic Christian doctrines that have managed to linger within the frail ethos of their fragmented evangelical

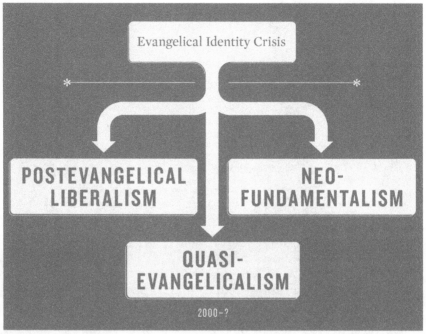

In the wake of the identity crisis, evangelicalism is fragmenting into a variety of movements.

communities. These "postevangelicals" have not only surrendered to the bullies they were groomed to withstand, but they are becoming the bullies themselves, increasingly adopting many of the presuppositions, methods, and conclusions of liberalism.

Other evangelicals handle the midlife crisis differently.[15] In an attempt to remain relevant in a rapidly changing culture, heirs of the evangelical movement are adopting a watered-down gospel, barely distinguishable from the feel-good messages of daytime talk shows. They think the fundamentals of the faith that once formed the DNA of evangelicalism are now failing to attract people in our postmodern, post-Christian culture. So, these quasi-evangelicals respond with an extreme makeover of evangelicalism itself. Christians are now called "Jesus followers." Conversion is "joining the journey." And evangelism is referred to as "cultural engagement."

Still others cope with the midlife crisis by desperately holding onto the past. A return to their roots means going back to the glory days of fundamentalism. These neofundamentalists clutch the beliefs and practices of their hundred-year-old movement with white knuckles. Though this group recognizes the dangers in the variety-show atmosphere of modern evangelicalism, their own solution is rather myopic. They don't often expend the effort to look past their own movement. If they did, they would realize that their own ways of doing things were once new and controversial.

Others are abandoning evangelicalism altogether, forsaking its strengths and heading back to pre-evangelical denominations, sometimes even pre-Protestant traditions. When they do this, though, they risk leaving behind an equally rich and lively legacy of personal faith, biblical fidelity, expository power, evangelistic zeal, and creative energy. I'm convinced that if the evangelical midlife crisis proves to be the end of evangelicalism as a Christian tradition, Christianity as a whole will lose something vital for its future.

Because the potential for disaster is so great, *intervention is needed.*

Relearning the Symphony: A Metaphor

The solution to the evangelical midlife crisis is to reclaim that aspect of its original identity it has lost, to reintroduce evangelicalism to the forgotten faith of its forsaken past. This brings me to a musical metaphor.

Almost twenty centuries ago the original disciples of Jesus received an inspired symphony from the Father, through the Son, and by the Holy Spirit. This was the faith once for all delivered to the saints. This original score, often called "the gospel," "the word," "the faith," "the way," or "the truth," spread rapidly throughout the Greek-speaking world. The harmonious parts of this symphony were written and preserved in apostolic and prophetic Scriptures, which were then bestowed upon the next generation of Christians—the disciples of the apostles. Along with this written score, however, the second Christian generation also had the apostolic melody still ringing in their ears. With the written documents, these early church fathers inherited from their teachers the heart and soul of the new song. In short, they not only knew how to read the music, but they also instinctively knew how it was meant to be played as they continued the work of performing the music for different cultures and languages.

During the medieval period, the skillful reading and artful performance of this original symphony declined. The tune was never completely lost, but in many places it had become so distorted through transposition, rearranging, reinterpretation, and variation that the original melody was in danger of slipping from memory. Even many of the records of the score's earliest performers had been forgotten.

However, during the Renaissance, scholars turned their attention back to the classics. After centuries of neglect, the original score was discovered as well as numerous early "recordings" that more closely approximated the apostles' own performance of the music. These came in the form of ancient manuscripts of Scripture, the writings of the early Fathers, and long-forgotten documents that restored a true picture of the original apostles and their teachings. This rediscovery ignited the Protestant Reformation. Passionate believers looked back in time to revitalize the Christian faith. To revive the faith, they argued, it must first be reclaimed. To reverse the church's decline, it had to return to its earliest sources.

Fast-forward five hundred years. Today the evangelical version of that same Protestant Reformation has lost its musical ear. Sadly, the beautiful symphony of classic Christianity has become increasingly difficult to discern in the carnival atmosphere of one-man-bands, competing orchestras, and amateur wannabes who all believe they can play God's original song better than both the Fathers and the Reformers. The problem? An increasing number of either arrogant or ignorant evangelical pastors and teachers have never learned how to read the original sheet music! The result? The new renditions of Christianity can be likened to amateur musicians performing Beethoven's Ninth Symphony on ukuleles . . . and missing half the notes!

The time has come for evangelicals to demand a more faithful performance of God's symphony. To do so we must return to the original score, to read it rightly, and to perform it in the way it was meant to be performed. The time has come for evangelicals to reclaim the forgotten faith. However, this means doing something many are reluctant to do. It means reflecting on the past to rethink the present and revitalize the future. It means, in short, to think not just biblically and theologically, *but also historically*.

Going Retro without Going Wrong

*Y*awn . . . history class . . . again . . .
Remember it? A stiff wooden chair, stale air, a ten-year-old-textbook that looks as if nobody ever read it. With the enthusiasm of a sloth, the football coach reads from a book about people, places, and events you care nothing about. If your classmates aren't doodling, they're drooling. The guy across the aisle stockpiles an arsenal of spitballs. The girl in front of you paints her fingernails. Somebody behind you is snoring. Even the teacher glances at the clock as he labors through the material like a prisoner chipping away at rocks in a quarry.

Finally the bell rings. Snatching your books, you leap from your seat and rush from the musty room into fresh air—the here and now of *real* life.

Though you can always find a few history buffs who love learning dates and details, most of us relate better to the more typical experience of the history class doldrums. Yes, rediscovering the forgotten past may be interesting to a precious few, but is it really *relevant* to our modern world? Okay, maybe American or European history has some important information to keep us from repeating the errors of our immediate past—but what about the *ancient* past?

After the last chapter you may agree that evangelicalism is in some kind of trouble. But what does church history have to do with the evangelical identity crisis? After all, some might ask, "Didn't Paul say,

'One thing I do: forgetting what lies behind and straining forward to what lies ahead' [Phil. 3:13]"? Why in the world would we return to what lies behind in order to find our way forward? Don't we have enough trouble making the Bible relevant to our postmodern world? Why complicate things with *history*?

These questions deserve answers.

Why Travel the Ancient Paths?

I've heard this question a lot over the years. In response, I've come up with a number of important reasons for looking into our rearview mirrors as we seek to drive forward into the future:

- It will *cure* our ignorance of the past.
- It will *curb* the arrogance of our present.
- It will *conserve* the faith for the future.
- It will *connect* us to a rich legacy.
- It will *counter* the claims of critics.
- It will *cultivate* Christian growth.
- It will *clarify* our interpretation of Scripture.

First, *looking back will cure our ignorance of the past.* Too many evangelicals are walking around in a constant state of what we might call *duja vé*. No, not *déja vu*—you know what that is: the odd feeling that this has happened before. *Duja vé*, on the other hand, is just the opposite: *it's that nagging feeling that none of this has ever happened before.* The truth is, throughout the church's history Christians have pretty much dealt with every kind of doctrinal and practical challenge you can imagine. Ecclesiastes 1:9–10 puts it this way: "What has been is what will be, and what has been done is what will be done, and there is nothing new under the sun. Is there a thing of which it is said, 'See, this is new'? It has been already in the ages before us."

Let me give an illustration. As a young believer, I was a member of a small community church in northern Minnesota. It was so small that the adult Sunday school class included everybody in the church except for the children and youth. As you might expect, in this mixed-generation class, the intergenerational conflict sometimes flared up. On one occasion the subject of church music came up, centered on the question of the use of various instruments like guitars and drums. In our church only the piano was used in Sunday morning worship.

One older man in the class spoke up in a deep, gruff voice, ranting against the use of anything but the piano in worship and complaining about "that satanic beat" of modern music using drums. In his mind, using instruments associated with contemporary secular music would be selling out to the culture. A little historical perspective would have helped here. Most people who resist musical and instrumental changes to the worship service fail to acknowledge that every style of music and musical instrument has, at some point, been adapted from the surrounding culture. In fact, when great hymn writers like Isaac Watts and Charles Wesley wrote their now classic hymns, the songs were rejected by many church leaders who believed Christians should sing only the inspired and inerrant Psalms. And instruments like the piano, the violin, and even the organ were all initially rejected for Christian worship because of their associations with secular music.

Though the ignorance of the past illustrated in this particular example did not drive our church into controversy and conflict, other cases of ignorance of the past could potentially lead to disaster. In order for Christians to make wise decisions, they must be able to draw from a depth of historical knowledge.

Second, *looking back will curb the arrogance of our present.* Some evangelicals could very well define "church history" as "the study of how everybody misinterpreted the Bible until *we* came along." In fact, on several occasions I've heard people actually say, "I don't care if I'm the first person in history to read the Bible this way. If that's what Scripture says, then I'm going to accept it." We should admire this confidence in Scripture. However, that statement places a lot of unquestioned confidence in one's own abilities to properly interpret the Bible. Don't get me wrong. I believe in the sufficiency of *Scripture*, but I don't believe in the sufficiency of *me.* The kind of arrogance that makes a person completely abandon the contributions from the past is what C. S. Lewis called "chronological snobbery."

He defined chronological snobbery as

the uncritical acceptance of the intellectual climate common to our own age and the assumption that whatever has gone out of date is on that account discredited. You must find why it went out of date. Was it ever refuted (and if so by whom, where, and how conclusively) or did it merely die away as fashions do? If the latter, this tells us nothing about its truth or falsehood.[1]

Grown men often look back over their lives and reflect on how far they've come and the progress they've made throughout. But poet Thomas S. Jones presents the opposite perspective: what if the younger version of me were to peer *forward* and see what kind of person I have become?

> Across the fields of yesterday
>   He sometimes comes to me,
> A little lad just back from play—
>   The lad I used to be.
>
> And yet he smiles so wistfully
>   Once he has crept within,
> I wonder he still hopes to see
>   The man I might have been.[2]

Those words haunt me. I often wonder what the bygone generations of Christianity might think if they could peer "across the fields of yesterday" and see what had become of the faith for which they lived and died. I constantly ask myself, "If the church fathers or Protestant Reformers were to show up at my church, would they worship . . . or run?" Sometimes I see such a pitch of "chronological snobbery" in our avant-garde churches that I wonder if we might intentionally drive them off, then brag about having done so!

Third, *looking back will conserve the faith for the future.* The Lord's brother, Jude, urged Christians "to contend for the faith that was once for all delivered to the saints" (Jude 1:3). The Greek verb translated "delivered" refers to a sacred trust or tradition. Paul described this tradition as he handed it down to the Corinthians: "Now I would remind you, brothers, of the gospel I preached to you, which you received, in which you stand. . . . For I delivered to you as of first importance what I also received" (1 Cor. 15:1, 3). Jude used the same language as Paul for receiving the tradition and sending it forward to the future. In this case the things "received" and "handed down" were the central truths of the Christian faith.

Paul also wrote letters to his younger disciple, Timothy, for the purpose of encouraging the next generation to faithfully convey the core Christian tradition into the future. Paul wrote, "Continue in what you have learned and have firmly believed, knowing from whom you learned it" (2 Tim. 3:14). He also said, "What you have heard from me in the presence of many witnesses entrust to faithful men who will be able to teach others also" (2 Tim. 2:2). By observing what our spiritual forefathers fought to preserve and pass on, we come to understand and appreciate the need to continue the pattern established by 2 Timothy 2:2. By looking back, evangelicals today can learn how to conserve and convey the timeless message through time-tested methods.

Fourth, *looking back will connect us to a rich legacy.* Picture Christianity throughout history as a giant tree that has continually grown for generations. Some of its branches have gone one way, some another. Some are more in line with their roots in the apostolic church and the straight trunk of the first few centuries. We might call this trunk the "ancient catholic church" as opposed to later developments in the Western (Roman) Catholic and Eastern Orthodox traditions.[3] Other branches, unworthy of the tree, have withered and fallen off.

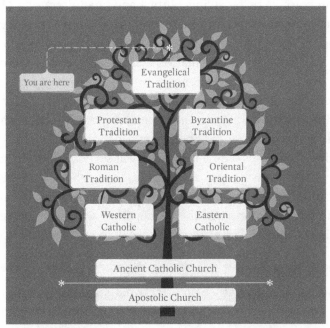

The history of Christianity can be illustrated by branches of a giant tree.

Now picture your place on this massive tree. Your own church is but a tiny leaf, hanging from a small twig, shooting from a thin branch, attached to a large limb, connected to a thick bough, growing from a massive trunk. The diverse Christian churches today (the various branches of the tree) are not necessarily united to each other through visible, institutional unity. However, every generation has been connected to the apostolic and ancient church by legitimately receiving its core beliefs and practices.

For example, every believer who has been baptized in the name of the Father, Son, and Holy Spirit was baptized by somebody who had also been baptized by a predecessor. This line of baptism, though it may have taken various forms throughout history, connects present-day believers to the church of the first century.[4]

The same may be said of ministry ordination. Those ministers today who have been tried, tested, and approved by other ordained ministers stand in a long and ancient line of those who themselves had been ordained by the "laying on of hands," a practice that reaches back to the apostles themselves.[5]

Finally, evangelicals are also connected to the rich legacy of their Christian heritage by receiving—intact and unadulterated—the apostolic and prophetic Scriptures as well as the core message of the Christian faith. Many participate further through orders of worship, hymns, liturgies, and denominational structures, which were passed down from previous generations.

In each case, evangelical Christians already participate in this historical tradition *passively, unconsciously,* and *uncritically.* That is, they have passively received these core beliefs and practices by virtue of being evangelical Christians. These things were absorbed, as it were, without much conscious awareness. As a result, evangelicals received them uncritically. This means that any distortions, additions, or omissions that may have accompanied their reception were also received without their knowledge. For example, those who received the Scriptures did so in a certain translation or accompanied by a particular pattern of interpretation. They learned the gospel message in a specific form or as part of a larger catechism, doctrinal statement, confession, or creed. Their approach to baptism took a certain form with regard to its candidates, timing, and mode. Their practice of ordination was either more or less formal, depending on their tradition. And their worship happened to reflect a certain style—liturgical or extemporaneous, traditional or contemporary. Many evangelicals have received these "traditions" without reflecting on how these things have connected them to people of the past about whom they know so little.

By looking back, evangelicals can connect to their own tradition *actively, consciously*, and *critically*. They can seek out their spiritual ancestors, experiencing familiarity and a feeling of kinship with the people of faith who preserved Scripture, took a stand for the gospel, reformed church practice, and glorified God with their words and works. They can see their own particular traditions in light of a broader spectrum of emphases and practices, understanding their own church's attitudes and actions in light of its history. By re-establishing an active and conscious connection to their rich legacy, they will also be equipped to sort through the positive, negative, and neutral aspects of their beliefs and practices, led by more than personal preference or thoughtless traditionalism.

Connecting to a rich legacy of the faith will therefore add a previously unknown depth to personal faith and corporate worship. It has the power to shape the identity of both individual believers and local churches. This identity will help us to transcend our own lonely and seemingly insignificant place on the greater tree, making us aware that we are all part of something far bigger than ourselves.

Fifth, *looking back will counter the claims of critics*. Prior to the eruption of World War II, between 1925 and 1935 a frantic France fortified the long border it shared with Germany. The "Maginot Line"—named after the man who conceived the idea—included a network of bunkers, forts, tunnels, and fortifications for thousands of soldiers. For all practical purposes, the Maginot Line was impenetrable. The French army had prepared to fend off a frontal assault by the Germans —and history proved that the defenses were successful.

But the Germans didn't bother to penetrate the Maginot Line. They went around it!

Because of a treaty with Belgium (which stood between France and Germany), the French had not anticipated that the Nazis would simply roll through Belgium to circumvent the Maginot Line. But they did. The Germans found the weakest point in France's defense and exploited it. They found, as it were, an unguarded back door.[6]

Maginot Line

As we saw in chapter 1, evangelicalism spent over a century building up its fortifications, first against the destructive skepticism of modernist liberalism and more recently against postmodern cynicism. To hold the line, they set guards on the borders of biblical inerrancy and secured the doctrines that directly related to the gospel message of salvation by grace through faith. At the same time they sent forth an army of evangelists, missionaries, apologists, and teachers to take new ground. But in the process of fortifying the obvious points of direct attacks, they neglected their heritage in the ancient and Reformation eras.

The result? In the last few decades clever critics and sneaky scholars have switched their assaults from attacks on the Bible, theology, and personal faith to an all-out assault on the Achilles' heel of evangelicalism: the history of Christianity. Their attacks have left Christians scrambling to defend a history they have forgotten and saints they have forsaken. Remember the panic over the silly and inaccurate historical claims in *The Da Vinci Code?* That is a minor blip on the radar of the advancing army of much more persuasive critics who are writing books, appearing on television programs, and teaching our college kids.

In the first thirty seconds of the movie *Braveheart*, we hear a line that summarizes the critics' view of church history: "History is written by those who have hanged heroes."[7] These scholars say the early church fathers changed the real human Jesus from a controversial rabbi and idealistic martyr into a risen Savior and God who bears no resemblance to the historical Jesus. They claim the early catholic Christians browbeat those who opposed them, selected Christian writings that agreed with their positions, and then rewrote history to make it look like theirs had been the original view of Jesus and the apostles. All other views were then unfairly declared to be "heretical."[8]

It all boils down to this: Did the early church fathers after the apostles *preserve and defend* the faith or did they *pervert and destroy* it? Did the Protestant Reformers restore Christianity to a condition similar to the early church, or did they create a new religion from scratch? Are the early fathers and later Reformers "heroes" or "villains"? Who are those people that we implicitly trust to have accepted the right Scriptures and rejected the wrong ones? How do we know they could discern the difference between *correct* teachings about Jesus and *false* doctrines? Most evangelicals have no idea how to respond to these questions in order to deflect the attacks and contend for the faith.

The time has come for evangelicals to refortify this vulnerable target, so when critics launch their inevitable attacks, we won't lose the battle on our own soil. We need to strengthen our levee, so when the storms of controversy rise, we won't be flooded with needless doubts. And we need to inspect our historical foundations, so we can adorn this two-thousand-year-old temple of the church with gold, silver, and precious stones instead of wood, hay, and straw (1 Cor. 3:12–13).

Sixth, *looking back will cultivate Christian growth*. Cicero wisely said, "To remain ignorant of what has happened before you were born is to remain always a child."[9] Christian growth requires knowledge not only of the changeless truths of Scripture, but also of how these truths were understood, applied, attacked, defended, and explained throughout history. This applies to the individual believer as well as to the whole body of Christ worldwide.

Imagine if every year over summer break a student forgets everything she has learned during the previous year of school. After kindergarten, her mind is wiped clean. Then, after struggling through first grade and barely keeping up, the next summer vacation clears her mind once more, and she starts over again for second grade. What would be the result? Although she might grow physically and keep advancing in grade levels, she would never have the necessary knowledge upon which to build in the higher grades. She would remain forever a child, needing somebody to instruct her over and over again about basic, foundational principles.

Similarly, the whole church must continue to pass along what she has learned throughout the past two thousand years of her growth and development. It only takes one negligent generation to forget the accumulated knowledge and wisdom of the entire history of the church. This corporate forgetfulness will result in a generation of Christians susceptible to the same kinds of struggles, errors, and deceptions successfully dealt with in the church's past. To prevent this kind of amnesia, the church must continually look back at its history in order to apply its amassed knowledge to present circumstances and to pass it on to the next generation.

Besides the benefit of corporate maturity, individuals can grow in both knowledge and wisdom by reflecting on the past. That is, history provides us with bad examples to avoid as well as good models to follow. We can rediscover errors to avoid, better ways to defend Christian truth, questionable interpretations or applications of Scripture, and time-tested approaches to the spiritual life. The more lessons we learn from the victories and defeats of those who have gone before us, the better off we'll be. This concept of looking back to the saints of old for inspiration goes all the way back to the first century.

After Hebrews 11 reviewed the lives of the Old Testament men and women of faith, the author concluded, "Therefore, since we are surrounded by so great a cloud of witnesses, let us also lay aside every weight, and sin which clings so closely, and let us run with endurance the race that is set before us" (12:1). The words and works of those saints who have gone before us still surround us like a cloud, inspiring us to follow their examples and avoid their mistakes. The apostle Paul also pointed out this truth:

> For I do not want you to be unaware, brothers, that our fathers were all under the cloud, and all passed through the sea. . . . Nevertheless, with most of them God was not pleased, for they were overthrown in the wilderness. Now these things took place as examples for us, that we might not desire evil as they did. . . . Now these things happened to

them as an example, but they were written down for our instruction.
(1 Cor. 10:1, 5–6, 11)

It should not surprise us that immediately after the age of the apostles, their disciples began to look to the apostles' lives as examples as well. We see this already by AD 95 in a letter from Clement of Rome, who could have been the same "Clement" Paul mentioned in Philippians 4:3. Clement wrote:

> But to pass from the examples of ancient times [the Old Testament], let us come to those champions who lived nearest to our time. Let us consider the noble examples that belong to our own generation. Because of jealousy and envy the greatest and most righteous pillars were persecuted and fought to the death. Let us set before our eyes the good apostles. There was Peter, who because of unrighteous jealousy endured not one or two but many trials, and thus having given his testimony went to his appointed place of glory. Because of jealousy and strife Paul showed the way to the prize for patient endurance. After he had been seven times in chains, had been driven into exile, had been stoned, and had preached in the east and in the west, he won the genuine glory for his faith, having taught righteousness to the whole world and having reached the farthest limits of the west. Finally, when he had given his testimony before the rulers, he thus departed from the world and went to the holy place, having become an outstanding example of patient endurance.[10]

Throughout church history, Christians continued to remember the examples and teachings of earlier believers who had followed Christ in both life and death. At first glance these believers may seem remote, distant, and completely irrelevant in our modern Christian context. However, a closer examination will reveal that these men and women struggled with faith, hope, endurance, suffering, persecution, patience, and other matters of spiritual growth common to every generation. Like objects in a rearview mirror, the Christians of the past are spiritually "closer" than they appear. Today we can also gain wisdom and inspiration from the lives of those saints who have gone before us: church fathers, theologians, Reformers, preachers, missionaries, and martyrs.

Seventh, *looking back will clarify our interpretation of Scripture.* Just get two or three believers together for a Bible study and you soon realize that not everybody interprets the Bible exactly the same way. Sometimes they come to completely opposite conclusions. Other times they emphasize certain passages or doctrines more than others. We evangelicals have no pope or infallible guide to govern how we read the Bible. Even when we follow the rules of methodical Bible study or the principles of exegesis, we sometimes come up with different interpretations.[11]

By looking back over church history, we can see the whole history of the Bible's interpretation and application.[12] Tradition and history can never replace Scripture as the final authority for faith and practice. However, gaining a historical perspective can aid our reading of Scripture in two ways that will help rule out dangerous interpretations while providing clear boundaries within which a variety of different interpretations can coexist.

First, *early testimony* can provide added insight into the historical and theological context within which the New Testament itself was written and read. By "early" I mean the writings of the period overlapping with and immediately following the New Testament apostles and prophets themselves, between about AD 50 and 150.

We have numerous writings from this period, many of which were written by students of the original writers of Scripture. Though these accounts aren't infallible and they are not Scripture, these early authors' interpretations, doctrines, and practices open a window into the teachings of the apostles themselves. The African church father, Tertullian, writing around AD 200, put it this way: "On the whole, then, if that is evidently more true which is earlier, if that is earlier which is from the very beginning, if that is from the beginning which has the apostles for its authors, then it will certainly be quite as evident, that that comes down from the apostles, which has been kept as a sacred deposit in the churches of the apostles."[13]

The figure on the next page shows that we have an unbroken testimony from the early churches established by the apostles. It's reasonable to conclude, for example, that Polycarp, a disciple of the apostle John, reflects much of John's theology and practice in his own letter to the church in Philippi, which he wrote around AD 110, a couple of decades or so after John wrote his Gospel, epistles, and Revelation. In fact, Irenaeus of Lyons, a disciple of Polycarp, wrote around AD 180: "For how should it be if the apostles themselves had not left us writings? Would it not be necessary . . . to follow the course of the tradition which they handed down to those whom they did commit the Churches?"[14] That is, many people were still alive throughout the second century who had the authentic words and theology of the original apostles and prophets still ringing in their ears.

The farther one progresses away from the first generation of apostles, however, the less reliable the church leaders become for preserving the general tenor of the apostles' teaching. So, although these earliest testimonies cannot be adopted *uncritically*, a reading of the New Testament in its historical context cannot afford to completely ignore these writings as tools to help us properly interpret the apostles' writings in their actual historical theological contexts.

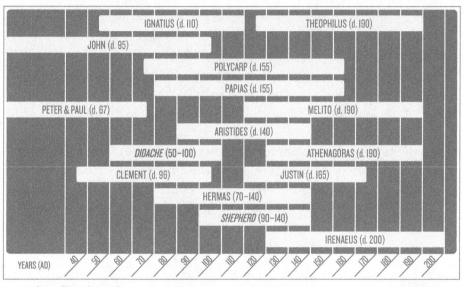

Earliest Church Leaders

Second, *enduring tradition* refers to those things that continue to be retained, reaffirmed, or restored in every generation of Christian history. Christ promised that he would never leave us, even to the end of the age (Matt. 28:20). He also promised that the gates of hell would not prevail against the church (Matt. 16:18).[15] We know that he is ever-present with the church by means of the person of the Holy Spirit (John 14:16–18). Also, through the Holy Spirit the ascended Christ has gifted the church with not only first-generation apostles and prophets, but also enduring leaders called evangelists, pastors, and teachers (Eph. 4:11). The implication is that the truth-telling and life-giving ministry of the Holy Spirit will prevail in the church against the hellish attacks of Satan.[16] So, if individual leaders, whole churches, or even most of the universal Christian church were to stray from the fundamental saving doctrines of the faith, the Holy Spirit would eventually shepherd the church back to a proclamation of the gospel in its purity.

What does this mean for our reading of Scripture as it relates to church history? Simply this: that we can discern certain core doctrines that have stood unchanged throughout the history of the church.[17] The degree of continuity in these matters is remarkable, as they include every generation, span every continent, and transcend all denominational lines. When we become aware of these central, unifying core truths of the faith that have endured throughout history, we can be constantly reminded of the boundaries of orthodoxy—the rules within which believers have freedom to responsibly interpret Scripture, but outside of which believers must never stray. As Vincent of Lérins wrote in AD 434, "All possible care must be taken, that we hold that faith which has been believed everywhere, always, by all."[18]

This rule of "orthodoxy" will be explored more completely in part 2. For the time being, it's important to note that looking back will help safeguard evangelical interpreters of the Bible from either denying central dogmas of the Christian faith (contracting the core), or from centralizing opinions about what the Bible says (expanding the core).

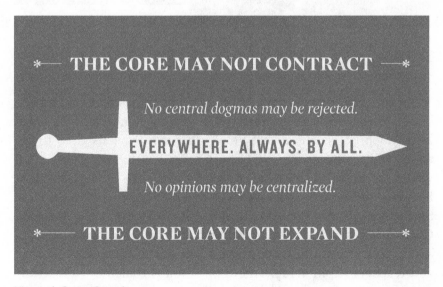

— THE CORE MAY NOT CONTRACT —

No central dogmas may be rejected.

EVERYWHERE. ALWAYS. BY ALL.

No opinions may be centralized.

— THE CORE MAY NOT EXPAND —

Vincent's Canon Sword

In other words, *the core teachings of the Christian faith must never change.* The faith has been once for all delivered to the saints (Jude 3). But in order for evangelicals to know the boundaries of their biblical interpretations, they must know which biblical doctrines are core. Looking back at the history of how the Spirit corrected, disciplined, pruned, and grew the church in its doctrinal understanding will help believers clarify their interpretation of Scripture.

Going Retro

Is It Biblical?

One great thing about us evangelicals is our insistence that everything we say and do, believe and teach, be *biblical.* The last thing we want to do is transgress what's clearly inscribed. One of our favorite verses is, "Do not go beyond what is written" (1 Cor. 4:6 NIV). Jesus himself complained that the Pharisees transgressed the command of God contained in Scripture for the sake of their man-made traditions (Matt. 15:3). The rule of Scripture plays a strong role in the history of the church as well. Saint Augustine (AD 354–428) said that the canonical Scripture "has paramount authority . . . to which we yield assent in all matters of which we ought not to be ignorant, and yet cannot know of ourselves."[19] Anselm of Canterbury (AD 1033–1109) once wrote, "For I am sure that, if I say anything which plainly opposes the Holy Scriptures, it is false; and if I am aware of it, I will no longer hold it."[20] I've heard this same kind of statement from many evangelicals: "Show me in the Bible that I'm wrong, and I'll stop believing it." The great Reformer, Martin Luther, himself stood his ground on the authority of God's Word when he famously responded to the Catholic Church's accusations of heresy, "Unless I am persuaded by Scripture and clear reason . . . I will not recant. My conscience is captive to the Word of God."

So, our evangelical insistence on Scripture as the final authority in all matters of faith and practice has strong historical roots. Understandably, then, when somebody suggests that we need to look back to the early church, or revive the Reformation, or retrieve the tradition, some evangelicals understandably get a little nervous. If history has taught us anything, it's that people can easily forsake the authority of God's Word for human opinion or man-made traditions.

However, this high view of Scripture as inerrant and authoritative doesn't settle the issue of proper and improper interpretations. If somebody argues that the Bible teaches this or that, he may believe and claim that it's biblical, but he might be reading the Bible wrongly. All sorts of things can lead to *seemingly* biblical but *untrue* teachings. We may fail to read the text carefully. Or we might assume something based on our translation that may not be true in the original Greek, Hebrew, or Aramaic text. Or we may read a verse out of its immediate literary context, its context in light of the whole Bible, or its historical context.

Evangelicals must never surrender their high view of Scripture. In fact, history demonstrates that the absolute authority of Scripture is, in fact, a fundamental view of the church that has been believed everywhere, always, and by all. Yet evangelicals should not be afraid of learning how to better interpret and apply those authoritative Scriptures by learning both good and bad interpretations from the past. By valuing the history of the Bible's interpretation, we actually value Scripture more.

Potential Hazards along the Way

Though I discussed seven reasons for looking back at the rich history of Christianity, the journey into the past is not without its hazards. In my experience, evangelicals who have never studied their Christian past generally fall into one of four categories: the jungle, the desert, the ruins, or the blastoff. Each has its own potential dangers we must seek to avoid.

The Jungle. When it comes to exploring the church's forgotten past, many evangelicals have the sense of setting out on a dangerous adventure through a dark jungle of tangled historical vines, slavering opponents, and doctrinal dangers. Bizarre people and places, wild ideas, and the bulky biases that students carry with them can make the study of church history seem just too treacherous. Ancient Christians used words like "catholic," "bishop," and "Eucharist" quite differently than we do today. And names like Ignatius, Augustine, and Aquinas frighten some people simply because they sound too, well, *Latin.*

This view of church history as a jungle can lead to anxiety. To some degree, though, a certain measure of anxiety is proper. It will lead to necessary caution. I have too often witnessed evangelicals carelessly reading church history and either rejecting it as useless rubbish or jumping headfirst into Roman Catholicism or Eastern Orthodoxy, wrongly assuming that those traditions better reflect the ancient faith. Both approaches are misguided. However, hacking through the some-times confusing vines is a necessary first step in exploring the richness of our Christian past.

The Desert. Many liken the study of church history to a vast desert of pointless speculations or doctrinal deviations in which only the discerning can discover the occasional oasis of insight. To be sure, as the church matured, philosophical discussions became more com-mon. These can often confuse or even alienate modern evangelicals who value a simple, biblical faith. Many approach such discussions with skepticism, unconvinced that they provide anything relevant or interesting for today's church.

I must admit, even as an interested scholar of church history, I've dozed off while reading Clement of Alexandria, skimmed over com-mentaries of Origen, and actually pushed aside some sermons of Luther, Calvin, or Spurgeon (which often can be inspiring). Not everything is exciting, and even the most interesting, illuminating, or practical writ-ings from church history have some unfortunate and even irrelevant digressions that modern editors would have cut. However, even the most arid treatises contain oases of truth to aid us in our journey. Don't give up, even when the landscape looks like a wasteland.

The Ruins. Others consider church history to be just overgrown ruins. Most people can appreciate the idea of well-preserved ruins of once thriving cities or castles. They're great places to tour by day, but we leave the digging to the experts and get back to civilization before sundown. True, the serious study of church history does require a lot of digging. It's often painstaking, dirty, and downright tiring work. Yet the world one discovers, the gems unearthed, the exciting stories that surface—these things make the work well worth the effort.

Let me encourage you, though, to go beyond mere idle curiosity. The goal of historical reflection is not to have a few trinkets to place on our shelves or shove into some musty corner of a museum. Our goal is to rediscover things about our Christian faith that can change our lives and our churches. Not only should we seek to correct earlier errors with our modern understanding, but we must allow the wisdom of the past to correct our contemporary mistakes as well.

The Blastoff. When I teach church history, I always have a few enthusiastic students who feel like they're blasting off on an exciting quest into another universe filled with fascinating and refreshing ideas, where few modern believers have gone before. They encounter intriguing new people and places, forgotten ideas that have been dormant for centuries, and a greater appreciation for the untiring witness of the earliest saints and martyrs. They land on a new understanding of how we got our Bible, why we interpret it the way we do, where the Christian church went wrong, and how they got things right.

However, sometimes these enthusiastic students can go overboard. Although this book is advocating an engagement with the past, its purpose is ultimately forward-looking. We must avoid the desire to travel back in time, to restore the church to some kind of primitive state. The goal is to *reclaim* the forgotten faith, not to neglect the present.

Anxiety . . . skepticism . . . curiosity . . . excitement—these are normal feelings as you take your first steps toward exploring the faith of people like the church fathers, theologians, Reformers, and great missionaries of the past. Yet, as you hack through the jungle, wander the desert, excavate the ruins, or visit strange worlds, anxiety should turn to *encouragement*, skepticism to *confidence*, curiosity to *satisfaction*, and excitement to *discernment*.

Retrofitting

Digging [Up] the Past?

It seems that church history is more popular than ever. I've noticed this both at the nondenominational seminary where I teach as well as at the independent Bible church where I worship. Evangelicals—especially of the "independent" variety—are yearning to uncover their historical roots. However, they're sometimes getting their information from less than reliable sources. The study of Christian history is a vast and varied field, and the quality of some materials available for lay readers ranges from tedious to tragic. Unbelieving scholars turn the historical narrative in one direction, denominational loyalists in another. There is no "neutral" history. Even hard facts can be the victims of prejudice.

This is a time when local churches—*especially evangelical churches*—must take the lead in providing their members resources for a balanced Christian perspective on history. Let me put it bluntly: if you don't take the initiative to quench this thirst in your local church, they'll get their fix somewhere else—and could end up swallowing poison! Here are a few suggestions of what you can do to harness the positive interest in church history in your own church.

1. Include courses on church history as part of your adult or small-group educational plan. I would advise against having a layperson untrained in church history lead such a class without proper preparation, as the landmines in Christian historical studies nowadays can be insidious. However, several curricula, video series, discussion guides, and other resources are available to help facilitate such groups. See "Suggested Resources" beginning on page 281 for suggestions.

2. Consider hosting special seminars on church history led by evangelical church historians. Many church history teachers are available to present on a variety of topics related to church history.

3. Consider facilitating small informal church history reading groups. Like book clubs, reading groups of five to seven people adopt a schedule for reading through particular writings from church history. They then engage in an open critical discussion of the reading, thinking through the issues and how they relate to contemporary life and ministry. Again, see "Suggested Resources."

4. Pastors and teachers can incorporate illustrations and quotations from various historical figures into their teaching and preaching to complement their biblical exposition. Various resources, including ancient commentaries on Scripture, topical quotations, and other links to church history are available. Pastors and teachers should intentionally draw on these historical resources in their own preparation and presentation to add historical perspective and depth.

5. If your church has passed at least the decade-marker, consider having a "church heritage celebration." Present your church's (or denomination's) story, describing its unique historical roots, where it connects to the broader Protestant theological tradition, and how God has worked through the ministry of the church over the years. Reflecting on your church's history can bring a greater appreciation for its present and future ministry.

More than ever, evangelicals both need and desire nourishment for their historical roots. If our local evangelical churches fail to meet this real need in a balanced way, many may go outside the safety of your community to get it. Don't miss this opportunity to equip the saints with a historically rooted identity.

What Is RetroChristianity?

Shakespeare's Juliet once mused about Romeo, "What's in a name?" The implied answer was, "Nothing." But she was wrong. (Sorry, Bill Shakespeare.) Assigning a name to something changes how we think about it, talk about it, and categorize it.

Despite knowing the risks involved in labeling, I named the cluster of ideas that describes my particular approach to reclaiming the forgotten faith:"RetroChristianity."[1] But before I provide a complete definition of this term, I need to introduce some others

Orthodoxy. The Greek original of our word "orthodox" means "correct opinion." In Christian theology it refers to the correct views on the essential truths of the Christian faith and the proper observance of central Christian practices. As a rule of thumb, orthodoxy is that which has been believed and practiced "everywhere, always, and by all." Orthodoxy thus means the right opinion about crucial doctrines and practices in keeping with what true Christians have always believed about these things.[2]

Some of the beliefs that pass the general rule of what has been believed everywhere, always, and by all include:

1. The triune God as Creator and Redeemer
2. The fall and resulting depravity
3. The person and work of Christ

4. Salvation by grace through faith
5. Inspiration and authority of Scripture
6. Redeemed humanity incorporated into Christ
7. The restoration of humanity and creation.

Many other things have been taught and practiced everywhere, always, and by all, but this brief sampling gives us an idea of the kinds of central doctrines that mark all evangelicals as "orthodox."

All this talk might make it sound like discerning the content of orthodoxy is always easy. Truth be told, some squinting is often required in order to overlook minor blemishes on an otherwise hopeful history of orthodoxy. Without constant cleaning and regular checkups, orthodoxy is subject to "truth decay." This can happen to individuals, to churches, to vast communities, and to entire generations. But don't despair! We will see that one of the main functions of the Spirit of truth is to restore the church to orthodoxy when she veers too far—and to breathe into her new life. The history of the church is filled with these revival movements that retrieve forgotten aspects of orthodoxy.

In short, orthodoxy can never be taken for granted. It must be constantly re-received and retaught. We will fail to pass orthodoxy down from one generation to another if we don't faithfully and intentionally teach it. There's no such thing as "orthodoxy by osmosis" or "trickle-down orthodoxy." It must be intentionally taught and actively learned in every generation.

Heterodoxy. We use the term "heterodoxy" to refer to different opinions. Heterodox teachings tend toward the margins of the received doctrines of the faith. In fact, they sometimes teeter at the very edges. Heterodox Christians still want to count themselves among the Christian tradition and still acknowledge the essential Christian truths. But they also want to be unique, innovative, and clever in their theology and practice. They feel comfortable recasting traditional truths in nontraditional language. They sometimes want to rearrange, reinvent, reinvigorate, and reformulate the things that have been handed down to them. They like to surf the waves of the margins, buck the system, and go against the grain.

For example, some evangelicals who uphold classic orthodoxy have exchanged Sunday morning worship for "seventh-day" Sabbath observance. Their study of Scripture apart from its historical early church context has led them to believe that true Christians must keep the Sabbath (and often other Jewish feast days). The truth is, unbiased church historians know that since the days of the apostles themselves, Christians have been worshiping on the *first* day of the week—Sunday—in constant commemoration of Christ's resurrection, and that the observance of "Sabbath" worship and the celebration of special Jewish festivals were never universal practices of the Gentile converts to Christianity. The historical records from the first and second centuries are quite clear on this. Thus, the opinions of these modern-day "Sabbatarians" are "heterodox"—deviating significantly from what was originally practiced by the apostolic churches. Yet their minority opinion is still within the bounds of orthodoxy, because it does not flatly contradict an essential doctrinal or practical core of the Christian faith.

However, because heterodoxy often results in teachers and churches distancing themselves from the normative center of Christian ortho-doxy, heterodox teachers run the risk of breaking free from ortho-doxy's gravitational pull and drifting off into the cold void of heresy. Heterodoxy is also often characterized by exaggerating a minor dis-tinctive and trying to jam it into the center of orthodoxy. To return to my example, I've known some Sabbatarians who actually believe non-Sabbath-keepers are sinning by worshiping on Sunday, thus essentially raising their marginal view to the level of orthodoxy. When a person's novel view becomes their focal point, the true center of orthodoxy becomes minimized. Thus, heterodoxy often develops because of a failure to keep the primary orthodox truths front and center. Division, dissension, and destruction often ensue.

Heresy. The term "heresy" describes the conscious, willful, and stub-born departure from the central core of Christian orthodoxy. As such, heresy alone is "damnable doctrine." Heretics by classic definition are false Christians. Though most heresy begins as a radicalized heterodoxy, not all heterodoxy ends up in heresy. Heresy differs from heterodoxy in that the heretic *consciously* (not ignorantly), *willfully* (not acciden-tally), and *stubbornly* (not momentarily) denies a key tenet or tenets of orthodox Christianity. He or she consciously rejects certain truths that have been believed everywhere, always, and by all.

For example, somebody who denies the full deity and humanity of Christ is a heretic. The belief that Jesus of Nazareth did not literally rise bodily from the dead is heretical. And the view that the Holy

Spirit is a created being and not a fully divine person is heresy. In other words, "heresy" is simply the direct denial of the core content of "orthodoxy."

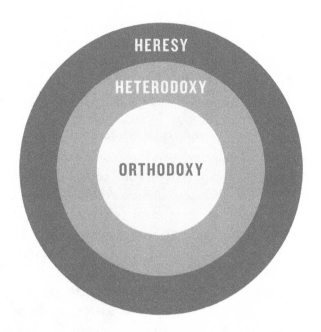

For the most part, evangelicals have consciously embraced classic orthodoxy and consistently rejected heresy. However, evangelicals have historically been less careful about avoiding the mucky mire of heterodoxy. In fact, lurking in the border land of heterodoxy, are two tendencies that I see among evangelicals today. I call these tendencies "metrodoxy" and "petridoxy."

Metrodoxy. I coined the term "metrodoxy" to describe trendy, faddish, and "cool" doctrines and practices that tend to take over contemporary churches—especially megachurches and all the megachurch wannabes. The message of metrodoxy says, if you want your church to have greater cultural impact, to draw media attention, and to place itself on the map of pop culture, you must live by metrodox values. Metrodox ministries value *personal relationships*, not impersonal religion . . . *contemporary praise*, not conventional worship . . . *relevant messages*, not ritualistic mumbling . . . *innovative technology*, not obsolete techniques . . . *fresh ministry*, not stale churchianity. The overarching mandate? Disassociate with the old ways of being Christian and change as often as necessary to keep things exciting.

Metrodoxy thrives in metropolitan areas, drawing from a pool of young, energetic men and women who have excess time and money. This group is often impressed by clever lingo, advanced technology, and trendy buzz. Anything perceived as boring, belabored, or bogged down gets snuffed. Amidst the excitement, though, metrodox churches tend to be in a constant state of identity crisis—especially when they lose their celebrity pastors who had once drawn the crowds. After the stars move on to bigger and better things, the metrodox churches need to rebrand themselves. Thus, metrodox churches tend to wave to and fro, like reeds in the wind, never achieving true stability.

Over the years, I've observed several churches go through this rebranding process. One in particular comes to mind. It started in the 1970s as a home fellowship—an unassuming church plant that emphasized a relaxed community and practical Bible teaching. In the 1980s the church bought an old office building off the highway and targeted young business men and women. In the 1990s they sold the office building and bought a movie theatre! In the course of its relatively short life, that evangelical church tended to flow with the culture, doing what worked, with little reflection on what's right in light of biblical, theological, and historical reflection. Don't misunderstand me: a church's architecture is the least of my concerns. But the zigzagging course that that church took is symptomatic of a metrodox mentality that almost always affects other aspects of theology and ministry.

If metrodox churches survive a few of these phoenix-like rebirths, they often find themselves adrift, unsure of what they're supposed to be doing or why. Of course, ready captains are always prepared to take over and steer the ship toward some new and trendy port of call, but these navigators are usually not looking to classic orthodox beliefs and practices as guides to lead them. These new leaders—often trained in business, leadership, or even entertainment—place little value on their ancient and enduring heritage as a stabilizing source of truth and wisdom. Instead, they draw on secular philosophies of leadership, sociologically driven ministry models, or their personal opinions and experiences. As such, metrodoxy is often antagonistic toward the ideas of RetroChristianity.

Petridoxy. On the other extreme we find what I call "petridoxy." If the metrodox are too trendy and willing to change everything, the petridox are frozen in time, unable and unwilling to change anything. They have been, as it were, petrified—stuck in one point of their tradition and scared to death to move forward. That point of solidification may be a sixteenth-century Lutheran form, a nineteenth-century Baptist model, or a twentieth-century independent Bible church mold. Regardless of the specific cluster of traditions they inaugurated as the "pure church" or "pure theology," petridox churches tend to regard change as being a great evil. They fail to realize that their own unique beliefs and practices were themselves once quite new (and likely quite controversial). If we could liken metrodox churches to reeds in the wind, petridox churches are petrified trees that can't bend without shattering.

Petridox evangelicals often have a myopic perspective on their own church's history, believing their way has stood and will continue to stand the test of time. They have no desire to critically examine their narrow perception of "orthodoxy" or to evaluate whether what they're doing actually does help to preserve and promote the real central orthodox beliefs and practices. Petridox churches would just as soon die as to make major adjustments, which they often view as compromising the gospel itself. Having lost sight of the fundamental goal of receiving, preserving, and passing on the faith once for all entrusted to the saints, petridox churches settle on one method of receiving, one manner of preserving, and one means of passing on their *version* of the faith.

Petridoxy therefore tends to be defensive, ultraconservative, and idealistically nostalgic. As such, it stands in opposition to RetroChristianity, which reminds every Christian tradition that it was once new and embraces a view of orthodoxy that allows for great diversity and development within its clear boundaries.

RetroChristianity

The basic contours of RetroChristianity have been taking shape, but a simple, compact description is now needed. The prefix "retro" means "involving, relating to, or reminiscent of things past." But in contemporary compound words, it indicates an attempt to recall the forgotten past and apply it to the present and future. This forms the basic definition of RetroChristianity:

RetroChristianity is an adjustment of the attitudes and actions of individuals and churches, retrieving ideas and practices from the whole Christian past, thus renewing personal and corporate identity and providing evangelicalism a positive path toward the future.

Having defined RetroChristianity, let me clear up a few potential misunderstandings. RetroChristianity is not another form of neofundamentalism. Though it seeks to reemphasize the "fundamentals" of the faith and although it takes a strong stand against theological liberalism, RetroChristianity is not old-school fundamentalism. Nor is RetroChristianity an attempt to secretly reroute evangelicals back to papal Rome, or along a pilgrimage to Eastern Orthodoxy, or into some multilane ecumenical highway that promotes a flaccid faith of generic "Christendom." Rather, RetroChristianity seeks to carefully navigate our received orthodox faith and practice through a precarious channel between metrodoxy and petridoxy, both of which can shipwreck the faith.

RetroChristianity wants to bridge the gap between the church of yesterday and the church of today without going to two extremes: (1) idealizing the past and condemning the present, or (2) ignoring the past and glorifying the present. (I call these two extremes "primitivism" and "progressivism.")RetroChristianity attempts to navigate between these two extremes, both of which are destructive to the future of evangelicalism.

RetroChristianity also seeks to strengthen evangelicalism, not undermine it. As we saw in the introduction to this book, many who engage in a retrieval of the past have been motivated to return to High Church traditions that, in their minds, better reflect the "historical church." As a result, some have shot like a bullet out of Protestant evangelicalism to Roman Catholicism or Eastern Orthodoxy. However, RetroChristianity sees this kind of movement as both unnecessary and ultimately unhelpful. Leaving evangelical churches for Rome or Constantinople neglects two important facts, which I will discuss more fully throughout this book as we examine specific issues.

First, the exodus out of evangelicalism fails to realize that the non-Protestant traditions do not actually represent the ancient church's beliefs and practices. In fact, as we begin to see in the discussion of "progressivism" below, in some important ways the Catholic and Orthodox traditions depart significantly from the original catholic church of the first and second centuries. They have *added* content to the core of the Christian faith, thereby failing to pass the test of the Vincentian Canon—that which has been believed everywhere, always, and by all.

Second, the flight from evangelicalism fails to consider the fixed and flexible elements of Christianity as well as the possibility of both doctrinal and practical development and deviation throughout church history. (These will be discussed in part 2.) Thus, departure from evangelical churches for "more ancient" or "more traditional" churches has not adequately answered the question of legitimate versus illegitimate development and diversity within orthodoxy. RetroChristianity addresses these issues.

I'm not attempting to criticize conservative High Church Protestant churches such as those found in the Episcopalian, Presbyterian, Lutheran, or Methodist denominations. Many churches in these denominations are solidly evangelical and do, in fact, reflect a particular aspect of the ancient and Reformation faith. However, some of these churches and denominations have a tendency toward petridoxy, declaring their own unique historical forms to be *the* historical faith. They often fail to acknowledge that their foundational documents, teachings, and liturgies were themselves once new. Their institutional forms therefore resist the acceptance of later growth and development in the broader church.

Let me also put a little distance between RetroChristianity and the "tradition fad" taking place in many young twenty-first-century churches: those trendy, postmodern, "emerging" churches that try to incorporate incense, candles, sacraments, icons, and other relics from the past into their dimly lit sanctuaries. Often the motivation behind these attempts at refashioning their worship space and experience with traditional elements is understandable. They have gotten fed up with the sometimes overly intellectual worship of some evangelical churches. To some believers of my generation, the rigid propositional truths and daunting dogmatism found in some parts of the evangelical tradition seem to have suppressed authentic spirituality, a vibrant relationship with God, and dynamic, loving relationships with other believers. These worshipers want a genuine Christian faith free from an oppressive Tradition, but incorporating a variety of "traditions."

This means drawing on images, symbols, and practices that often have ancient pedigrees.

However, I find the all-too-frequent "buffet-style" approach to borrowing from past traditions to be rather arbitrary. I have nothing against incense and candles, but picking and choosing which "traditions" from two thousand years of church history to use in today's worship seems a little ridiculous if we detach them from the history, culture, and theology in which they originally developed and were ultimately understood. If I bought a high-end piece of antique furniture from an estate sale and placed it in my Ikea-fashioned living room, it would look silly. In the same way, I've seen evangelicals try to incorporate ancient rites and rituals into their worship in ways that make me cringe. Some things just don't fit.

Labyrinths, icons, stations of the cross, and other practices associated with Roman Catholicism or Eastern Orthodox mysticism are suddenly enjoying a new audience among some Christians seeking a different type of spiritual devotion—a deep, authentic, meaningful Christian experience that incorporates all five senses. RetroChristianity understands and appreciates this desire. However, most attempts at actually putting this together lack a sense of theological coherence, a clear notion of what is central, or a grasp of the stories these symbols try to tell. I see experience without explanation, image without interpretation, ritual without revelation. What's more, when Christians try to weave together ancient practices, they often apply me-centered criteria of individual preference. That is, the method used to determine which traditions to import into the modern world is usually "whatever works" for *me* or "whatever feels good" to *me*.

The result of harvesting "traditions" from church history is not much more appealing to me than the old-style zoo (zoological societies have tried to change over the last several decades). Remember when we used to rip God's creatures from their natural habitats and cram them into rows and rows of jail cells for spectators to "enjoy"? In many ways today's rip-offs of ancient traditions are worse. Some unthinking evangelicals and churches have gone on a "bring 'em back alive" safari, snared a handful of appealing practices from the jungles of church history, and now display them in their two-year-old churches. That's not RetroChristianity. That's sloppy mishandling and misappropriation of beliefs and practices.

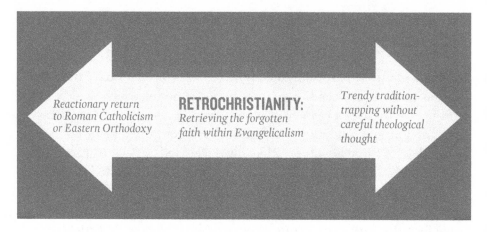

Reactionary return
to Roman Catholicism
or Eastern Orthodoxy

RETROCHRISTIANITY:
Retrieving the forgotten
faith within Evangelicalism

Trendy tradition-
trapping without
careful theological
thought

RetroChristianity favors carrying on a constant dialogue with the past, but it also requires an actual practical connection with the present and an orientation toward the future. Therefore, it asks how we can and ought to teach and practice orthodoxy everywhere (that is, in every kind of church and ministry around the world), always (in every ministry opportunity, outreach, or service), and to all (young and old, rich and poor, educated and uneducated, men and women).

RetroChristianity also demands that the past first be reckoned with on its own terms. It can't settle for picking through Christian history for relevant bits and pieces that will make us feel more "connected" to our roots. It can't stand for politely consulting church history to make us look sophisticated. And it can't naively transplant the past into the present as if the intervening centuries of development never occurred. As such, the dialogue is a complex, time-consuming, strenuous work that requires the input of many. This includes Patristic, medieval, and Reformation scholars; pastors, teachers, and laypeople; denominational and independent churches; and numerous others interested in genuinely engaging in real transformation and unashamed preservation.

RetroChristianity tries to address the practical questions of how we can clearly teach and live the enduring orthodox faith and practice in today's evangelical churches. It seeks first to change attitudes, orienting hearts and minds toward a more classically Christian approach to the faith. Then it challenges believers, including church leaders, to move in practical steps toward implementing real and lasting changes in their individual and corporate practices that will more accurately reflect the historical faith. As we will discover, in most cases these changes are not radical. Sometimes they don't even affect *what* an individual or church is doing, but *how* and *why* they are doing it.

In sum, RetroChristianity means *revitalization, not reaction*. God works in every age, so pendulum-swinging away from our own generation or particular church or denomination is both unwise and unnecessary. Our task is to revive evangelicalism to move ahead, not return to some mythological golden age of the past. RetroChristianity also involves *rejuvenation, not revolt*. The Protestant Reformers themselves were trying to return the Catholic Church's errant theology back to the Patristic theology of the first several centuries; they were not trying to revolt against the fathers of the church.[3] We're living at a time in which a similar reformation of faith and life must occur for Christianity to face the future. Finally, RetroChristianity seeks *restoration, not reconstruction*. Local evangelical churches in all their diversity take center stage in the restoration process. While radical reconstruction would require destruction, healthy restoration seeks preservation and improvement based on an earlier standard. RetroChristianity does not call for a realignment of church or denominational loyalty, but for adjustments in attitudes and actions within present congregations and realignment among evangelical churches.

Primitivism, Progressivism, or RetroChristianity

Evangelicals who dive into the deep waters of church history often make one of two mistakes. They either embrace certain periods as ideal, believing the modern church ought to return to the "good ol' days" of the ancient period, the Reformation era, or their own denominational roots. Or they regard the past negatively, believing today's churches ought to keep up with the times, stay culturally relevant, and forget the worn-out traditions of the past. I call the first view *primitivism*, which resonates with the words of the Judds's country ballad, "Grandpa, Tell Me 'Bout the Good Old Days." That song drips with nostalgia, pondering doubtfully about all the changes occurring in society and culture. The opposite of primitivism is *progressivism*, a view that finds a kindred spirit in Bob Dylan's "The Times They Are A-Changin'." Instead of looking back at the "good ol' days," Dylan and a whole generation rejected the "old road" of traditional ways of thinking and living, and shoved aside all those who got in the way of progress.

Primitivism: Its Radical, Moderate, Patristic, and Protestant Forms

Generally speaking, primitivism seeks to *adopt* the forms, methods, and practices of the historical church, transforming our current forms to match—as closely as possible—the way earlier Christians did things. If the ancient church seems just too *ancient* to be workable, some want to at least return to the Reformation, seeking refuge in the writings of Reformers like Martin Luther or John Calvin. But if late medieval doesn't do it for you, some primitivists seek to go back to the golden age of their own denomination or church—back to the glory years when everything seemed so much better.[4]

However, such a primitivistic approach fails to realize the unique historical and cultural situation every generation faces. Our twenty-first-century church doesn't exist in the same world as the first century, or the sixteenth, or even the twentieth. To some degree, we all need to come to grips with the basic truth behind Dylan's song: "the times they are a-changin'." Without a time machine, literally going back is not merely undesirable—*it's impossible.*

Primitivism has been a major force among "biblicist" evangelicals, who have strived to base their church structure, practices, and methods *strictly* on the Bible. This has led many to completely ignore the history of the church between the first generation and the rise of the Protestant Reformation. This kind of primitivism has been a potent influence on much popular Christianity. In fact, I'm convinced that if the average evangelical were to make a movie based on his or her paltry knowledge of church history, the first act would cover Christ and the apostles. Then, as the camera slowly zoomed in to the apostle John lifting his pen from the last word of the book of Revelation, the scene would suddenly cut to Martin Luther nailing his *Ninety-Five Theses* to the door at the church in Wittenberg on the eve of the Reformation—October 31, 1517. Between the first-century apostles and the sixteenth-century Reformers, many Christians picture a dark abyss, a pointless period of time often dismissed as the "dark ages."

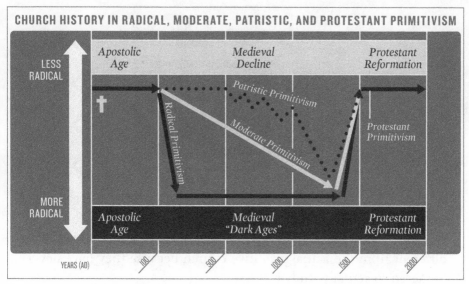

CHURCH HISTORY IN RADICAL, MODERATE, PATRISTIC, AND PROTESTANT PRIMITIVISM

Common Evangelical Views of Church History

When did these "dark ages" begin? To many, the pure apostolic church fell into error immediately after the apostles. After all, didn't Paul warn the Ephesians, "Savage wolves will come in among you and will not spare the flock" (Acts 20:29 NIV)? That's the view expressed in the steep black line in the chart above. Such *radical primitivists* regard every early Christian pastor and teacher outside the New Testament as not only untrustworthy, but even downright dangerous.

Radical primitivists' reforming or restoration movements more or less circumvent all church history after the first century. These believers act as though they are themselves the immediate heirs of the apostles. "We're a New Testament church," they claim. "We get our church order, theology, and practice only from the Bible. The one source of everything we do comes from the Bible alone." They may call themselves "Bible churches" or "apostolic churches" or even "primitive churches."

I always have one question for Christians who claim that their church or denomination stands in direct continuity with the New Testament church: "If that's true," I ask, "then why doesn't your church actually *look* like the early church?" We have enough firsthand documents from early church history to draw the general contours of the earliest churches led by the disciples of the apostles themselves. If our present day "New Testament" or "Bible" churches are really standing in direct continuity with the apostles, shouldn't we expect them to look at least

The Radical Primitivist View of Apostolic
Continuity

a little like the historical churches that the apostles actually founded? Of course, most primitivists wouldn't know that their churches look different from the actual primitive church because they have never bothered to actually study it.[5]

The gray line in the chart on page 73 represents the view of more *moderate primitivists*, who believe the church began a gradual decline immediately after the apostolic age. Moderates therefore hold that the early church fathers might have some insights that are helpful for modern Christians, such as the content of the New Testament canon of Scripture. However, with regard to actual doctrine and practice, moderate primitivists regard the early church fathers as having no more insight than any modern interpreters of Scripture. The Fathers, they say, were subject to serious error and corruption. As with the radical primitivists, then, the Bible alone is the only necessary source for Christian doctrine and practice. In the mind of some moderate primitivists, the church continued to be relatively healthy for several centuries until Emperor Constantine "hijacked" the faith in AD 325 for political reasons, merging church and state and altering everything from basic doctrines to sacred Scriptures. Others simply see the church's coddling with the state as symptomatic of the steady secularization of Christianity that progressively worsened through the centuries.

The radical and moderate primitivists have something in common. Their pessimistic view of church history leads them to a method of theology that begins and ends with the Bible. There is no real need to leave the New Testament either to aid their interpretation of Scripture or to gain insight into Christian doctrine and practice through the contribution of the church fathers. They would be unimpressed with most of the seven reasons for looking back discussed in chapter 2. In fact, to look back too much could be regarded as challenging the authority of God's Word or adopting man-made traditions. Those who view the history of the church according to this model usually end up excusing themselves from actually reading anything written after the first or second century.

A third kind of primitivism, represented in the chart by the dotted line, is much more common among pastors and scholars interested in a "retrieval of the tradition" or an "ancient-future renewal" of evangelicalism.[6] I call this *Patristic primitivism*, and though I personally find some things in common with this perspective, it does not fully reflect the view of RetroChristianity. The word "Patristic" means "related to the church fathers." It refers generally to the period of early church history from about AD 100 to 500. Patristic primitivists believe that the first few centuries of the church faithfully carried on the written and oral teachings of the apostles. These early saints also contributed positively to the discernment of the New Testament canon, the defense of fundamental Christian theology, the dissemination of the true gospel message of Christ's person and work, and the development of important structures of the church that guaranteed its survival through persecution from without and false teaching from within. Thus, the Fathers of the first five centuries—including Polycarp, Ignatius, Irenaeus, Clement, Cyprian, Athanasius, Gregory of Nazianzus, John Chrysostom, and Augustine—loom large as heroes of the faith for Patristic primitivists. Were these early church fathers infallible? No. But those luminaries carried the essential truths of the gospel like torchbearers through the darkness of the first few centuries, lighting the path for the future.

As I will show in part 2, the Patristic primitivists are correct that the Christian church did not suddenly apostatize from the apostolic faith. It affected changes, to be sure. These changes included both legitimate and necessary growth in doctrinal understanding as well as gradual deviations that required corrections and reforms. However, the first-century apostolic era gave birth to a new Spirit-filled community of Christ, a dynamic, growing sanctuary for protecting the truth once for all delivered to the saints, and a legacy of pastors and teachers gifted to the church for the equipping of the saints (Eph. 4:11–13). Of course, the history of Christianity—even the church we see in the

New Testament period itself—is characterized by good, bad, and, yes, even ugly people and events. Every age has those, including our own.

However, the problem with Patristic primitivism is its tendency to forget that the same Spirit that empowered the early church fathers continued to revive, restore, and reform the church throughout history. Thus, we must recognize the reality of advancement in understanding and application of God's unchanging revelation beyond the Patristic period. In fact, the same Spirit has built upon or even corrected developments of the early church. Just as church history did not cease with the apostolic age, neither did it end in the Patristic period. The Reformation, too, contributed importantly to the development of the church's doctrinal and practical legacy, as did the centuries following. Thus, even though Patristic primitivism is a great improvement over radical and moderate primitivisms, it must be tempered with a biblical perspective on Spirit-led doctrinal growth, which will be discussed in greater detail in part 2.

Finally, and briefly, let me mention *Protestant primitivism*, represented in the chart at the far right. In this approach, "going back" to our evangelical roots means a return to the Reformation, and no farther. Thus, revival is sought by returning to the five "solas"—*sola Scriptura, sola gratia, sola fide, solus Cristus*, and *soli Deo Gloria* (Scripture alone, grace alone, faith alone, Christ alone, to God's glory alone).[7] Or they want to restore their wayward denomination to its foundational Protestant confession. Or they desire to return to the methods of preaching, missions, or revival that characterized the First Great Awakening . . . or the Second . . . or the Third.

In any case, Protestant primitivism cares little about what great or horrible things may have happened prior to the Reformation itself. Instead, it tends to regard the Protestant Reformation as "Christianity reloaded," and therefore it sees little need to go back before the birth of one's own Protestant denomination. The problem with Protestant primitivism is that every Protestant Reformer was influenced by the previous models of primitivism—radical, moderate, or patristic. Thus, to the degree that the original Reformers' models of church history prove to be inaccurate, their resulting Protestant traditions prove to be inadequate guideposts for "looking back" and correcting the errors, excesses, and omissions of contemporary evangelicalism.

Progressivism: Its Conservative, Moderate, and Radical Forms

In contrast to all forms of primitivism, *progressivism* is open-minded when it comes to development, growth, and even change in the Christian faith. Like its primitivist counterpart, progressivism has a variety of forms. For the sake of simplicity, I will deal with three: conservative, moderate, and radical progressivism.

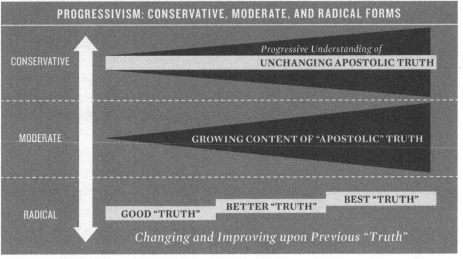

Progressivism's Forms

Though it may sound like a contradiction in terms, *conservative progressivism* is found among many conservative evangelical denominations and theologians. They tend to describe their progressivism as the church's gradual, progressive understanding or illumination of God's once-for-all truth contained in Scripture.[8] So, the Spirit may progressively illumine the church as a whole with regard to the meaning and application of Scripture. Through trial, testing, error, and correction—all based on Scripture—the Spirit roots out poor interpretations or brings to light aspects of the truth that had been overlooked or forgotten. However, this form of progressivism relates only to uncovering truths already revealed in Scripture, not to creating new doctrines or practices outside of the apostolic writings. As I will describe in part 2, a form of conservative progressivism is not only observable in the history of the church, but it is also anticipated by the apostolic writings themselves. So, conservative progressivism—tempered with Patristic primitivism—will contribute to an application of RetroChristianity.

The second form, *moderate progressivism*, views genuine development of new doctrine in the church as God-ordained, Spirit-led, positive growth. That is, moderates view original apostolic truth as a seed planted in the early church, which then grows throughout the centuries into a large tree.[9] Or they believe the apostles delivered an infant faith into the world, which was meant to grow through trial and tribulation into a mature adult.

Exactly when the tree began bearing its fruit or when the child reached adulthood depends on the particular church tradition. Roman Catholicism views the progressive nature of theology as ever-growing, so that certain doctrines and practices may develop in the Catholic Church—such as purgatory or the assumption of Mary—even though there is no hint of such doctrines in the Bible or the early church. In its view, the Spirit has simply guided the church into greater discoveries of truth, generally through its bishops, but particularly through the pope. On the other hand, the Eastern Orthodox Church tends to view the progress in theological development as having died down, more or less, by the eighth century. The Spirit, speaking through the unified voice of the Orthodox fathers of the church, faithfully led the church into all truth—resulting in the growth of a mature Orthodox communion represented by the seven Ecumenical Councils: Nicaea (325), Constantinople I (381), Ephesus (431), Chalcedon (451), Constantinople II (553), Constantinople III (680–681), and Nicaea II (787). In the Eastern Orthodox view, like that of the Roman Catholics, progress is meant to stand in continuity with what has gone before—from the apostolic age onward—but it may contribute legitimate new doctrines and practices to the Orthodox Church.

The third perspective, *radical progressivism*, is embodied in the various liberal and heretical forms of "Christianity" that have arisen through the centuries.[10] These include the Marcionites and Gnostics of the second and third centuries, the Arians and Pelagians of the fourth and fifth centuries, the Muslims in the seventh century, the neo-Pelagian scholastics in the fourteenth and fifteenth centuries, the classic American cults like Mormonism or Christian Science in the nineteenth century, and the modern liberal theologians of the eighteenth and nineteenth centuries. In one way or another, these heresies or new religions all started as attempts to conform Christianity to some new standard, caring little or nothing for the original apostolic faith as it was handed down by the apostles and preserved in the early church.

Of course, not all radical progressivists begin their path of destruction by saying, "Let's completely overhaul Christianity to the degree that it looks nothing like the historical church and everything like our own culture or our leader's revolutionary ideas!" Rather, most radical progressivists begin with a more moderate progressivist mode of thinking, trying to "help" Christianity or "save it" from its outdated form. They seek to reinvent Christian forms and structures for each new generation. In the process, they begin to examine everything—theology, worship, authority, morality. For a while they continue to try to hold on to the essence of Christianity. They contend that the message remains *timeless*, but that the medium must be *timely*. They insist that the methods of communicating the "old, old story" must be new, fresh, and innovative.[11]

But these less radical progressivists sometimes forget that the message is never understood apart from its method of communication. Without some kind of mechanism for quality control, certain progressive methods of communication begin to severely undercut essential Christian doctrines and values. In the end, unleashed progressivism leads to a radical departure from the Christian faith.

The Judds make an important observation that we should remember as we are tempted to harness our Christian message and method too tightly to the prevailing culture: "Everything is changing fast; we call it progress, but I just don't know."

RetroChristianity: Balancing Primitivism and Progressivism, Metrodoxy and Petridoxy

In light of the strengths and weaknesses of primitivism and progressivism described above, RetroChristianity seeks to strike a balance between these two generally opposing forces.

RetroChristianity seeks to *adapt* the methods of the past for our unique twenty-first-century context—the whole past: not just the

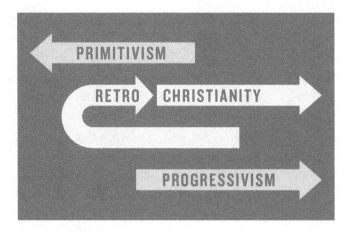

apostolic age but also the Patristic, medieval, Reformation, and modern periods. Rather than retreating into the past, we look back for inspiration and insight. We learn from past mistakes, but we also find forgotten truths that can help correct present errors. We can glean priceless wisdom for today's postmodern world from the ancient, premodern world. We can make future course corrections as we glance back at the original Reformation trajectory. And we can learn from our own local church traditions as we seek to remain faithful to our past while we become fruitful in our present.

At the same time, RetroChristianity acknowledges that some things from the past simply don't fit our current culture. But like old hats or ties that suddenly come back in style, sometimes forsaken forms of ministry can feel fresh and innovative, addressing neglected needs. Moving forward by looking back can be a difficult process requiring time, study, deliberation, and constant reevaluation, but it can provide necessary balance between the extremes of wide-eyed primitivism and wild-eyed progressivism.

While balancing primitivism and progressivism, RetroChristianity also challenges the practices of otherwise orthodox evangelicals stuck in either a metrodox or a petridox mode. We remind petridoxy that reflective change is necessary and healthy—within the standards of orthodoxy and drawing on the guidelines of both Patristic primitivism and conservative progressivism. At the same time, we try to put the brakes on out-of-control, thoughtless metrodoxy, which is in a constant state of revolution according to changing trends rather than changeless truth. So, within the boundaries of primitivism, progressivism, metro-doxy, and petridoxy, RetroChristianity carries on its necessary dialogue.

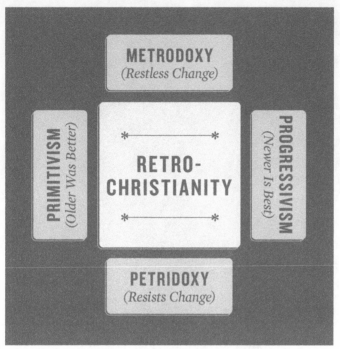

Balance of RetroChristianity between Metrodoxy, Petridoxy, Primitivism, and Progressivism

No doubt about it, the times they are a-changin'. But instead of getting crushed by the rising tide of radical change, we can face the future equipped with the wisdom of countless generations that have gone before.

Part 2

RetroOrthodoxy: Preserving the Faith for the Future

Contend for the faith that was once for all delivered to the saints. — Jude 1:3

So then, brothers, stand firm and hold to the traditions that you were taught by us. —2 Thessalonians 2:15

Engagement in the age-old duel between orthodoxy and heresy has fallen out of favor among many evangelicals today. Perhaps we're suffering from battle fatigue as a result of the friendly fire we endured when stern-faced preachers and dogmatic theologians gave a bad name to fundamentalism—a movement that originally wanted to refocus on the fundamentals or foundational truths of the faith. Nevertheless, we evangelicals still need a proper understanding of orthodoxy and heresy if we will reclaim the forgotten faith for the future.

However, in the jumbled diversity of overlapping "Christianities" today, how can we trace the contours of orthodoxy? Is orthodoxy found in just one church or denomination? Is it something we can actually define? Is it expressed in confessions, creeds, or doctrinal statements? How can the various churches all be orthodox when they disagree on so many things?

In the midst of an evangelical culture in which everybody's brand of orthodoxy appeals to the Bible as the ultimate source and final authority, RetroChristianity answers these questions by first gaining some historical perspective. As we examine the history of the church, we can discern the essential truths or enduring fundamentals of the faith once for all delivered to the saints (Jude 1:3). Along the way we'll also discover that the majority of evangelical denominations and traditions reflect the legitimate facets of an orthodox faith as they center on the core doctrines and practices of classic Christianity. At the same time, however, these orthodox evangelical churches differ from each other in startling ways—and every church tradition reflects developments that have occurred since the period of the apostles.

This leads to an important overarching question: *How can the unchanging truths of orthodoxy allow for diversity of doctrinal opinions as well as development of doctrinal understanding?* Hence the theme of the following three chapters: the three "canons" of RetroOrthodoxy.

A canon is defined as "a fundamental principle or general rule." You may have heard of "canons of architecture," "canons of rhetoric," or "canons of science." Canons constitute foundational principles necessary for understanding a particular philosophical system or technical structure. RetroOrthodoxy has three simple canons that are easy to remember:[1]

Canon 1: Some things never change and never should.
Canon 2: Some things have never been the same and never will be.
Canon 3: Some things grow clear through trial and error.

If you get these three canons down, it will make the rest of this overview of RetroChristianity easier to follow. So, let's look a little more closely at these three fundamental canons.

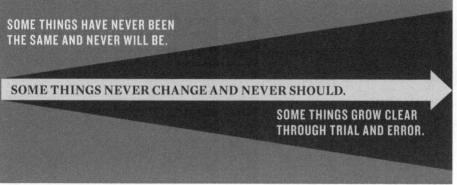

SOME THINGS HAVE NEVER BEEN THE SAME AND NEVER WILL BE.

SOME THINGS NEVER CHANGE AND NEVER SHOULD.

SOME THINGS GROW CLEAR THROUGH TRIAL AND ERROR.

The Three Canons of RetroOrthodoxy

The First Canon
of RetroOrthodoxy

Some Things Never Change and Never Should

For some evangelicals, the word "orthodox" conjures up images of icons, incense, altars, and priests rattling off ancient liturgies in Greek or Russian. Over the centuries, the Eastern Orthodox Church has developed numerous rites that seem strange to most evangelicals, who view such "orthodoxy" as out-dated, irrelevant, or even creepy. With this perspective, some may consider "orthodoxy" to be a stale, worn-out, top-down, and overbearing system that evangelicals need to flee from rather than embrace.

In another vein, some evangelicals associate the term "orthodox" with their own doctrinal systems. That is, they believe the detailed beliefs of their particular church or denomination alone represent orthodoxy. This is especially true of complex theological systems expressed in doctrinal statements, confessions, catechisms, or consistent patterns of interpretation. Too often evangelicals believe that their seemingly airtight systems perfectly express both the big picture and the details of the Bible, rendering their system alone as *pure* theology. This means, of course, that everything else is heresy—or at least polluted doctrine.

The result of this kind of narrow orthodoxy is often a graceless dogmatism leading to mean-spirited debates over every minor point of disagreement.[1]

So, what is "orthodoxy"? How do we define it?

I wish it were as easy as holding up the Bible, pointing, and saying, "That's it. *That's* orthodoxy. Doubt it at your peril." That would be a misunderstanding of the term "orthodoxy." The word means "correct opinion," and relates specifically to the tried and true *interpretations* of the Bible's major theme, its overarching story, and its foundational truths. These are the fundamental beliefs of the Christian faith that never change—and never should. They correspond to that cluster of teachings Vincent of Lérins had in mind when he wrote in AD 434, "We hold that faith which has been believed everywhere, always, by all."[2] These core truths of Christianity, which have endured throughout history, constitute the essence of orthodoxy. Practically, orthodoxy becomes the framework within which we faithfully read the Bible as Christians. Before we spend some time actually tracing these truths throughout church history, let me suggest that a firm grasp of orthodoxy provides us with three distinct but related standards:

> **The Center.** Orthodoxy continually points us to the person and work of Christ in his first and second coming as the central theme of the Bible, theology, Christian life, and all reality.

> **The Story.** Orthodoxy reminds us of the overarching biblical narrative of creation, redemption, and ultimate restoration effected by the harmonious work of the triune God: *from* the Father, *through* the Son, and *by* the Holy Spirit.

> **The Markers.** Orthodoxy provides specific and memorable markers that help us determine when our doctrine is out of bounds while providing a fenced field in which Christians can think and act.

The Standards of Orthodoxy: The Center, the Story, and the Markers

As we saw in part 1, nineteenth-century America was beset with a major theological crisis in its churches and seminaries. Liberals began questioning—then abandoning—the Christ-centered orthodox creeds and authoritative Scriptures in exchange for a man-centered religion

The center (Christ), the story (Trinitarian creation and redemption narrative), and the markers (doctrinal definitions as points of reference)

of morality, personal feeling, and cultural relevance. Evangelicalism originally sprang up as a defense of the fundamentals of the Christian faith. Though this response was characterized by extremes and over-reactions, it ought to be viewed as a necessary corrective against very real threats to classic Christianity. However, since its initial identity as the guardian of classic Protestant orthodoxy, evangelicalism itself has changed and developed over the decades. In some cases the pendulum has swung so far in one direction that it has gotten stuck!

In the twentieth century the center of evangelicalism began to materialize into a more solid core of beliefs and values. These included an emphasis on Scripture as the center, source, and norm of the faith, sometimes to the complete exclusion of other sources of theological understanding and reflection. Ironically, as occurred in the liberal-ism of the previous century, the creeds, theological traditions, and historical continuity became less important—until in many branches of evangelical tradition they became irrelevant distractions or even signs of heterodox or heretical thinking. As long as a belief or practice appeared to conform to Scripture, it was accepted—even if it went against all of church history and every theological tradition.

Other values also took evangelicalism's center stage—practical theology, expository teaching and preaching, a revivalist view of the gospel, an unrelenting emphasis on free will and personal choice in conversion, a psychologically satisfying approach to the Christian life, and militant conservative social and political agendas. In many sectors of evangelicalism, if somebody were to challenge these priorities, they would be labeled nonevangelicals, liberals, or even heretics!

As strange as it may sound, the center of some branches of evangelicalism seems to have moved toward the fringe of classic orthodox Christianity. In short, many evangelical churches are appearing increasingly more evangelical, but increasingly less Christian.

You see, the center of Christianity has always been Jesus Christ. It is not the Bible. It is not expository preaching. It is not a personal response to the gospel message. As important as all of these are for supporting the center, the focal point of right Christian faith is God the Son who became man, lived a life of perfect righteousness, revealed the Father, died for our sins, rose from the dead, ascended into heaven, bequeathed the Spirit, and will come again. Through Christ we understand the Bible as the inspired and inerrant Word of God that points us to him. Through Christ we encounter the triune God of Father, Son, and Holy Spirit. Through Christ we have salvation and forgiveness of sins by grace through faith alone. Through Christ we are empowered to live a regenerate life by his Spirit. Through Christ we are incorporated into the church and receive instruction and power to carry out its mission. Through Christ we have a proper view of the depravity and neediness of fallen humanity as well as the ideal model and ultimate pattern of redeemed humanity. Through Christ we can anticipate the new world to come, when this fallen cosmos will be redeemed by his power and glory.

Don't misunderstand me. I love the inerrant Word of God, powerful expository preaching, a clear presentation of the gospel of grace through faith, and all the things that mark me as an evangelical. Nevertheless, to the degree that evangelicalism has put "me and my Bible" at the center of the Christian worldview, it has removed Jesus Christ from the center. To the degree that it has focused on a personal, voluntary, and free-will response to a bare-bones gospel presentation, evangelicalism has reduced the profound person and work of Jesus Christ to mere propositions to be preached and data to be processed. To the degree that evangelicals have modeled their methods and structures after cultural forms supported by a few proof-texts, they have failed to measure them against the one model of all things human and perfect: Jesus Christ.

What if evangelicalism has unwittingly drifted not into heresy *per se*, but into a heterodox emphasis on things that were always meant to orbit *around* Jesus Christ and point *to* him? What if twenty-first-century evangelicals have replaced the Christ-centered community of faith and faithfulness with an insidious me-centered individualistic philosophy? What if the means of expressing the faith has become the faith itself? What if evangelicals have gone the way of nineteenth-century liberalism and have drifted from a conscious continuity with the great tradition of the church that has always placed Jesus Christ at the center of all things? What if we've gone so far astray that everything I'm writing now actually sounds liberal to you? In short, what if the "center" of much evangelicalism has actually migrated toward the "fringe" of authentic, historical, orthodox Christianity?

When I ask believers, "What is the center of your theology," some Christians firmly footed in churches that strive to maintain biblical fidelity answer, "the Bible." After all, the Bible is the written Word of God, the only inerrant and infallible source of truth, the treasure trove of spiritual wisdom and divine revelation. What else could stand as the center of our theology?

Nevertheless, back in 1883 C. I. Scofield—fundamentalist pastor, Bible teacher, and editor of the *Scofield Reference Bible*—declared, "Jesus of Nazareth is the center and source of my theology." Scofield accepted the divine origin and authority of Scripture "because Jesus did."[3] Even if people answer the question concerning the center of their theology in the same way as Scofield, is Jesus Christ *really* the center of our theology? That is, does our practice of theology actually *indicate* that Jesus is the center?

The doctrinal statement at the seminary where I teach says, "We believe that all the Scriptures center about the Lord Jesus Christ in his person and work in his first and second coming, and hence that no portion, even of the Old Testament, is properly read, or understood, until it leads to him."[4] Our evangelical tradition has long strived to place the person and work of Jesus Christ at the center of the Bible and therefore at the center of our theology and practice. This Christ-centered tradition goes back farther than C. I. Scofield. In fact, its origins are found with Jesus and the apostles, throughout the apostolic period, through the Reformation, and into our own evangelical tradition.

Christ said, "You search the Scriptures because you think that in them you have eternal life; and it is they that bear witness about me" (John 5:39). Luke gives this account of Christ's instruction after his resurrection: "And beginning with Moses and all the Prophets, he interpreted to them in all the Scriptures the things concerning himself" (Luke 24:27). Paul uses the same Old Testament to convince people that Jesus was the Messiah who died and rose again (Acts 17:2–3). Later he declared in his letters that the gospel of the person and work of Christ was foreshadowed in Old Testament Scripture (Rom. 1:1–4; 1 Cor. 15:1–5). Clearly, the center of Scripture is Jesus Christ.

The generation following the disciples also saw Jesus Christ as the center. Around the year AD 110, while being transported by soldiers to Rome for execution, Ignatius, pastor of Antioch, passed through the city of Philadelphia in Asia Minor. During his brief visit there, he had a run-in with some Judaizers who refused to accept the Christian teachings about Jesus unless they could find them clearly spelled out in the Old Testament.[5] The very issue was whether Jesus Christ stood at the center of revealed truth—old and new. The exchange went something like this:

JUDAIZERS: If we can't see it plainly written in the Old Testament, we won't believe it in the gospel.

IGNATIUS: Well, then, let's just look at what the Old Testament says. If you look at this passage here, you'll see what's written about Christ . . .

JUDAIZERS: Ha! That's precisely the question! You're reading Jesus into the Bible! The Scriptures alone must be the standard of truth.

IGNATIUS: Quite right! But for me the standard of interpreting the Bible is Jesus Christ. The unbreakable standard is his cross, death, resurrection, and the faith that comes through him. These are the things by which we are justified.

In short, for Ignatius the question was not whether Scripture was authoritative, inerrant, and the source of inviolable truth. All true

Christians believed that. The issue was how to read Scripture correctly.[6] Ignatius's response reveals that the person and work of Jesus Christ stood at the center of his theology. Similarly, Irenaeus of Lyons emphasized Christ as the central theme of Scripture when he wrote, "If any one, therefore, reads the Scriptures with attention, he will find in them an account of Christ, and a foreshadowing of the new calling. For Christ is the treasure which was hid in the field, that is, in this world (for "the field is the world"); but the treasure hid in the Scriptures is Christ, since He was pointed out by means of types and parables."[7]

As the history of the church unfolded in the first several centuries, the church worldwide continued to emphasize Christ as the center of Christian identity. The triune creation, redemption, and consummation *story* climaxes with Jesus Christ. The historic *markers* of orthodoxy—the confession and creedal definitions, driven deep into the soil of Christianity in the early centuries of the church—all supported Jesus Christ.

When Irenaeus at the end of the second century summed up the story of Christian truth as the "rule of faith," it focused heavily on the person and work of Jesus Christ:[8]

> This then is the order of the rule of our faith, and the foundation of the building, and the stability of our conversation: God, the Father, not made, not material, invisible; one God, the creator of all things: this is the first point of our faith. The second point is: The Word of God, Son of God, Christ Jesus our Lord, who was manifested to the prophets according to the form of their prophesying and according to the method of the dispensation of the Father: through whom all things were made; who also at the end of the times, to complete and gather up all things, was made man among men, visible and tangible, in order to abolish death and show forth life and produce a community of union between God and man. And the third point is: The Holy Spirit, through whom the prophets prophesied, and the fathers learned the things of God, and the righteous were led forth into the way of righteousness; and who in the end of the times was poured out in a new way upon mankind in all the earth, renewing man unto God.[9]

This same basic story of creation, redemption, and consummation is sung in our hymns, portrayed in our children's picture Bibles, expressed through art, and remembered through worship. In fact, through the observance of baptism and the Lord's Supper, the church has continued to confess the centrality of the incarnation, death, and resurrection of Christ as the crux of Christianity. It is true that this clear centrality of Christ's person and work became increasingly obscured as less Christ-centered sacraments, beliefs, and practices accumulated throughout the medieval period. But the central core of Christian identity could be found in every age of the church, even in the so-called dark ages.

In addition to constantly retelling the old, old story, the church developed important language to serve as explicit *markers* of orthodoxy. Through purifying fires of persecution and intense scrutiny, the church fathers settled on time-tested language that precisely articulated fundamental truths of Christian orthodoxy. Patristic scholar D. H. Williams has rightly stated, "Like guideposts along a precipitous mountain pass, the consensual creeds and theological writings of Patristic Christianity were meant to mark the path of doctrinal trustworthiness and theological constancy, as they still do, for every subsequent generation of pilgrims."[10]

The four major markers, to which all future generations must refer, are summed up by four church councils. As the churches faced new challenges and encountered new questions, they responded decisively by calling councils of church leaders from all over the world to deliberate on the issues. The first ecumenical council of Nicaea (325) rejected the heresy of Arius, who taught that Jesus was a created being. The second council, held at Constantinople in 381, defended the deity of Christ and the distinct person and deity of the Holy Spirit. The result of the work of the first two councils was the Nicene-Constantinopolitan Creed. This creed expresses the consensus of orthodoxy handed down from the apostles and defended in the churches. It tells the basic Christian story and centers on the person and work of Jesus Christ:

> I believe in one God, the Father Almighty, Maker of heaven and earth, and of all things visible and invisible.
>
> And in one Lord Jesus Christ, the only-begotten Son of God, begotten of the Father before all worlds; God of God, Light of Light, very God of very God; begotten, not made, being of one substance with the Father, by whom all things were made.
>
> Who, for us men and for our salvation, came down from heaven, and was incarnate by the Holy Spirit of the virgin Mary, and was made man;

and was crucified also for us under Pontius Pilate; he suffered and was buried; and the third day he rose again, according to the Scriptures; and ascended into heaven, and sits on the right hand of the Father; and he shall come again, with glory, to judge the quick and the dead; whose kingdom shall have no end.

And I believe in the Holy Spirit, the Lord and Giver of life; who proceeds from the Father; who with the Father and the Son together is worshiped and glorified; who spoke by the prophets.

And I believe in one holy catholic and apostolic church. I acknowledge one baptism for the remission of sins; and I look for the resurrection of the dead, and the life of the world to come. Amen.

Having affirmed that Jesus is fully God, the next issue with which the early church wrestled was how Jesus could be both God and man. The doctrine of the incarnation became a precarious balancing act, as some wanted to relieve the tension by emphasizing either Christ's divinity or his humanity or by denying a real union between the two natures. The third and fourth markers of orthodoxy came to us in the fifth century. The Council of Ephesus (431) condemned the teaching of the Nestorians, who divided Christ into two separate persons—one divine, the other human. This council also condemned the doctrine of the Pelagians, who taught that human beings could choose good without divine grace. Twenty years later, the Council of Chalcedon (451) condemned the teaching that Christ's divine nature and human nature were mixed and blurred into only one new nature, neither fully human nor purely divine. The "Definition of Chalcedon" represents a mature and complete expression of the doctrine of Christ's person and work, the substance of which is accepted by all orthodox Christians:

> Therefore, following the holy fathers, we all with one accord teach men to acknowledge one and the same Son, our Lord Jesus Christ, at once complete in Godhead and complete in manhood, truly God and truly man, consisting also of a reasonable soul and body; of one substance with the Father as regards his Godhead, and at the same time of one substance with us as regards his manhood; like us in all respects, apart from sin; as regards his Godhead, begotten of the Father before the ages, but yet as regards his manhood begotten, for us men and for our salvation, of Mary the virgin, the God-bearer; one and the same Christ, Son, Lord, only-begotten, recognized in two natures, without

confusion, without change, without division, without separation; the distinction of natures being in no way annulled by the union, but rather the characteristics of each nature being preserved and coming together to form one person and subsistence, not as parted or separated into two persons, but one and the same Son and only-begotten God the Word, Lord Jesus Christ; even as the prophets from earliest times spoke of him, and our Lord Jesus Christ himself taught us, and the creed of the fathers has handed down to us.

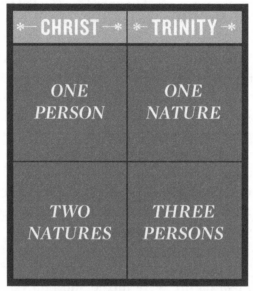

The Trinitarian and Christological language resulting from the first four ecumenical councils

In the Protestant Reformation, the Christ-centered message again took center stage. Reformers like Luther, Zwingli, and Calvin reaffirmed the centrality of the two sacraments of baptism and the Lord's Supper that emphasized Christ's person and work. They clarified and proclaimed the simple good news of God's saving work through Christ by the power of the Spirit. They boldly reformed the church's theology and practice in line with this centering principle. Theologian and church historian, Timothy George, writes concerning the theology of the Reformers: "The revelation of God in Jesus Christ is the only foundation, the only compelling and exclusive criterion, for Christian life and Christian theology."[11]

Besides reviving the *center* and the *story*, Protestant Reformers also accepted the *markers* established by the early church councils and the standard interpretations of the early fathers—not as inspired sources to revelation, but as authentic and enduring expressions of Christian truth handed down from the apostolic times. Thus, the Lutheran *Augsburg Confession* of 1530 states: "The churches, with common consent among us, do teach that the decree of the Nicene Synod concerning the unity of the divine essence and of the three persons is true, and without doubt to be believed."[12] Likewise, the Swiss *Second Helvetic Confession* of 1566 said:

> And, to speak many things in a few words, with a sincere heart we believe, and with liberty of speech we freely profess, whatsoever things are defined out of the Holy Scriptures, and comprehended in the creeds, and in the decrees of those four first and most excellent councils—held at Nicaea, Constantinople, Ephesus, and Chalcedon—together with blessed Athanasius's creed and all other creeds like to these, touching the mystery of the incarnation of our Lord Jesus Christ; and we condemn all things contrary to the same.[13]

Evangelicals inherited this biblical and historical center of Christian orthodoxy, but over the last century they have increasingly neglected the centrality of Christ's person and work as the gravitational center of Christian faith. In doing so, two extremes seem to have evolved. On the one hand some believe that every statement in the Bible must be treated as potential marks of orthodoxy, from the nature of angels to the order of end-time events. On the other hand certain doctrinal issues have worked their ways into the center, displacing the centrality of Christ. Both poles serve to distract from the center of Christian orthodoxy: Jesus Christ's person and work.

Of course, the Bible is the only inerrant source of information we have today about the person and work of Jesus Christ. However, to reiterate a point I've made throughout this chapter, just because we accept the supreme *doctrinal* authority of Scripture as revelation, this doesn't guarantee that we always interpret it correctly. Like the Jews in the days of Jesus and the Judaizers in the days of Ignatius, we will misinterpret the Bible if Jesus Christ does not stand at the center. If we read the Bible in isolation from the person and work of Christ, we've handled it wrongly.

The Content of Orthodoxy: Seven Basic Doctrines in Retrospect

The first canon of RetroOrthodoxy points to the backbone of Christianity—the content of the faith once for all delivered to the saints. This content has been described with a number of terms: fixed elements, central truths, normative dogmas, foundational doctrines, fundamentals of the faith, essential marks. Whatever we call them, these are the core doctrines of the Christian faith that mark a person or church as truly "Christian." The following is a brief summary of these basic beliefs of orthodoxy.

1. The Doctrine of God: The Triune God as Creator and Redeemer

True Christians have always shared a basic view of God—called "theology proper." *Theology* comes from a Greek word that means "the study of God." We use this term generally to refer to the study of any subject related to Christian teaching, but when we use the phrase "theology proper," we narrow the discussion specifically to God as God—the divine being. With few exceptions, the Christian concept of God has remained rather stable over the centuries. Summing up the two thousand year consensus on the nature of God, Thomas C. Oden writes:

> God is the source and end of all things, that than which nothing greater can be conceived; uncreated, sufficient, necessary being; infinite, unmeasurable, eternal One, Father, Son, and Spirit; all-present, all-knowing, all-powerful, and all-empowering creator, redeemer, and consummator of all things; immanent without ceasing to be transcendent, Holy One present in our midst; whose way of personal being is incomparably free, self-determining, spiritual, responsive, and self-congruent; whose activity is incomparably good, holy, righteous, just, benevolent, loving, gracious, merciful, forbearing, kind; hence eternally blessed, eternally rejoicing, whose holiness is incomparable in beauty.[14]

Though non-Christian philosophies and religions might share many of these descriptions of divinity, Christianity is unique in its doctrine of the triunity of God—one God in three persons. Though ancient heretics, modern liberal theologians, and rogue "evangelicals" have occasionally departed from the doctrine of the Trinity, it is a central part of the church's unbroken tradition from the apostolic period to the present. The Lutheran *Augsburg Confession* of 1530 sums up the historical doctrine well:

> The churches, with common consent among us, do teach that the decree of the Nicene Synod concerning the unity of the divine essence and of the three persons is true, and without doubt to be believed: to wit, that there is one divine essence which is called and is God, eternal, without body, indivisible [without part], of infinite power, wisdom, goodness, the Creator and Preserver of all things, visible and invisible; and that yet there are three persons of the same essence and power, who also are co-eternal, the Father, the Son, and the Holy Ghost.[15]

2. Humanity and Sin: The Fall and Resulting Depravity

The doctrine of God includes his work as Creator, including the unique creation of humanity according to the image of God (Gen. 1:26–27). Many other religions also teach that humans were created by God or gods. However, the Christian faith uniquely teaches that Adam and Eve fell from a state of innocence through an abuse of their free will, resulting in the "total depravity" of human nature. That is, apart from God's divine grace, humanity is completely lost and without hope of salvation.

Though it's not politically, socially, or philosophically popular to speak of the innate sinfulness of humanity, the essential badness of the human race is a fundamental doctrine of the Christian faith. It's a doctrine reflected in the official teaching of every generation of orthodox Christianity. The *Brief Statement of the Reformed Faith* of 1902 accurately sums up the general orthodox teaching on the fall and depravity of humanity:

> We believe that our first parents, being tempted, chose evil, and so fell away from God and came under the power of sin, the penalty of which is eternal death; and we confess that, by reason of this disobedience, we and all men are born with a sinful nature, that we have broken God's law, and that no man can be saved but by His grace.[16]

3. The Gospel of God the Son: The Person and Work of Christ

The person and work of Jesus Christ constitutes the substance of the saving gospel message. Two key passages describe the gospel in the New Testament: Romans 1:1–3 and 1 Corinthians 15:1–5. The first focuses on the *person* of Christ—his divine and human origins. The second focuses on the *work* of Christ—his atoning death as payment for sin and his glorious resurrection from the dead. All four Gospels also emphasize these two sides of the good news about Jesus. They seek to convince readers that Jesus is a man, but more than just a man, the unique Son of God. They also spend more time on the last week of Jesus's ministry than on any other period of his life—emphasizing his suffering, death, and resurrection.

Throughout church history, pastors and teachers maintained the centrality of the person and work of Christ. Though they sometimes differed on exactly *how* the death of Christ saved a person, *that* it saved was never disputed. The true humanity and true deity of Christ, along with his saving death and resurrection, have been the central message of the church's unbroken tradition from the apostolic period to the present. *The Doctrinal Basis of the Evangelical Alliance* (1846) synthesizes Christianity's basic teaching concerning Christ's person and work: "And we do more especially affirm our belief in the Divine-human person and atoning work of our Lord and Saviour Jesus Christ, as the only and sufficient source of salvation, as the heart and soul of Christianity, and as the centre of all true Christian union and fellowship."[17]

4. The Doctrine of Salvation: Salvation by Grace through Faith

When it comes to historical continuities regarding the doctrine of salvation, things can get a bit mucky. Soteriology (the doctrine of salvation) was the main doctrinal dispute that split Christianity into Protestant and Catholic branches. Neither regards the other as reflecting the original apostolic teaching on exactly *how* God saves us by his grace.

Roman Catholics view the Protestant doctrine of salvation by grace through faith *alone* apart from any contribution of good works as a heretical deviation from what the church has believed everywhere, always, and by all. However, Protestants argue just the opposite: that the medieval Roman Catholic doctrine of salvation by grace distributed through the sacramental system represents a deviation from the original teaching of the apostles. To weigh in on this debate would take volumes—or at least one large, dense volume.[18] However, many treatments of the history of doctrine, from a variety of denominational backgrounds, note a major departure from the apostolic and Patristic emphasis on salvation by grace through faith.[19] In fact, late medieval theologians taught that "God does not deny grace to the person who does what is in him." That is, several teachers of the medieval period taught that God gives grace *as a reward* to those who do their best! McGrath writes, "The medieval period saw this axiom become a dogma, part of the received tradition concerning justification."[20]

From a historical perspective, this represents deviation from—not continuity with—the classic Christian tradition. It's no wonder that during this late medieval period we begin to see that attempts at reforming the theology of the Roman Church ultimately result in the Protestant Reformation. Thus came to pass Vincent of Lérins's once hypothetical universal crisis, which he anticipated in AD 434: "What if some novel contagion seek to infect not merely an insignificant portion of the Church, but the whole? Then it will be his care to cleave to antiquity, which at this day cannot possibly be seduced by any fraud of novelty."[21] When medieval scholars led the theology of the church away from salvation by grace through faith, Reformers responded by "cleaving to antiquity," demonstrated in Scripture and the Patristic period.

However, if we were to step back and focus on the *continuity* of the Christian tradition, we would see that a long and stable emphasis on *grace* undergirds the entire history of the doctrine of salvation. That is, all branches of Christianity agree that fallen, sinful humans are saved *by grace through faith*, that no person can do enough to earn God's favor, and that ultimately God—not human ability—is responsible for a person's salvation.[22] Roman Catholic Cardinal Gasparo Contarini illustrates this point well:

> Because Luther has said various things about the grace of God and free will, . . . [the Roman Catholic scholars] now oppose anyone who preaches and teaches about the grandeur of grace and human infirmity. Believing that they are contradicting Luther, they contradict Saints Augustine, Ambrose, Bernard, Jerome, and Thomas—in brief, moved by commendable zeal . . . they do not realize that they deviate from Catholic truth, move toward the Pelagian heresy, and cause disturbances among the people.[23]

5. The Bible: Inspiration and Authority of Scripture

Among evangelicals today, the doctrine of the inspiration and authority of Scripture appears to be slipping. Some regard it as a nonessential, a doctrine helpful for the health of the church, but not an *essential* plank of orthodoxy.[24] Others have considered the absolute authority of Scripture to be a modern novelty, a deviation from the teachings of the early church and even the Reformers.[25]

However, even a cursory perusal of the past two millennia of church history will demonstrate that the apostles, church fathers, theologians, scholars, and Reformers regarded Scripture as given by the inspiration of God and therefore without error. The absolute authority of the Bible is a doctrine that has been believed everywhere, always, and by all.[26] This is not only observed in how the Christians of the past treat Scripture in their theology and practice, but it is also seen in their explicit statements regarding the doctrine of Scripture. Saint Augustine, in a letter to Jerome around AD 420, sums up the Christian estimation of Scripture's authority relative to other writings quite well: "I have learned to yield this respect and honour only to the canonical books of Scripture: of these alone do I most firmly believe that the authors were completely free from error."[27]

6. The Church: Redeemed Humanity Incorporated into Christ

Like the doctrine of salvation, until the time of the Reformation, the doctrine of the church never received a detailed and full treatment in Christian theology.[28] In many ways these two doctrines were joined at the hip. As the medieval Roman Catholic Church viewed its sacramental system as the means of receiving saving grace, the nature and function of the church and her offices would be seen in increasingly loftier terms. Also, as the church transitioned from a persecuted illegal religion to the official religion of the Roman Empire, it amassed great power, prestige, wealth, and political clout. This, too, affected how the church viewed itself and its place in the world.

In the medieval period we can discern several developments that differed significantly from the apostolic and early Patristic periods. These included, among others, ascent of the power of the bishops, the rise of the papacy, the fixing of liturgical worship, and the development of numerous sacraments as means of saving grace. Eventually, political and moral corruption set in, threatening to undo the Christian world. The Council of Constantinople in AD 381 confessed belief in "one, holy, catholic, and apostolic church."[29] However, as Euan Cameron notes, "Every traditional epithet applied to the Church, 'one, holy, catholic, and apostolic', had been somehow put in doubt in the fifteenth century: unity by schisms, holiness by moral failings, catholicity by lack of general agreement, apostolicity by doubts about individual popes."[30] The Protestant Reformation responded to this deterioration of the Roman Catholic Church by challenging the Roman Catholic doctrine of the church itself as a heavenly-earthly institution headed by the pope and vested with the sole power to forgive sins.[31]

As with the doctrine of salvation, if we were to focus on common themes in the doctrine of the church throughout its history, we would discern an emphasis on the unity, holiness, apostolicity, and universality of the church, with Jesus Christ as its head and foundation. We also see a very high view of the church in the life of the believer—from conversion to spiritual growth. Closely connected to the importance of the church is the administration of its sacred practices of baptism and the Lord's Supper, both of which contribute to a believer's sanctification. By all accounts, the church is *necessary* for a person's spiritual life, not an optional appendage to a personal relationship with God. Theologian Thomas Oden sums up the church's two millennia of teaching on the church in the following way:

> The church is one, finding its oneness in Christ. The church is holy, set apart from the world to mediate life to the world and bring forth the fruits of the Spirit amid the life of the world. The church is catholic in that it is whole, for all, and embracing all times and places. The church is apostolic in that it is grounded in the testimony of the first witnesses to Jesus' life and resurrection, and depends upon and continues their ministry.[32]

7. The Future: The Restoration of Humanity and Creation

Probably no area of Christian theology has promoted more controversy and disunity among otherwise unified believers than the doctrine of the end times. Debates raged in the early church about the proper interpretation of the millennial kingdom in Revelation 20. Protestant Reformers renewed that debate, adding to it the identification of the Antichrist: Was it the pope? Luther? The Anabaptists? The Muslims? Still more detailed and almost trivial debates over the order of end-time events and the interpretation of symbols in Daniel and Revelation have divided evangelicals for decades.

However, if we step back and examine the major issues emphasized throughout the history of the church, we discover that all Christians have sung the same basic tune without missing a note. All orthodox Christians have anticipated the future literal, bodily return of Christ as Judge and King. All believe in the physical, bodily resurrection of the righteous and the wicked, the one to everlasting life, the other to everlasting damnation. And all hold to an ultimate restoration of creation in which only righteousness dwells. John of Damascus, the great eighth-century theologian of the Eastern Church, summarizes the basic Christian teaching concerning future things this way:

> We shall therefore rise again, our souls being once more united with our bodies, now made incorruptible and having put off corruption. . . . Those who have done good will shine forth as the sun with the angels into life eternal, with our Lord Jesus Christ, ever seeing Him and being in His sight and deriving unceasing joy from Him, praising Him with the Father and the Holy Spirit throughout the limitless ages of ages.[33]

Conclusion: Some Things Never Change

These seven areas of doctrinal continuity demonstrate that the basic contours of orthodoxy can be discerned throughout the history of the church.

The Triune God as Creator and Redeemer. God is a trinity—one divine essence in three persons: Father, Son, and Holy Spirit. All things have been created and will be redeemed from the Father, through the Son, and by the Spirit.

The Fall and Resulting Depravity. Due to the disobedience of the first man and woman, all humanity and creation fell into a state of depravity, unable to save themselves.

The Person and Work of Christ. The eternal Son of God became incarnate through the Virgin Mary and was born Jesus Christ, fully God and fully human, two distinct natures in one unique person. He died as a holy substitute for sinners, rose victoriously from the dead, ascended into heaven, and will come again as Judge.

Salvation by Grace through Faith. Because of humanity's depravity, people are unable to save themselves. Therefore, grace is absolutely essential to salvation, resulting in faith in God and eternal life.

Inspiration and Authority of Scripture. The Holy Spirit moved the prophets and apostles to compose the Holy Scriptures of the Old and New Testaments, the inspired, authoritative norm for the Christian faith.

Redeemed Humanity Incorporated into Christ. The church is Christ's body of elect, redeemed, baptized saints who by faith partake of the life and communion with God through Jesus Christ in the new community of the Spirit.

The Restoration of Humanity and Creation. One day yet future, Jesus Christ will physically return to earth as Judge and King. All humanity will be resurrected bodily—those saved by Christ unto everlasting blessing, the wicked unto everlasting condemnation. The physical creation itself will also be renewed, and sin, death, and evil will be eternally vanquished.

Together, these seven essential truths tell a compelling *story* of creation, fall, revelation, redemption, and ultimate consummation from the Father, through the Son, and by the Holy Spirit. This narrative focuses on the immovable *center* of Jesus Christ, whose incarnation, death, and resurrection destroyed death and brought the hope of salvation. Finally, along the way the church has re-emphasized the *markers* of orthodoxy—councils and creeds that defended the Christian concepts of the Trinity, Christ's person and work, sin and grace, and the basic content of Christian orthodoxy.

In short, some things never change . . . *and never should.*

The Second Canon
of RetroOrthodoxy

Some Things Have Never Been the Same
and Never Will Be

As I drive every day from home to work, I pass more than a dozen churches: Shiloh Terrace Baptist Church, New Life Tabernacle, Second Baptist Church, New Covenant Presbyterian Church, Greater Golden Gate Baptist Church, Bethel Baptist Church, Evangelic Temple Assembly of God, White Rock Church of Christ, First Community Church, New Creation Bible Church, Westglen Baptist Church, Trinity Lutheran Church, and Lakewood Presbyterian Church. All of these churches are Protestant, and most of them would adhere to the essential truths of the classic orthodox faith described in the previous chapter.

Interestingly, every one of these churches stands within walking distance to at least one of the others. Some are an earshot away from another. And at least two of the churches seem to occupy the same building! I know for a fact that most of these churches aren't actually filled to capacity. That is, several of these churches could easily merge into one church with little or no physical discomfort.

So if most of them agree on the orthodox essentials we explored in chapter 4, what's keeping these churches apart? The answer is simple: doctrinal and practical diversity. While unity on the core doctrines of orthodoxy has failed to result in practical unity, doctrinal diversity has fragmented evangelicalism into smaller competing communities. The number of distinct Protestant denominations worldwide—including independent churches—easily reaches into the tens of thousands.[1] With new independent churches or denominations being founded each year, it's literally impossible to keep up with accurate statistics. The numbers are staggering.

This leads me to the second canon of RetroOrthodoxy, a fact we all need to acknowledge: *Some things have never been the same and never will be*. This means that doctrinal and practical *differences* have always characterized the orthodox Christian faith. There have been diverse, distinct, and even contradictory opinions from the beginning of the church until today. Even amidst doctrinal agreement on the essentials, every period of church history has experienced sometimes *radical* diversity. This chapter explores the history of doctrinal differences to encourage evangelicals to properly navigate between essential orthodox unity and healthy confessional diversity. It serves as a warning against the dangers of an extreme tolerance of diversity, leading to the acceptance of heretical views within evangelicalism.

Some things have never been the same and never will be. Diversity among the Christian tradition is not only real, it's actually healthy. We should embrace diversity in nonessentials with liberty toward those who disagree. Yet we must never let our liberty turn to doctrinal license, accepting major deviations outside the core of Christianity.

Doctrinal Diversity Yesterday and Today

In the Patristic period (to about AD 500), diversity seems to have been accepted even as the early church fathers focused on the same center, told the same story, and agreed upon the same markers. However, during the medieval period (500–1500), church leaders appreciated and tolerated doctrinal and practical diversity less and less. This intolerance eventually exploded in the Protestant period (1500–1700), fragmenting the Christian tradition into numerous competing traditions clamoring for converts. Only with the dawn of evangelicalism did orthodox Christianity renew the possibility of essential unity amidst celebrated diversity. But today this hope, too, is threatened by a forgetfulness of the core of orthodoxy and an overemphasis on confessional distinctives.

Diversity in the Patristic Period (AD 90–500)

In the early church, we can discern numerous cases of doctrinal and practical diversity. Several examples illustrate the types of diversity amidst essential unity.

Diversity of Practice

The *Didache*, a manual of church order drafted sometime during the first and second generations of Christianity (c. 50–100), included instructions regarding water baptism. The following process was to be followed:

> And concerning baptism, thus baptize: Having first said all these things [instructions regarding Christian living], baptize into the name of the Father, and of the Son, and of the Holy Spirit, in running water. But if you do not have running water, baptize into other water; and if you cannot in cold, in warm. But if you have neither, pour out water three times upon the head into the name of Father and Son and Holy Spirit.[2]

In this early church manual, the common formula, "in the name of the Father, and of the Son, and of the Holy Spirit" remains the same. However, rather than prescribing one single mode of baptism, the *Didache* actually allows for several acceptable methods. It should not surprise us that even during the apostolic period no single form of baptism was universally followed. Rather, we see diversity of practices, sometimes even within the same church![3]

One early controversy that threatened to separate the Roman Christians from the Christians of Asia Minor concerned whether the celebration of Christ's resurrection should be aligned with the Jewish celebration of the Passover or fixed to a specific Roman calendar date.[4] Polycarp of Smyrna, a disciple of the apostle John, argued for the celebration of Easter during the time of the Jewish Passover. Anicetus, leader of the church in Rome, argued for a different timing of the celebration to avoid celebrating the feast twice in the same Roman calendar year. The following description notes the outcome of this debate:

And when the blessed Polycarp was at Rome in the time of Anicetus, and they disagreed a little about certain other things, they immediately made peace with one another, not caring to quarrel over this matter. For neither could Anicetus persuade Polycarp not to observe what he had always observed with John the disciple of our Lord, and the other apostles with whom he had associated; neither could Polycarp persuade Anicetus to observe it as he said that he ought to follow the customs of the presbyters that had preceded him. But though matters were in this shape, they communed together, and Anicetus conceded the administration of the eucharist in the church to Polycarp, manifestly as a mark of respect.[5]

In other words, although the two bishops could not come to an agreement regarding the proper day for the annual celebration of the resurrection, they nevertheless "agreed to disagree." The differences of opinion and practice they clearly held over minor issues did not distract them from major issues for which they were in full agreement. Their willingness to celebrate the Lord's Supper together proves their unity amidst diversity, for no church leader at the time would have communed in this manner with people they regarded as heretics.

Church historian J. N. D. Kelly sums up the situation of diversity among the churches in the midst of unity of the global church this way: "Looked at from the outside, primitive Christianity has the appearance of a vast diffusion of local congregations, each leading its separate life with its own constitutional structure and officers and each called a 'church'. In a deeper sense, however, all these communities are conscious of being parts of one universal Church."[6] On any given Sunday, the external forms and functions of each local church may have appeared vastly different. But sometimes the differences went deeper than practices to actual doctrines.

Diversity of Doctrine

We also observe in the early church doctrinal diversity, that is, differences of opinion over areas of theology. Though orthodox teachers always held to the essential truths of the Christian faith, they had diverse opinions on a number of issues. For example, with regard to the doctrine of the nature and origin of angelic beings, Origen of Alexandria (early third century) makes the following points:

This also is a part of the teaching of the Church, that there are certain angels of God, and certain good influences, which are His servants in accomplishing the salvation of men. When these, however, were created, or of what nature they are, or how they exist, is not clearly stated. . . . Every one, therefore, must make use of elements and foundations of this sort, according to the precept, "Enlighten yourselves with the light of knowledge," if he would desire to form a connected series and body of truths agreeably to the reason of all these things.[7]

Origen's point seems to be that because there was no general consensus regarding the details of angelology, Christian theologians must attempt to work out these details through a careful study of Scripture.

Not surprisingly, we also find differences of opinion in the early church regarding the end times. Though we see clear examples of a view similar to modern-day premillennialism, there are also hints of amillennial perspectives among orthodox Christians by the second century.[8] Justin Martyr, a representative of ancient premillennial thought, recounts a debate he had with unbelieving Jews sometime around AD 140. In that debate he said:

I and many others are of this [millennial] opinion, and believe that such [end-time events] will take place, as you assuredly are aware; but, on the other hand, I signified to you that many who belong to the pure and pious faith, and are true Christians, think otherwise. . . . But I and others, who are right-minded Christians on all points, are assured that there will be a resurrection of the dead, and a thousand years in Jerusalem, which will then be built, adorned, and enlarged.[9]

Elsewhere, Justin also explains the radical diversity of opinions that existed regarding whether truly saved Christians can keep the Law of Moses as a form of personal devotion, or if such a legalistic approach to the Christian life indicated a lack of salvation. Justin admits to his Jewish friend, Trypho, that orthodox Christians do not all agree on every point of doctrine, though they all share the same orthodox faith. Justin writes:

And Trypho again inquired, "But if someone . . . after he recognizes that this man is Christ, and has believed in and obeys Him, wishes, however, to observe these [institutions of the Law], will he be saved?"

I said, "In my opinion, Trypho, such a one will be saved, if he does
not strive in every way to persuade other men. . . ."
Then he replied, "Why then have you said, 'In my opinion, such a
one will be saved,' unless there are some who affirm that such will not
be saved?"
"There are such people, Trypho," I answered; ". . . but I do not agree
with them."[10]

These several examples serve to illustrate that within early orthodox Christianity we could find diversity and even debate. Distinctive
prayers, liturgies, doctrinal emphases, and ways of expressing basic
truths could be seen among the early church fathers. Diversity was
especially evident in less central theological issues such as end times
and angels, but sometimes diversity touched on issues related to
salvation! This lack of general doctrinal consensus made room for a
variety of answers as pastors and teachers examined the Scriptures
and tried to wrestle with what God had revealed. We see diverse
views on the Lord's Supper, the order of worship, the nature of pre-
destination and free will, and other issues. Both unity and diversity
were characteristic features of orthodox Christianity in its early
centuries.

In the early sixth century, at the twilight of the Patristic period, the
Christian philosopher and theologian, Boethius, described the unity
and diversity of catholic Christianity in the following way:

The Catholic Church, then, spread throughout the world, is known
by three particular marks: whatever is believed and taught in it has
the authority of the Scripture, or of universal tradition, or at least of
its own and proper usage. And this authority is binding on the whole
Church as is also the universal tradition of the Fathers, while each
separate church exists and is governed by its private constitution
and its proper rites according to difference of locality and the good
judgment of each.[11]

However, this openness to the "good judgment of each" church
regarding issues that were not clearly marked by universal consensus and clear biblical teaching eventually fell out of favor. The
early church's appreciation of "unity and diversity" gave way to
an attempted "hostile takeover" by those in favor of monolithic
uniformity.

The Medieval Attempt at Doctrinal Consensus (AD 500–1500)

The unity and diversity enjoyed in the early church continued throughout the medieval period in both East and West. The idea of a monolithic, perfectly uniform, and all-encompassing Global Catholic Church is a myth. Great diversity could be seen between Eastern and Western Christianity in their liturgies and theological emphases. These differences eventually led to the Great Schism between East and West in 1054, a breach between the Roman Catholic Church and the Eastern Orthodox churches that continues to this day.

However, in the midst of these radically diverse opinions, some made attempts at synthesizing the diversity of the earlier church leaders. Instead of being content with unity and diversity, church leaders became increasingly concerned about the oneness of the Catholic Church, believing the church should have spoken unanimously on all matters in every age. For them, everything became central, and they saw it as their duty to explain "apparent contradictions" between earlier church fathers. They did this in three ways:

- Some rejected as "heterodox" or "heretical" the diverse teachings of those who had at one time been accepted as orthodox.[12]
- Some simply copied and promoted the portions of orthodox fathers they agreed with, leaving other portions of their writings hidden.[13]
- Some tried to explain the diverse opinions as merely "apparent contradictions," as one would explain apparent discrepancies between equally inspired biblical narratives.

To this end, Jean Gerson, in 1363, wrote:

If there is "one Lord, one faith," and one law, and if, moreover, the truth is common to all and comes from the Holy Spirit, regardless of who expresses it, what will be the outcome of this violent controversy between various classes and orders of Christians, when a theologian is defended, cherished, and preferred by one group but not by another?[14]

Gerson's assumption was that just as the Holy Spirit moved the prophets of the Old and New Testaments to write Holy Scripture (2 Pet. 1:21), the same Holy Spirit was guiding the Roman Catholic Church into all truth. This would necessarily result in doctrinal uniformity as the Spirit inspired the Church's official teachers to speak with one unified voice. Therefore, to harmonize the "apparent" contradictions or even diverse views on such things as the Eucharist, the authority of the pope, and the assumption of the Virgin Mary, some scholars in the Roman Catholic Church felt compelled to reconcile the entire preceding Christian tradition! Such a grandiose venture—rejecting the classic view of unity on essentials and diversity on nonessentials—was bound to fail. With a heightened view of the spiritual authority of the bishops, and especially of the pope, the Roman Catholic theologians failed to recognize that only the apostles and prophets of the first century carried absolute divine authority as the doctrinal foundations of the church (Eph. 2:20).

However, that's not how the Roman Catholic Church saw things. Instead, they believed that the officially ordained bishops of their tradition, and especially the pope, had inherited the authority of the apostles. Therefore, they sought a *uniform* pattern of teaching among the official teachers of the church throughout its history. The alternative—unity at the core, diversity in the margins—would undermine the Roman Church's own claim to have a monopoly on truth.

The more the Roman Catholic Church pushed their claims of infallibility and doctrinal purity, the more early Reformers pushed back. Early Protestants like John Wycliffe and John Huss in the fourteenth and fifteenth centuries argued that the apostles and prophets had far superior authority to anybody after them. The writings of the New Testament were the foundation of Christian theology and practice, to which nothing more could be added. The early Reformers could point to both the New Testament and the theology of the early church to demonstrate the Roman Catholic Church's shortcomings. They could prove not only that the teachings of the pope were at variance with the first few centuries of Christianity, but that the Roman Catholic insistence on absolute doctrinal uniformity and conformity was itself a novelty. As ironic as it may sound, the Roman Catholic Church in the medieval period failed to meet St. Vincent of Lérins's standard of orthodoxy—what has been believed everywhere, always, and by all. By attempting to force its novel doctrines into the unchangeable core of essentials, the Roman Catholic Church became less and less "catholic"!

Protestant Fragmenting from Diversity to Conflict (AD 1500–1700)

We have seen that the early church's emphasis on the unifying, unchanging truths of orthodoxy (the story, the center, and the markers) allowed for a rich and tolerable diversity of teachings and traditions. The Roman Catholic Church threatened this perspective of unity amidst diversity by attempting to enforce a worldwide uniformity in doctrine and practice and then to force this uniformity into the center of orthodoxy. Thus, the ancient church's unity and diversity were threatened by an emphasis on unity at the expense of diversity.

The Protestant Reformation also failed to restore the early church's balance between unity and diversity. They emphasized diversity at the expense of unity. So diverse were the new traditions that arose (and continued to arise) in the wake of the Reformation that theological, political, and military conflict ensued. Caspar Schwenkfeld summed up the situation well when he wrote in 1530, "The Papists damn the Lutherans; the Lutherans damn the Zwinglians . . . ; the Zwinglians damn the Anabaptists and the Anabaptists damn all others."[15]

The Protestant Reformers and several generations of leaders following them split the Christian tradition first into dozens, then hundreds, and ultimately thousands of squabbling churches. Armed with an overly optimistic view of their own abilities to interpret everything in the Scriptures with clear, unclouded glasses, Protestants tended to turn every interpretation into a dogmatic proposition. Propositions became catechisms. Catechisms became confessions. Confessions formed denominations. And the process continued to reproduce itself like an uncontrollable chain reaction.

For all the good the Reformation did to break up the hardening concrete of Roman Catholic dogma, it erred by replacing it with hard, sharp, and fragmented rubble! In all this conflict, the clear unity of the early orthodox faith was buried by the debris of diversity and conflict. This divisive denominationalism and conflicted confessionalism continued for several centuries, until a new hope of unity and diversity emerged in the late nineteenth and early twentieth centuries.

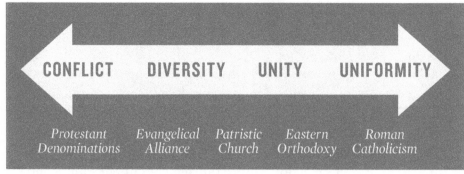

General tendencies of unity and diversity in historical Christian traditions

The Evangelical Experiment: Unity and Diversity (1700–Present)

Evangelicalism is nothing if not diverse. The broad term "evangelical" includes the orthodox, conservative, Bible-believing, gospel-preaching, mission-minded branches of numerous denominations and independent churches. Sometimes uninformed people stamp certain denominations as either "conservative" or "liberal." But these labels are virtually meaningless when you step foot into a particular church, because pastors or individual members of any church may align themselves with evangelical ideals.

For instance, if you were to walk into a PCA (Presbyterian Church in America) church on any given Sunday, you'd likely encounter a conservative, traditional, orthodox Presbyterian service; but if you were to go to lunch with one of its more nonconforming members, you might find a borderline heretic! When visiting a church in the Presbyterian Church (USA), however, you can't be sure what you'll find even in the pulpit. Some PC (USA) churches are very conservative and orthodox in their theology and practice. Others are very left-leaning socially, morally, and theologically. Others have liberal leadership, but a strong conservative membership, or vice versa. In other words, whereas the conservative versions of traditional Protestant denominations are more consistently evangelical, the liberal versions are unpredictably broad.

This is an important point to make, because it highlights the potential strength that accompanied an interdenominational, interconfessional movement like evangelicalism in the late nineteenth and early twentieth centuries. Because of its popular appeal, its simple message, and its role in strengthening the faith and piety of individual believers across denominational lines, evangelicalism as a movement served to unite rather than divide previously conflicting Protestant churches and traditions.

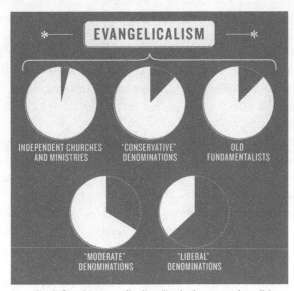

Broadly defined, "evangelicalism" includes several traditions to varying degrees: (1) Almost all independent churches and ministries; (2) The majority of "conservative" denominations; (3) Most old fundamentalists, though some think evangelicals are too "liberal"; (4) Many "moderate" denominations; and (5) Some members of "liberal" denominations.

One very early example is the American branch of the Evangelical Alliance—a loose interdenominational association that attempted to emphasize the essentials of orthodox Protestant doctrine (while downplaying nonessentials) as a basis for unity, fellowship, and cooperation. I quote extensively from the preamble of their "Doctrinal Basis" adopted in 1867:

> *Resolved,* That in forming an Evangelical Alliance for the United States, in co-operative union with other Branches of the Alliance, we have no intention or desire to give rise to a new denomination or sect; nor to affect an amalgamation of Churches, except in the way of facilitating personal Christian intercourse and a mutual good understanding; nor to interfere in any way whatever with the internal affairs of the various denominations; but, simply, to bring individual Christians into closer fellowship and co-operation, on the basis of the spiritual union

which already exists in the vital relation of Christ to the members of his body in all ages and countries.

Resolved, That in the same spirit we propose no new creed; but, taking broad, historical, and evangelical catholic ground, we solemnly reaffirm and profess our faith in all the doctrines of the inspired Word of God, and the consensus of doctrines as held by all true Christians from the beginning. And we do more especially affirm our belief in the Divine-human person and atoning work of our Lord and Saviour Jesus Christ, as the only and sufficient source of salvation, as the heart and soul of Christianity, and as the centre of all true Christian union and fellowship.

Resolved, That, with this explanation, and in the spirit of a just Christian liberality in regard to the minor differences of theological schools and religious denominations, we also adopt, as a summary of the consensus of the various Evangelical Confessions of Faith, the Articles and Explanatory Statement set forth and agreed on by the Evangelical Alliance at its formation in London, 1846, and approved by the separate European organizations; which articles are as follows:

1. The Divine inspiration, authority, and sufficiency of the Holy Scriptures.
2. The right and duty of private judgment in the interpretation of the Holy Scriptures.
3. The Unity of the Godhead, and the Trinity of the persons therein.
4. The utter depravity of human nature in consequence of the Fall.
5. The incarnation of the Son of God, his work of atonement for the sins of mankind, and his mediatorial intercession and reign.
6. The justification of the sinner by faith alone.
7. The work of the Holy Spirit in the conversion and sanctification of the sinner.
8. The immortality of the soul, the resurrection of the body, the judgment of the world by our Lord Jesus Christ, with the eternal blessedness of the righteous, and the eternal punishment of the wicked.
9. The divine institution of the Christian ministry, and the obligation and perpetuity of the ordinances of Baptism and the Lord's Supper.[16]

Another example of this move toward a restoration of unity with diversity is seen in the Evangelical Theological Society (ETS), an organization of professing evangelical scholars who hold graduate degrees in biblical and theological studies. Members gather regionally and nationally to present papers, discuss and debate theological issues, and address contemporary trends in evangelical theology. Formed in 1949, the ETS strives for evangelical unity amidst confessional and denominational diversity. As a doctrinal basis, it originally adopted only a simple statement on the inerrancy of Scripture: "The Bible alone, and the Bible in its entirety, is the Word of God written and is therefore inerrant in the autographs [original writings]." Sometime later, however, it expanded the doctrinal basis for membership to include the Trinity: "God is a Trinity, Father, Son, and Holy Spirit, each an uncreated person, one in essence, equal in power and glory." Within these broadly orthodox and evangelical doctrinal boundaries, scholars are encouraged to present numerous perspectives in biblical, theological, and historical studies.

However, the unity with diversity that twentieth-century evangelicals strived for never achieved anything like the balance of the earliest church. In many cases, instead of a big tent revival, organizations like the Evangelical Alliance and the Evangelical Theological Society looked more like three-ring circuses. Campy, defensive, and agenda-driven theologians simply used the opportunity to debate their theological positions with scholars they otherwise rarely saw and barely liked. Nothing like a broad doctrinal consensus was ever achieved, and practical unity that trickled down to the churches was never part of the agenda.

Parachurch ministries, seminaries, mission agencies, and other organizations served to build bridges or networks between previously disunited parts, but even these tended toward specific constituencies, communities, and circles of friends. Now, instead of a broad unity around essential truths, evangelicalism continues to consist of interlocking, concentric, adjacent, and overlapping circles. These circles do not center on the historical center, story, and markers of orthodoxy, but around individual doctrinal and practical issues like the inerrancy of Scripture, the proclamation of the gospel, personal conversion experiences, and other issues that have taken the spotlight away from a full, balanced orthodoxy.

Of course, most of those who call themselves "evangelicals" also hold to the orthodox center, but the core doctrines of orthodoxy do not always have a pronounced place in their doctrinal statements, nor do they play a large part in their official teaching and preaching. In any case, orthodoxy has not served as the clear, unambiguous, and conscious norm of the evangelical tradition as it did for the early Christians in the Patristic period. In this kind of situation, the threat of doctrinal diversity leading to doctrinal deviancy looms like dark clouds on the horizon. Without a broader accountability to historical orthodoxy and a more general fellowship between orthodox churches and traditions, evangelicalism is in danger of being blown about by the winds of strange doctrine—or uprooted altogether, only to wither away and vanish.

From Healthy Diversity to Heretical Deviancy

Granting freedom on nonessential doctrinal and practical issues is great, and tolerating diversity can be both healthy and stimulating among evangelicals who hold firmly to the foundations of Protestant orthodoxy. However, in their quest for peace and unity, evangelicals can sometimes be tempted to collapse the core, fudge on the fundamentals, or ease up on the essentials. The threat of extreme heterodoxy or even heresy is always lurking in the dark corners of evangelicalism where people have failed to come to terms with the tension between central and peripheral issues.

We have many historical examples and contemporary expressions of doctrinal diversity that have gone too far, flinging teachers and traditions into false Christian and even anti-Christian heresies. Numerous cults, denominations, teachers, and movements yesterday and today have sometimes ignorantly and sometimes knowingly rejected or redefined the center, the person and work of Jesus Christ. Or they have twisted the story of the Trinitarian creation and redemption narrative. Or they have ignored the historical markers of orthodoxy established during the first four ecumenical councils. In so doing, these "evangelicals" find themselves wandering out of bounds with no doctrinal discernment.

Chapter 4 emphasized the need for a biblically and historically faithful Christianity in which Christ's person and work stand at the center of the Trinitarian creation and redemption narrative. Now we need to consider the alternative. What would happen if we were to adopt a *different* "Jesus" as our center or to push the real Jesus to the margins? What if we were to tamper with the triune God's nature or to create a different plotline for his story of redemption? Or what if we moved markers of orthodoxy like pieces of furniture that can be placed, displaced, or replaced at will?

Simply put, if evangelicals overemphasize their distinctive doctrines or practices without maintaining the identifying norms of the Christian faith, they will begin to drift from orthodoxy, through heterodoxy, and toward gross heresy—*the conscious, willful, and stubborn departure from the central core of Christian orthodoxy.* Heresy is "damnable doctrine." As such, we should be very careful about labeling people who disagree with us "heretics," because this is the same as saying, "You're damned to hell." However, we shouldn't hesitate to call false teachers "heretics" if they knowingly, willingly, and persistently reject a key tenet or tenets of historical Christian orthodoxy—truths that have been believed everywhere, always, and by all.

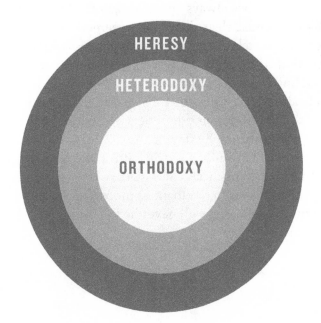

As noted earlier, most heresy begins as a radicalized heterodoxy—novel and idiosyncratic teachings that tend toward the margins or teeter on the edges of mainstream Christian truth. For example, denying the conscious existence of the soul after physical death while awaiting resurrection is heterodoxy. Rejecting the existence of hell is heterodoxy. Accepting authoritative apostles or prophets in the church today is heterodoxy. That is, in light of the entire Christian tradition, these beliefs are fringe. Taken to extremes, they may be quite dangerous. The denial of an immaterial soul could result in the belief in an immaterial resurrection rather than the orthodox view of a bodily resurrection. The rejection of the existence of hell may lead to the belief in universalism, a rejection of evangelism, a downplaying of the unique person and work of Christ, and an unbalanced perception of God's holiness and justice. The acceptance of authoritative apostles and prophets in the church today could yield additional revelations that contradict the orthodox interpretations of inspired Scripture.

In short, while doctrinal diversity amidst orthodox unity is healthy, deviant heterodoxy is dangerous, and heresy is downright deadly.

Conclusion: Some Things Will Never Be the Same

Doctrinal diversity has always characterized the orthodox Christian faith. *Always.* Amidst clear doctrinal agreement with regard to the orthodox fundamentals, every period of church history has experienced sometimes *radical* diversity. However, embracing diversity does not mean tolerating heresy or toying with heterodoxy.

Evangelicals must reclaim the forgotten faith of classic orthodoxy and reject the heterodox and heretical accretions that have led so many astray for centuries. By staying true to classic orthodoxy, we can equip ourselves to faithfully pass the faith to the next generation. At the same time, we evangelicals can excuse ourselves from the need to agree on everything. Full agreement is impossible. It always has been.

Simply put, some things will never be the same.

The Third Canon
of RetroOrthodoxy

Some Things Grow Clear through Trial and Error

In AD 410, on a French coastal island one mile long and half a mile wide, a monk named Honoratus founded a monastery. He originally intended to "get away from it all" and live as a hermit. But he apparently had such a magnetic spirituality that he attracted countless followers who wanted to withdraw from what many viewed as an increasingly political and troubled church to an island of peace and tranquility. The tiny island of Lérins afforded a perfect retreat from the theological upheavals that were occurring around the Mediterranean countries.

The events that had taken place in the church over the preceding century would have driven any spiritually minded saint to seek a refuge from the raging seas of controversy. A hundred years earlier Christians throughout the Roman Empire had endured the greatest persecution in their three centuries of suffering. This time of physical trial ended with the Edict of Milan in 313, when Emperor Constantine made Christianity a legal religion. In 325, the Council of Nicaea gathered bishops from throughout the Empire to settle a major theological rift brought on by the teachings of Arius of Alexandria. This resulted in the Nicene Creed. Yet political turmoil brought doctrinal confusion, as emperors favored Arian bishops, sent Nicene supporters into exile, and put orthodoxy on the run.

This political takeover by the Arian heretics ended in 381 at the Council of Constantinople, when the orthodox agreed on clearer language to describe the relationship of the Father, Son, and Holy Spirit. They also defeated the heresy of Apollinarius, who taught that Christ had a human body, but not a human soul. However, the nature of Christ's incarnation continued to pester the church, and in 431 the Council of Ephesus met to condemn the teachings of Nestorius and Pelagius—the former for denying the unity of the divine and human natures of Christ, the latter for denying the depravity of humanity and the necessity of grace in salvation. Then, in 451, the last of the four great ecumenical councils convened to condemn Eutyches, whose theology mixed the two natures of Christ into one mongrel nature, neither human nor divine.

In the midst of these doctrinal storms, the tranquil island monastery of Lérins flourished. Yet even the monks on that Mediterranean paradise couldn't escape the theological and political tidal waves that swept through Europe and Africa. In 434, a monk of Lérins named Vincent wrote a brief but potent account of the heresies that had brought numerous trials on orthodoxy. All of the heretics had appealed to Scripture as the source of their doctrines. Vincent wrote:

> Do heretics also appeal to Scripture? They do indeed, and with a vengeance; for you may see them scamper through every single book of Holy Scripture,—through the books of Moses, the books of Kings, the Psalms, the Epistles, the Gospels, the Prophets. Whether among their own people, or among strangers, in private or in public, in speaking or in writing, at convivial meetings, or in the streets, hardly ever do they bring forward anything of their own which they do not endeavour to shelter under words of Scripture.[1]

The problem among the heretics was not that they neglected Scripture, but that they misinterpreted it. The heretics failed to read the inspired, authoritative Word of God in light of the apostolic teaching passed down from the apostles generation after generation. In response, Vincent of Lérins coined his famous rule of orthodoxy:

Moreover, in the Catholic Church itself, all possible care must be taken, that we hold that faith which has been believed everywhere, always, by all. For that is truly and in the strictest sense "Catholic," which, as the name itself and the reason of the thing declare, comprehends all universally. This rule we shall observe if we follow universality, antiquity, consent.[2]

That is, deviant interpretations of Scripture concerning major issues like those rejected at the ecumenical councils can be judged as heretical based on the principle that *some things never change and never should*—the first canon of RetroOrthodoxy. However, this brings up an important question: Is there any room for learning, growing, or developing? Vincent himself asked this question in the *Commonitory*. His answer is insightful:

> But someone will say, perhaps, Shall there, then, be no progress in Christ's Church? Certainly; all possible progress. . . . Yet on condition that it be real progress, not alteration of the faith. For progress requires that the subject be enlarged in itself, [but] alteration [requires] that it be transformed into something else. The intelligence, then, the knowledge, the wisdom, as well of individuals as of all, as well of one man as of the whole Church, ought, in the course of ages and centuries, to increase and make much and vigorous progress; but yet only in its own kind; that is to say, in the same doctrine, in the same sense, and in the same meaning.[3]

That is, progress in Christian understanding is to be expected, even embraced. Yet this development must never contradict the core content of the Christian faith. In fact, legitimate growth and progress ought to make the essentials of the faith even stronger. Vincent continues with several analogies of legitimate doctrinal growth in the church:

> This, then, is undoubtedly the true and legitimate rule of progress, this the established and most beautiful order of growth, that mature age ever develops in the man those parts and forms which the wisdom of the Creator had already framed beforehand in the infant. Whereas, if the human form were changed into some shape belonging to another kind, or at any rate, if the number of its limbs were increased or diminished, the result would be that the whole body would become either a wreck or a monster, or, at the least, would be impaired and enfeebled. In like manner, it behooves Christian doctrine to follow the same laws

of progress, so as to be consolidated by years, enlarged by time, refined by age, and yet, withal, to continue uncorrupt and unadulterate, complete and perfect in all the measurement of its parts, and, so to speak, in all its proper members and senses, admitting no change, no waste of its distinctive property, no variation in its limits.[4]

This reality—even necessity and desirability—of doctrinal development and theological progress leads to the third canon of RetroOrthodoxy: "Some things grow clear through trial and error." That is, RetroChristianity acknowledges that real progress in doctrine and practice is part of the Christian faith. Twenty-first century Christians can benefit from the growth of knowledge and wisdom that has occurred over the previous twenty centuries, most often through trial and error—overcoming challenges to orthodoxy and learning from past mistakes. Those who reject doctrinal development forsake Spirit-led growth spurts of the body of Christ and squander the God-given wisdom that has helped to mature the Christian faith. However, like all principles of RetroOrthodoxy, the third canon must maintain a balance between several extremes.

Buttons, Duddies, and Coués: Three Extreme Responses to Doctrinal Development

Evangelicals can sometimes have extreme reactions to the idea of doctrinal development and theological progress: extreme primitivism, extreme stagnation, and extreme progressivism. We looked at the tension between primitivism and progressivism in chapter 3 as we defined the overall approach of RetroChristianity as neither primitivistic nor progressivistic. However, specifically related to the concept of doctrinal development, let's revisit this tension and add a third reaction: extreme stagnation.

These extreme positions can be likened to three devastating medical syndromes. If they linger untreated in churches for too long, they will cause great damage to the body of Christ. In keeping with the medical analogy, I've given these three diagnoses distinct names: *The Benjamin Button Syndrome* (extreme primitivism), *The Fuddy-Duddy Syndrome* (extreme stagnation), and *The Émile Coué Syndrome* (extreme progressivism). RetroChristianity seeks to avoid all three extremes, while acknowledging a healthy consideration of historical perspective, confessional stability, and legitimate development.

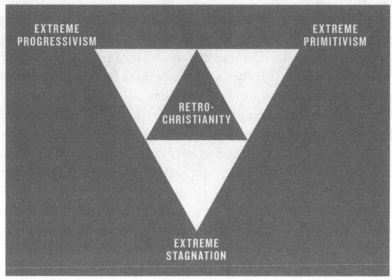

While acknowledging the value of historical perspective, confessional stability, and legitimate development, RetroChristianity seeks to avoid extreme progressivism, extreme primitivism, and extreme stagnation.

The Benjamin Button Syndrome (Extreme Primitivism)

The film *The Curious Case of Benjamin Button* (based on a short story by F. Scott Fitzgerald) tells an intriguing story of a man born with all the signs of extreme old age—wrinkles, arthritis, frailness, senility. Over the course of his life, Benjamin grows progressively *younger*, passing through the normal stages of human growth *in reverse*. From old age, to midlife, to young adulthood, to teenage years, to childhood—he eventually regresses into infancy, ending his life where the rest of us begin it.

This fantastic tale illustrates the condition of extreme primitivism common among many evangelicals, which I call "the Benjamin Button Syndrome." This refers to Christians who would like nothing more than to return to a past form of Christianity, turning back the clock of development that has occurred over the previous centuries. Like a writer who is utterly dissatisfied with the path her novel has taken might revert to a previous version of the story and take it in another direction, many Christians want to undo the course of Christian history, returning to a better past.

Bryan Singer's film, *Superman Returns*, illustrates this well. When Singer sought to jump-start the burned-out Superman series for the twenty-first century, he surveyed the previous four Superman films starring Christopher Reeve and, like most fans, decided the low-budget *Superman III* and *IV* simply didn't measure up to the first two films. What did he do about it? Singer proceeded as if parts three and four had never been made! In other words, *Superman Returns* was produced as the *Superman III* that should have been.

Let me state this unequivocally: *RetroChristianity is not in favor of literally returning to past forms of Christianity.* To avoid misunderstanding, let me put this another way. Evangelicals cannot embrace any ancient-future, primitivistic, or reactionary approaches to current Christian life and ministry that attempt to "go back" to an earlier era of Christian history as if the previous centuries hadn't happened. Such an approach to Christianity is no more reasonable than trying to restore the feudal system, or bring back horse and buggy, or erase the medical breakthroughs over the last hundred years.

Even if "going back" were something we actually desired to do, without a time machine and a mechanism to erase our memories, it's simply impossible. In fact, it's even impossible for twenty-first century evangelicals to adopt the New Testament patterns of church and ministry. Why? Because our current historical, cultural, and theological context is *radically different* from that of the first century. We don't have hand-selected apostles who were eye witnesses to the resurrection and ascension and who had absolute authority in the churches. That was the situation in the first century; it is not the situation today. Also, today we have a complete Old and New Testament canon, which the first-century church didn't have. The New Testament church described in the book of Acts is an era inaccessible to us. We can read about it and learn from it, but we cannot return to it. We must, of course, base our theology and ministry upon biblical *principles*, but we cannot always adopt New Testament *patterns*.

Nor should we favor an attempted return to the Patristic period— that era of the church that culminated in a clearly defined orthodox doctrine of the Trinity, christology, sin, grace, a complete biblical canon, and an organized Christian identity in the world. Who would want to trade the mature theology hammered out in that era for an approach that tries to reinvent orthodoxy from scratch? Neither do we want to exchange our complete collection of Holy Scripture for a confusing open canon of generic early Christian writings. In other words, we want to *build upon* the advances made in the Patristic period, not demolish them.

We definitely don't want to return to medieval Christendom. We should have no desire to revive the vast gulf between the church hierarchy and laypeople that alienated Christians from a mature faith and an informed piety. We don't want to re-adopt a confusing sacramental system, a complex liturgical calendar, and a worldview that places each of us in a teetering uncertainty between heaven and hell. And none of us relish the idea of returning to a relationship between church and state that sanctioned the execution of heretics and the slaughter of infidels under the banner of the cross. (Few of us would last long under that system!) Instead, we desire to *learn from* the excesses of the medieval period, not relive them.

Similarly, we shouldn't yearn for a return to the Protestant era—the age of the Reformers like Zwingli, Luther, and Calvin. Too often we forget that the major Reformers defined themselves, their theology, and their practice in direct contrast to medieval Roman Catholic errors. In so doing, they often "pendulum swung" by exaggerating some aspects of the Christian faith to the detriment of others. The medieval church exalted the altar and downplayed the pulpit; Protestants swung to the opposite extreme, downplaying the spiritual blessings associated with the Lord's Supper. Roman Catholics emphasized tradition at the expense of Scripture; Protestants threw off the shackles of tradition, leaving the Bible open to almost *any* interpretation. The pope and his bishops emphasized their essential role in salvation at the expense of personal faith and conversion; Protestants downplayed the physical church and its leadership, emphasizing an individualistic and private approach to salvation and the Christian life. In other words, we should strive to *reverse* the overreaction of the Reformation, retrieving a balanced approach to faith and life.

Finally, none of us should seek a way to go back to the "good ol' days" of fundamentalist evangelicalism. We should never desire to retreat from culture. I'm uninterested in whipping large crowds into a frenzy to manipulate them with psychological tricks or manmade methods of "revival." We should be unimpressed by a movement that wants to fight about every detail of doctrine until it alienates even orthodox allies. In other words, we should strive to *get over* the militant and isolationist mentalities of early evangelicalism, focusing on advancing the kingdom in the twenty-first century.

In sum, RetroChristianity's approach to reclaiming the forgotten faith is not the same as "returning to the past faith." Rather, RetroChristianity advocates a conscious continuity with the past that incorporates the positive contributions of all eras—the Patristic, medieval, Protestant, and evangelical phases of the church, all in light of the biblical revelation. However, we must always strive to avoid the negative elements that also came from these periods.

I mentioned Singer's *Superman Returns* as a Hollywood example of the Benjamin Button Syndrome. Let me give a contrasting Hollywood example that illustrates RetroChristianity's approach to the past. When the brilliant filmmaker J. J. Abrams wanted to relaunch the Star Trek film series, he appeared to have two options. He could have produced a *remake*, starting the franchise afresh with new actors, as Christopher Nolan did with *Batman Begins*. Or he could have produced another *sequel*, somehow digging up the retired cast of the classic Star Trek series or building upon one of its many spin-offs (*Next Generation, Deep Space Nine, Voyager, Enterprise*). Instead, Abrams did something remarkable. He created a true sequel that simultaneously relaunched the series with a new cast playing the original characters. Through extreme cleverness (as well as a heavy dependence on intrusive time travel and a resulting alternate history), Abrams both honored the original story arc of all the television series and films while successfully reinventing the franchise for a new generation. That's the approach of RetroChristianity. It's not returning to the past, but retrieving the past for the present. It's not rewinding to a more favorable era, but reclaiming the forgotten faith for the future.

The Fuddy-Duddy Syndrome (Extreme Stagnation)

By using the word "fuddy-duddy," some might very well accuse me of being one. However, the fact that I need to define it means it's the perfect word for illustrating the second syndrome relating to evangelical responses to doctrinal development.

"Fuddy-duddy" is an almost obsolete term that refers to a person— usually a man past middle age—who has more or less plateaued in his cultural and social development. In other words, at some point in his life he froze in time. Perhaps through his thirties or forties he kept on top of the latest advances in technology, updated his wardrobe, and at least knew the names of the endless parade of pop culture icons. However, at some point this development froze. For the second forty years of his life, a fuddy-duddy continues to comb back his thinning hair, listen to the same cassette tapes over and over, wear three-piece suits to special occasions, have the newspaper delivered to his door, and type letters on an electric typewriter.

Now, there's nothing wrong with such a person. I'm sure one day we'll all be called "fuddy-duddies" by the younger generations. But the fact is that the fuddy-duddy loses his voice in an ever-changing, constantly evolving culture. In a world of e-mails, interoffice memos just don't cut it. In the business-casual office environment, coats and ties appear out of touch. In the information age of cable or Internet news networks, newspapers appear either quaint or wasteful. All of these earlier forms and norms were at one time cutting edge and commonplace. But to cling to them as the world passes us by is to peter out in the growth process.

In the realm of evangelicalism, the Fuddy-Duddy Syndrome relates to the problem of extreme stagnation. Those plagued by this paralyzing disease suffer from arrested development. Some rigid denominations or inflexible confessional traditions tend toward this extreme, but independent churches unable or unwilling to break from their past also fit the bill.

Sadly, Christians plagued by the Fuddy-Duddy Syndrome forget that *everything* unique to their tradition reflects doctrinal and practical developments that had occurred in the past until a previous generation of leaders decreed, "This far and no farther!" At some point in their doctrinal evolution, they put a stop to further growth and codified their doctrines and practices in an unchanging form. Generations later, the form persists, even though continued biblical, historical, theological, and practical reflection might have improved the tradition.

Let me illustrate the Fuddy-Duddy Syndrome first with an extreme example, then one that hits a little closer to home for some evangelicals. The extreme stagnation of the Amish suits our purposes well. At some point in the early nineteenth century the Old Order Mennonites decided that they would no longer keep up with the technological advances of the modern world. So, at the horse-and-buggy stage they disconnected themselves from progress, living to this day following the beliefs, values, customs, and technology of a bygone generation. This approach to life differs from the Benjamin Button Syndrome in that it doesn't seek to go backward. Rather, *it resists moving forward*.

The same is true of the fundamentalist, separationist, and isolationist churches we can still find here and there. Many have never improved upon a single doctrine or practice for fifty years. They sing the same hymns from a dusty, cracking hymnal. They follow the same week-to-week ritual of Sunday morning, Sunday evening, Wednesday night meetings, with the occasional week-long revival or missions conference breaking up the calendar. Suspicious of tweaks to any part of their comfortable style of being Christian, they condemn evangelicals that escape from that fundamentalist mindset.

Those beset with the Fuddy-Duddy Syndrome need to break up their fallow ground. They need to realize that the traditional music they love to sing was once cutting edge, contemporary, and, yes, controversial. They need to realize that some methods of preaching, teaching, and evangelizing that may have worked splendidly in bygone generations simply do not work in today's culture. And they need to learn that some of the minor doctrinal views they codified may have turned out to be untrue or incomplete in light of new discoveries or improved methods of research.

The Émile Coué Syndrome (Extreme Progressivism)

Most people today have never heard of the French psychologist Émile Coué. He lived from 1857 to 1926, and toward the end of his life he published a book that helped launch the modern "power of positive thinking" movement.[5] Coué's most famous quotation illustrates the disease of extreme progressivism rather well. As part of his program of optimistic autosuggestion, Coué followers were expected to tell themselves repeatedly, both morning and evening, "Every day, in every way, I'm getting better and better."[6]

By simply telling yourself that you were making progress, experiencing improvement, and growing incrementally, such growth and development was sure to take place. This represents an ambitious, overly optimistic (and extremely unrealistic) view of one's progress in the world. The truth is, a person can tell himself that everything's getting better and better, while his whole psyche is collapsing!

Evangelicals suffering from the Émile Coué Syndrome wholeheart-edly believe that every day, in every way, evangelicalism is getting better and better. They clamor for the latest church growth strategies. They drool over the newest outreach, evangelism, missionary, or assimilation methods. They're on the lookout for the "rising stars" of young and dynamic evangelical leaders. They try to emulate cutting-edge culture. Why? Because to keep fresh, stay alive, and continue to progress, *every-thing must change*! Constantly. Repeatedly. Endlessly. Thoroughly. After all, every day, in every way, we're getting better and better!

The problem is, evangelicals plagued by the Émile Coué Syndrome rarely think of the guidelines for change, the limits of growth, or the direction of legitimate development. They simply assume, without question, that a larger congregation and a bigger building is the natural next step in becoming better and better. They assume that if a book was written more than ten years ago, it's no longer relevant. They believe that almost everything in the Christian faith is subject to updating—even the essentials of orthodoxy themselves. Never will they actually stop to think through changes biblically, theologically, and historically. Instead, they run ideas through a pragmatically prejudiced biblical grid. The demands of *progress*—not the principles of orthodoxy—govern their interpretation and application of Scripture.

The Émile Coué Syndrome can be cured when evangelicals real-ize that *some things never change and never should*. They also need to discover that the world's standards of growth, development, success, and progress are not identical to Christ's standards of growth, develop-ment, success, and progress. And they must come to realize that not all changes are positive, even though they may for a season appear to produce stunning positive results. Some forms of "development" are simply deviation and destruction in the guise of progress.

Building, Growing, and Adapting: Biblical Images of Doctrinal Development

Given the inherent conservative nature of the Christian faith and the church's task of receiving, preserving, and passing on orthodoxy to the next generation (Jude 1:3; 2 Tim. 2:2), is it even possible for believers to discover previously unknown doctrines in the Scriptures? By "doctrine" I mean teachings of Scripture that warrant belief and obedience. We have already seen that the foundation of Christianity includes essential, unchanging, clear teachings that have required belief and obedience from the very beginning (the first canon of RetroOrthodoxy). We have also seen that different Christian traditions have different teachings that result in different beliefs and practices (the second canon of RetroOrthodoxy). Now we discuss the concept of teachings that warrant faith and obedience even though their discovery in Scripture came later as a result of study, discussion, scholarship, experience, reflection, and the Spirit's illuminating grace given to the church. So the question is, as the church studies the revelation of God in Scripture, can the Spirit lead it to additional insights that are in continuity with the central apostolic teaching but altogether new in content?

Scripture teaches that the answer to this question is *yes.*

However, first let me clarify what is *not* meant by the concept of doctrinal development. First, we don't mean *the good and necessary retrieval of forgotten doctrines.* It is entirely possible that doctrines previously taught in church history—even very early church history—can be forgotten by subsequent generations and later rediscovered. In fact, this is what occurred during the Protestant Reformation. Though the Reformers did contribute new insights to the Christian tradition with regard to the doctrines of Scripture, justification, and the church, most of the key insights of the Reformation came from a retrieval of forgotten doctrines and practices of the Patristic period.

Second, by doctrinal development we don't mean *the healthy and inevitable rearticulation of apostolic doctrine.* To "rearticulate" means to say the same thing with different words. The Bible itself teaches the same truths using a variety of terms and images, so we should expect that unchanging doctrines will be explained, expressed, or illustrated differently as the church enters new cultural and language contexts. Saying things with new language is not itself doctrinal development.

Third, by doctrinal development we don't mean *the impossible and devastating inspiration of new doctrine.* The ancient heresies of Gnosticism and Montanism—and their modern counterparts in cults and new religious movements—have erred by believing that new authoritative revelations or even Scriptures can be added to the apostolic faith. The canon of Scripture is closed, and the era of the apostles and prophets has come to an end. Any new insights into God's revelation will come through their discovery in the Scriptures themselves, not through added information gained from so-called prophets.

By the very nature of the Christian faith, the developments that come as a result of progressive illumination cannot be regarded as necessary for maintaining orthodoxy. By definition, previously unknown doctrines discovered through the study of Scripture cannot pass the test of the Vincentian canon—what has been believed everywhere, always, and by all. So, for example, neither covenant theology's theological covenants nor dispensationalism's distinct stages in God's program can ever be held as central to orthodox truth. Neither perspective was passed down from the apostles. Both represent the church's later reflection on Old and New Testament revelation studied as a complete inspired canon.

Doctrinal development refers to the positive, Spirit-led illumination of the meaning of Scripture throughout history, resulting in a deeper or clearer understanding of God's truth. This concept also includes the idea of *practical* development—coming to terms with how to best live out the Christian faith in changing cultural contexts. Thus, some practical developments that benefited the church in one era may cease to benefit the church in later times.

But on what biblical basis can evangelicals anticipate positive development of doctrinal understanding, articulation, and application? Let me share three New Testament images that clearly anticipate the idea of progress in doctrine and practice. These illustrations include building (1 Cor. 3:10–17), growing (Eph. 4:11–16), and adapting (1 Cor. 9:20–23).

Building

In 1 Corinthians 3:10–15, the apostle Paul refers to doctrinal development following his foundation-laying apostolic ministry.

> According to the grace of God given to me, like a skilled master builder I laid a foundation, and someone else is building upon it. Let each one take care how he builds upon it. For no one can lay a foundation other than that which is laid, which is Jesus Christ. Now if anyone builds on the foundation with gold, silver, precious stones, wood, hay, straw—each one's work will become manifest, for the Day will disclose it, because it will be revealed by fire, and the fire will test what sort of work each one has done. If the work that anyone has built on the foundation survives,

he will receive a reward. If anyone's work is burned up, he will suffer loss, though he himself will be saved, but only as through fire.

At first glance, the casual reader may not notice exactly what Paul is suggesting here. However, if we examine the text and its context closely, we realize that Paul likens the Corinthian church to a building project. He laid the unchangeable doctrinal foundation of the person and work of Jesus Christ (3:10–11). No other foundation can legitimately be laid; to do so would establish a separate building project, deviating from the orthodox faith.

Upon that apostolic foundation, others will be called to build. In Corinth, Apollos and other teachers had already contributed to the building up of the church. They were not themselves apostles but believers trained and ordained to contribute to the building up of the body of Christ. That development and growth would include both doctrinal and practical development—all in conformity with the original apostolic teaching concerning Christ. Historically, the early church continued to build upon the foundation of the apostles, resulting in the recognition and defense of the Old and New Testament canon, the establishment of a stable system of church leadership and succession, and the enduring confessional language universally adopted by orthodox churches.

However, Paul acknowledges the possibility that some teachers who would come after him would fail to contribute to the stable Christian tradition with quality, enduring materials—gold, silver, and precious stones (3:12). Instead, they would use cheap, temporary building materials—wood, hay, and straw (3:12). Paul suggests, then, that when a purifying fire comes, only those quality additions to the building would survive the purging flames. Most readers take this as referring exclusively to the judgment seat of Christ. This may be true in the ultimate sense, yet throughout church history God has used periods of trial and challenges in order to purge the church. In fact, Peter himself notes that "it is time for judgment to begin at the household of God" (1 Pet. 4:17). Likewise, Jesus warns local churches in Revelation 2–3 of the real danger of judgment meted out to individual believers, churches, and traditions that fail to measure up to his standards of doctrine and practice, resulting either positively in purging and purifying or negatively in a complete removal of their "lampstands" from their original places of prominence (Rev. 2:5). Thus, just as individual believers can experience times of purging in their Christian lives, local churches, regional churches, and even the whole global church should expect to experience times of purifying fire sent to purge and to cleanse.

We see purifying challenges like this occurring during times of persecution and times of influence by false teachers. Doctrinal debates and other events like the Great Schism of 1054, the Protestant Reformation in the sixteenth century, and the Modernist-Fundamentalist crisis in the twentieth century were also purifying for the church. These periods of purging serve to reveal the quality of the work that had been wrought on the original foundation and historical framework of the church. As church history unfolds, the purging serves to weed out worthless contributions to the Christian tradition while purifying and preserving quality work. St. Augustine in the fifth century puts it well:

> For while the hot restlessness of heretics stirs questions about many articles of the catholic faith, the necessity of defending them forces us both to investigate them more accurately, to understand them more clearly, and to proclaim them more earnestly; and the question mooted by an adversary becomes the occasion of instruction.[7]

A person's quality work that positively and permanently contributes to the doctrine and practice of the church would be preserved and passed forward. On the other hand, poor quality work would be burned up and demonstrated to be useless. The quality work remains a valuable part of the authentic Christian tradition and the basis of further development.

Note that in 1 Corinthians 3 Paul foresees both positive development and negative deviation in the building of the church. We must never forget this point. Not all construction on the foundation is valuable and enduring. Much of it is worthless, or at least *temporary*. Whatever remains from the test will be counted worthy to be preserved and passed on to the next generation of workers. However, whatever is burned away will come to nothing, contributing only a bad example to the enduring tradition.

One final note of warning. Those who believe the Spirit speaks equally authoritatively through all of the subsequent pastors, teachers, bishops, and theologians of the church since the apostles stand on shaky ground. The Bible extends no such promise to *all* leaders that they will be right in everything. Simply put, time will tell whether a person's contribution to doctrine and practice in the church will be worthy of preservation . . . or destruction.

Paul's image of *building* in 1 Corinthians 3 cures all three extreme reactions against the concept of doctrinal development described earlier. Those who suffer from the Benjamin Button Syndrome (extreme primitivism) desire to wipe the foundation clean, discarding even the gold, silver, and precious stones that contribute positively and permanently to the Christian faith. Victims of the Fuddy-Duddy Syndrome (extreme stagnation) abandon the building project and resist future purification; they benefit from *some* of the positive growth, but dwell in a structure that is not only half-finished but also needs repairs and updates. Finally, the Émile Coué Syndrome (extreme progressivism) blinds believers into thinking that every contribution to the building is positive, and because low-quality materials can be incorporated *cheaply and quickly*, these worthless materials tend to pile up, obscuring even the glory of the priceless treasures of the church's rich history.[8]

Growing

In Ephesians 4:11–16, Paul illustrates the anticipated increase of doctrinal stability with the image of physical growth.

> And he gave the apostles, the prophets, the evangelists, the shepherds and teachers, to equip the saints for the work of ministry, for building up the body of Christ, until we all attain to the unity of the faith and of the knowledge of the Son of God, to mature manhood, to the measure of the stature of the fullness of Christ, so that we may no longer be children, tossed to and fro by the waves and carried about by every wind of doctrine, by human cunning, by craftiness in deceitful schemes. Rather, speaking the truth in love, we are to grow up in every way into him who is the head, into Christ, from whom the whole body, joined and held together by every joint with which it is equipped, when each part is working properly, makes the body grow so that it builds itself up in love.

In this context Paul describes a variety of leaders given as gifts to the church (in this context, the whole body of Christ worldwide). This passage relates to our understanding of Spirit-led doctrinal development. By the Holy Spirit working through gifted leaders, the church should experience growth in knowledge, stability, and unity, no longer tossed to and fro by strange doctrine. The infant church, under the original ministry of the apostles and prophets, grew more and more through the work of their successors—evangelists, shepherds (pastors), and teachers. The latter ministries of pastors and teachers extend beyond the apostolic period, through the Patristic, medieval, Protestant, and modern eras, indicating that the growth of the body of Christ toward maturity occurs throughout church history.

If we put Paul's image of growing in Ephesians 4 alongside his image of building in 1 Corinthians 3, we'll recognize the potential for both good pastors and teachers contributing quality instruction and bad pastors and teachers contributing poor instruction.[9] As the church grew through the centuries, it passed through several stages toward maturity. In matters related directly to orthodoxy (the center, the story, and the markers), the end of the Patristic period around AD 500 represents a milestone of maturity. However, from a Protestant perspective, though Christianity achieved maturity in many core doctrines, it still had several areas that required development, and in some places the medieval period led to degeneration and decay in certain areas that had reached a level of maturity.[10] Reformation was necessary to rejuvenate and revive the ailing church and contribute to its further maturity.

In Paul's growing body analogy, the image is organic rather than mechanical. So we should be able to perceive real development, not just historically contextualized developments that work for a season and must be modified later. This development heads toward greater doctrinal and practical maturity and unity that affect the entire church. However, the possibility always remains that the growth experienced in previous generations may be neglected, forgotten, or reversed if the mature church fails to pass on its acquired wisdom to the next generation. If one generation backslides in this way, the answer is not to return to the church's youth and start the process all over again, but to look back and reclaim the forgotten faith for the future.

This brings up the concept of "life cycles" in both individual congregations and the church universal. Many experts on church ministry point out that churches go through predictable life cycles: birth, infancy, childhood, adolescence, adulthood, maturity, empty nest, retirement, old age, and death.[11] During the declining years of a church, the Spirit of God must bring revival and renewal to restore vitality to the church. Many leaders abandon churches at this stage, finding it easier to start a new church plant and work toward maturity than to renew an existing church. However, church renewal can draw on the positive contributions of a church's past and build toward a new and exciting future. What can be said about the local church's life cycle and need for periodic renewal can also be said of the universal church.

Paul's image of *growing* in Ephesians 4 cures all three extreme reactions against the concept of doctrinal development. The Benjamin Button Syndrome (extreme primitivism) is cured by the fact that positive growth *toward maturity*—not reaction *toward infancy*—is the Spirit-led trajectory for churches and the body of Christ. The Fuddy-Duddy Syndrome (extreme stagnation) is remedied when churches and denominations realize that God not only led their sacred tradition to its current form, but that the same God *continues* to lead the church in doctrinal and practical development. Finally, the Émile Coué Syndrome (extreme progressivism) can be treated when we're reminded that growth of the body requires *continuity* with its past, not a *disconnection* from it. The Émile Coué Syndrome often takes theological growth to an unbalanced extreme, with an overly optimistic view of almost all official, dogmatic, ecclesiastical developments as Spirit-led and therefore binding. Among Roman Catholic, Eastern Orthodox, and some Anglican thinkers, the Christian church continually grew organically in ways consistent with its original spirit, message, and momentum. However, the tendency is to accept all developments as legitimate because of a theological presupposition that the Spirit of God always prevents deviations. Adherents often fail to take seriously the history of the church as always a mixture of legitimate developments (gold, silver, precious stones) and illegitimate developments (wood, hay, straw).[12]

Adapting

We've talked about *building* on a sure apostolic foundation and *growing* toward maturity in faith and practice. Yet Paul also allows for *temporary* and *contextual* development and change by adapting his ministry methods to his present circumstances. Paul describes this approach of adapting ourselves to various ministry contexts in 1 Corinthians 9:20–22.

> To the Jews I became as a Jew, in order to win Jews. To those under the law I became as one under the law (though not being myself under the

law) that I might win those under the law. To those outside the law I became as one outside the law (not being outside the law of God but under the law of Christ) that I might win those outside the law. To the weak I became weak, that I might win the weak. I have become all things to all people, that by all means I might save some.

Paul introduces the possibility of developments that are less doctrinal and more practical. These developments include methods of ministry and forms of communication that are necessary and appropriate for a given period of time, but that are defined by a particular geographical and historical ministry context. They include traditions that develop and endure for a season but are not to be confused with the unchanging foundation or legitimate growth of the faith.

To use Paul's analogy of building, we might liken the traditions developed through adapting as the décor, furniture, or fixtures of the structure—features that often need updating and remodeling as fashions and needs change. In relation to Paul's illustration of the growing body of Christ, we might liken the adaptations to articles of clothing, hairstyle, jewelry, or even technology that must be periodically changed or updated.

Obviously, the many attempts at adapting our ministries to various cultural, geographical, and historical contexts will lead to diverse forms of worship, leadership style, preaching, evangelism, discipleship, education, and communication. These diverse developments must never be allowed to damage the building or alter the body. Wisdom and discernment are crucial. In Paul's case, he adopted neutral Jewish customs when he ministered in Jewish contexts in order to avoid becoming a stumbling block for potential Jewish converts (Acts 16:1–3; 18:18; 21:20–26; 1 Cor. 9:20). Similarly, when his ministry focused on the Gentiles, he saw no need to keep the Law, from which he had been liberated (Gal. 2:11–21; 1 Cor. 9:21). Throughout history, as the church sought to minister to Romans, Armenians, Germans, Salvadorans, Chinese, or Americans, the outer expressions of the faith had to be adapted to new peoples, languages, and cultures.

Like the building and growing images, the adapting principle also addresses some of the extreme reactions against doctrinal development. Those afflicted by the Benjamin Button Syndrome (extreme primitivism) need to be encouraged that old, forgotten ways of doing things can *legitimately* be revived in present contexts without having to return to the past. That is, we need to remember that just as wide ties or bell-bottom jeans might come back into fashion, certain bygone approaches to ministry might find new life in our changing cultural contexts, countering extreme primitivism with a balanced appreciation for the past. Churches suffering from the Fuddy-Duddy Syndrome (extreme stagnation) must be reminded that although certain forms they hold dear once had a relevant place in the historical context in which they were formed, those forms may no longer be relevant in today's context. For example, highly liturgical worship fit quite nicely in the Greco-Roman world, in which incense, altars, images, candles, and bells were part of what it meant to *worship*. Today they may not communicate the same things they did in their original contexts. On the other hand, these forms may still serve a function for certain segments of the population or for certain cultures. Finally, victims of the Émile Coué Syndrome (extreme progressivism) need to rethink *how* and *how quickly* they apply changes to their methods of ministry and forms of worship. Change for change's sake is ridiculous. Paul became a Jew to the Jews and a Greek to the Greeks. He didn't say, "I've been acting like a Jew long enough; it's time for something completely different." Paul was motivated by ministry, not by change. Christians need to slow down to pray and think through change biblically, theologically, and historically, not just practically and experientially.

Conclusion: Some Things Grow Clear

Together the three images of *building, growing,* and *adapting* help us to think wisely about our approach to "tradition," realizing that there are three kinds of possible tradition. *Good tradition* refers to the unchanging truths of the Christian faith and the positive and enduring developments of the faith that have grown throughout history as a result of Spirit-led development through trial and error. *Bad tradition* includes the negative incursions of errors, distortions of truth, and illegitimate developments of doctrine or practice that need to be purged through God's purifying fires. *Neutral tradition* includes those helpful, but not essential, developments in ministry methods that come and go as the church seeks to adapt its means of communication to changing cultural contexts.

In the preceding three chapters we have set forth the three canons of RetroOrthodoxy:

1. Some things never change and never should.
2. Some things have never been the same and never will be.
3. Some things grow clear through trial and error.

With these three principles as our guide, we now can tackle two of the most vital areas affecting evangelicalism today: the church and the Christian life.

Part 3

RetroClesiology: Beyond the Preference-Driven Church

And I tell you, you are Peter, and on this rock I will build my church, and the gates of hell shall not prevail against it. —Matthew 16:18

Do you not know that you are God's temple and that God's Spirit dwells in you? If anyone destroys God's temple, God will destroy him. For God's temple is holy, and you are that temple. —1 Corinthians 3:16–17

We're steeped in a culture where preferences rule. As a result, many evangelicals treat church like malleable clay to be molded and shaped into whatever form *they* think it should take. Our expectations for what a church *is* and what a church *does* too often reflect our personal preferences. We may prefer contemporary music or traditional hymns, dynamic youth activities or deep discipleship, personable pastors or powerful preachers, state-of-the-art facilities or stunning sanctuaries. But do preference-driven churches reflect the biblical and historical marks and works of a church?

The solution to a preference-driven church mentality isn't to compose a new "me-centered" wish list, but to identify and adopt the classic marks and works for an authentic and healthy church. Then we'll be equipped to focus on our church's central strengths and address inevitable weaknesses, establishing reliable criteria for recovering a lost identity. But first we need to remind ourselves of the fundamental marks and works of the church. And to do this, we need to have a biblical and historical perspective.

For too long evangelicals have been trying to update the church. Today they have tamed it by removing its offensive countercultural elements and replacing them with comfortable cultural equivalents. The result is not an improvement to the church, but a weakening of the it. In this third part of our exploration of RetroChristianity, I first want to dispel four common myths about the church and describe four classic marks of the historical body of Christ (chap. 7). Then we explore in some detail the essential marks (chap. 8) and works (chap. 9) of a true local church from a biblical and historical perspective. By the time we're finished, we will not only appreciate our place in the universal "catholic" church, but also value the components of an authentic local church—including its nature, purpose, leadership, organization, ministries, and worship.

Seven

Church Classic

Four Common Myths and Four Classic Marks

W hen people encounter new things, their first tendency is to fit them into existing categories. If truth be told, most of us shy away from strange and unusual things that don't fit our expectations. It reminds me of a Northerner who ate his first tamale by peeling down the husk and eating it like a banana. I saw another try to actually eat the corn husk with a knife and fork! If we don't know better, we'll draw wrong conclusions about the true nature of things based on personal experiences or cultural norms.

The Bible portrays the church as something strange and unusual. When the Spirit gave life to the church on Pentecost (Acts 2), it bore little resemblance to what had come before it. In Jeremiah 31:32, God described the future new covenant in terms of what it was *not* going to be like; it was *"not* like the covenant that I made with their fathers on the day when I took them by the hand to bring them out of the land of Egypt." And in Ephesians 2:15, Paul tells us that from the two distinct groups of the Old Testament age—Jews and Gentiles—God created the church as "one *new* man." God didn't just *reboot an old program*; he *revealed a new people*.

At the same time, the church was meant to be different from the rest of the world. Christ said of his disciples, "The world has hated them because they are not of the world, just as I am not of the world" (John 17:14). The church shouldn't mimic the patterns of this world system, but should conform to God's unique design. This truth has direct implications for the lives of believers. Paul tells us in Romans 12:1–2, "I appeal to you therefore, brothers, by the mercies of God, to present your bodies as a living sacrifice, holy and acceptable to God, which is your spiritual worship. Do not be conformed to this world, but be transformed by the renewal of your mind, that by testing you may discern what is the will of God, what is good and acceptable and perfect." When I look around, I see that many Christians approach the local church in ways that conform more to the patterns of the world than to the pattern of God's Word.

We saw in the previous chapter that Christians are meant to *adapt* their message and methods to cultural forms without betraying orthodox beliefs and practices. But today an unclear understanding of the church's central marks and works has led to a gradual peeling away of the very core of church identity. Ill-informed pastors, entrepreneurial church planters, misguided church growth experts, and unlearned laypeople have too quickly abandoned classic church doctrines and practices that had either been part of the unchanging core of Christianity or had grown clear, through the fires of trial and error.

The result? Like mad scientists piecing together a monster from countless incompatible pieces without a clear pattern or guiding principles, too many Christians today have re-created the church after their *own* imaginations, according to their own likes and dislikes. Clustered around this mutant creature falsely called "church," proponents propagate four common myths that help keep the beast alive—four untruths that have become so accepted by many evangelicals that they believe them without question. But the time has come to refute the myths and slay the monster, replacing it with a corporate body reflecting marks and works of authenticity and created according to *God's* image for the church.

Four Common Myths Concerning the Church

Over the last several decades, too many evangelicals have conformed the church to the patterns of this world, transforming it from something miraculous and countercultural into something mundane and culturally comfortable.¹ In keeping with this tendency, several myths have developed regarding the church. As these myths become more deeply ingrained in our evangelical church culture, they weaken the church. It's important that we not only become aware of these myths, but that we challenge and overcome them.

Myth 1: The Church Is Merely a Human Organization

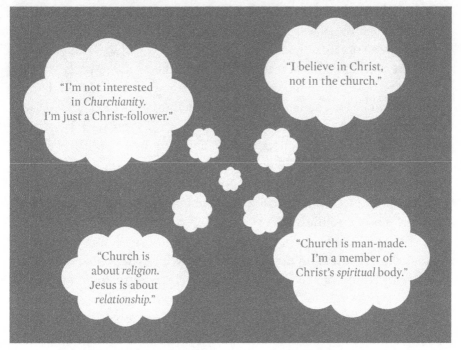

Though comprised of humans, the church itself is not *merely* a human organization. Jesus Christ is the head of the church, and the church is mystically his spiritual and physical body on earth (Eph. 1:22–23; 5:23; Col. 1:18). So intimate is this association of Christ and the church that to persecute the church is to persecute Christ himself (Acts 9:4). The church's relationship with Christ is so close that to be "in him" means that we are reckoned as raised up with him and enthroned with him in the heavenly places (Eph. 2:6).

A Christ-centered doctrine of the church means that just as Christ is simultaneously human and divine, earthly and heavenly, physical and spiritual, so also the church—his body—is both human and divine, earthly and heavenly, physical and spiritual. While we may distinguish these spiritual and physical aspects of the church, we must never separate them. Too often evangelicals have divorced the spiritual, heavenly, invisible, and eternal church from its physical, earthly, visible, historical manifestation. Having separated these into two completely different categories, they have downplayed the physical and emphasized the spiritual.[2] The result has been to treat local, visible churches as merely human organizations rather than as unique conduits through which God works his heavenly, spiritual purposes in history. Such dichotomizing has allowed Christians to treat their churches as they treat other human organizations—like a political party, a club, or a business.

In the world's political realm, if we don't like what our party stands for or if we lose confidence in its candidates, we just run against them, vote them out, or change the platform. If things get too bad, we can join another party or start our own. But in 1 Corinthians 3:3–4, Paul reprimands the church for taking sides and forming parties: "For while there is jealousy and strife among you, are you not of the flesh and behaving only in a human way? For when one says, 'I follow Paul,' and another, 'I follow Apollos,' are you not being merely human?" The church is not a political party.

Neither should we treat the church like a club, with members who direct the organization according to the will of the majority. These Latin words are engraved in the Minnesota state capitol building: *VOX POPULI, VOX DEI*—"The Voice of the People Is the Voice of God." Many Christians act like the church should be run by majority rule. However, after Israel demanded a king "like all the nations" to rule over them (1 Sam. 8:20), God told his prophet Samuel, "Obey their voice and make them a king" (8:22). By listening to the voice of the people, Israel ended up with just what they asked for: a king like the nations' rather than a king of God's own choosing, a king "after his own heart" (1 Sam. 13:14). In the case of King Saul, the voice of the people was *not* the voice of God. The church is not a club ruled by its members.

Finally, in contrast to what many so-called church growth experts and evangelical entrepreneurs advocate, the church is not a business, in which the bottom line dictates its decisions, investments are measured by their returns, and everything boils down to cost-benefit, risk management, and revenue. While we are all incorporated into the body of Christ, the body of Christ is not a corporation. First

Corinthians 12:13–14 says, "For in one Spirit we were all baptized into one body—Jews or Greeks, slaves or free—and all were made to drink of one Spirit. For the body does not consist of one member but of many." The church is not a business.

If the church is not merely a human organization like a political party, a club, or a business, what is it? Simply put, *the church is a physical-spiritual organism.* Certainly, there is something supernatural about the church. It's not merely a human organization. It's made up of people who have otherwise nothing in common. It's not united by political constitutions, common interests, or corporate bylaws. It's united by the Spirit of God around the person and work of Jesus Christ pursuing a common mission in the world.

Do you treat your local church like a mere human organization? Do you look for the complaint department every time something doesn't go your way? Do you start taking sides when you see a fight brewing? Do you pull out your capital when it appears that your investment might not pay off like you wanted? Do you vote with your feet when the leadership moves in a direction you don't understand? Or, have you completely dismissed the church as a merely man-made institution, opting for a totally spiritual, other-worldly approach to Christianity?

That may be how we behave in political parties, clubs, or businesses, but that's not how we should behave in the church. The church is *not* merely a human organization, but the spiritual-physical body of Christ.

Myth 2: The Church Is a Supermarket of Spiritual Groceries

In the world of supermarkets, we like options, variety, and freedom to choose. Few of us have heartfelt commitments to a particular grocery store. We may shop at one until the prices get too high, jump to another until the workers get too rude, then flee to a new one where the prices are better and the people are nicer. That may be how we make our shopping decisions, but is this attitude right for the church? Sadly, we often treat the church as if it were just one of many supermarkets that provide us with spiritual groceries. Consequently, we're living in a Christian culture that regards church shopping, hopping, and dropping as normal.

The problem of church shopping. Our supermarket mentality and the plethora of differing churches make our modern situation both unique and dangerous. We never seem to find just the right church,

and this dissatisfaction can lead to a never-ending church shopping spree. I once knew a seminary student who, after six months of living in Dallas, still hadn't settled down at a local church. Each Sunday he would try out a different church, then move on to another the following Sunday. Eventually he began following a well-known Christian preacher who didn't have a church at the time but guest-preached at a different church each Sunday. So, like a groupie following a rock band, this wandering sheep followed that celebrity preacher from church to church. This is an example of an indefinite church shopping spree turned into an extreme case of "church hopping."

The problem of church hopping. We believers sometimes stick around one church until something goes awry or until we just don't feel like we fit anymore. Then we hop to the next church, spend some time, get involved, and again prance off when things don't *feel* right.

I once knew a man of retirement age who had at least four church memberships at the same time! He started out at a Baptist church, which began having trouble when their life-long pastor retired. He moved to a small independent Bible church, which began to experience growth pains when the congregation grew too big and a decision had to be made to move to a new building. He then switched to a different Bible church closer to home, where he became a member and attended actively for about a year. Then, at the invitation of his son, he began attending a very small start-up church with a contemporary service, where he decided to stay for a while. Four memberships, no commitments. Unfortunately, that seems like the evangelical way.

The problem of church dropping. Church dropping disturbs me the most. This is the practice of not simply leaving a church for another, but quitting church altogether, staying home Sunday mornings to watch preachers on TV or to listen to worship services by radio or podcast. This believer tries to live the Christian life outside a living local, physical church community. We see this trend in the so-called "virtual church," where phony relationships are forged in simulated online communities without real, physical, body and soul commitment.[3]

This is not the New Testament picture of the Christian life. Whenever possible after baptizing new believers, the disciples incorporated them into the life of the local church. They didn't leave new believers alone in the world to fend for themselves without teaching and guidance (Acts 2:41–44). We would be alarmed if people decided to starve to death rather than visit another grocery store. The same should be true about those who drop out of the local church and attempt to "go it alone" with their spiritual lives completely isolated from others.

Our relationship to a local church is like our relationship to a family. Like a marriage, it's a covenantal relationship designed for the purpose of building each other up and exhorting each other to love and good works (Eph. 4:10–13; 1 Corinthians 12–14; Heb. 10:23–25). If we look at our pathetic commitments to the local church through the lens of covenant commitment, the picture isn't pretty. The church shopper is like the reckless romantic who wanders from woman to woman, never finding the ideal mate because his standard is unrealistic perfection. The church hopper is like the unfaithful spouse who, having become bored with his bride or fed up with his family, abandons his home and joins a new one. The church dropper is the absentee parent or the deadbeat dad who drops out of sight and relevance, leaving his responsibilities to others.

Are you treating the local church like a supermarket? Have you been influenced so much by our consumer culture that you've made church shopping, church hopping, and church dropping normal habits? Because these attitudes and actions are so common among Christians today, you may have never paused to consider whether such an approach is healthy, wise, or even right.

The solution? Start treating the local church less like a shopping mall and more like a family, less like a convenience store and more like a covenant community. The church is *not* a supermarket of spiritual groceries, but a family with covenant commitments.

Myth 3: The Church Is Just a Gathering of a Few Believers

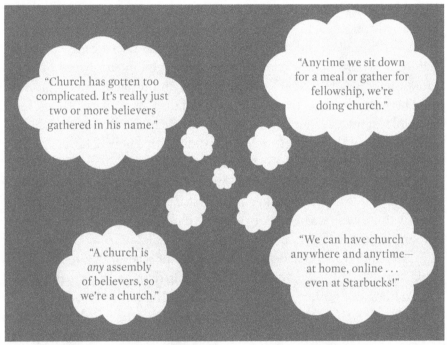

Several years ago when some of my friends and I prayed over our food at a fast-food joint, two scraggly men approached from across the restaurant and introduced themselves as a church. They explained that after visiting all the churches in the area they decided that none of them was preaching the true gospel, so those two men got together and decided, "We'll be our own church." I'll never forget that encounter. There they stood, like the Lone Ranger and Tonto, grinning triumphantly in the bright fluorescent light, obviously proud of their do-it-yourself church. Sadly, those men were to Christianity what witch doctors are to medicine. Whatever they were, they were *not* a church.

Today some Christians have dropped out of established churches in favor of "home churches" or "family churches." While the concept of a church meeting in a home has biblical and historical precedence (Rom. 16:5; 1 Cor. 16:19), many times an organization that calls itself a "house church" today is not a church at all, but just a bunch of disgruntled believers who couldn't (or wouldn't) make it work in a real established community of Christians.[4] But groups of Christians must have certain biblical marks and works to be regarded as authentic local churches.

Let's be clear. A Bible study is not a church. It's a Bible study. Getting together in the home for prayer is not a church. It's a prayer meeting. A herd of Christians with a guitar and tambourine is not a church. It's a sing-along. A man or woman opening the Bible and preaching at a willing crowd is not a church. It's an exercise of free speech. A gathering of saints for eating and gossiping (often misconstrued as "fellowship") is not a church. It's a party. The church is not just any gathering of a few believers.

Nevertheless, people often invoke Matthew 18:20 to support the idea that informal gatherings of a few saintly lambs count as a church: "For where two or three are gathered in my name, there am I among them." But Jesus didn't say, "Where two or three have gathered, there is the church." From a biblical, historical, and theological perspective, an authentic church must consist of certain marks and works. Though pastors and theologians have categorized and listed the marks and works of authentic local churches in a variety of ways throughout history, they have generally been in agreement on what the Bible says about what constitutes a true church.[5]

The essential marks of a local church include:

1. **Orthodoxy:** the proclamation of the central truths of the Christian faith regarding God, the person and work of Christ, and salvation
2. **Order:** the positions of biblically qualified and properly appointed leaders
3. **Ordinances:** the practice of baptism as the rite of initiation into the covenant community, and the Lord's Supper as the rite of sustained fellowship.

Besides these three marks, three essential works of a church include:

1. **Evangelism:** gathering others to God by the gospel of salvation by grace through faith in Jesus Christ
2. **Edification:** growing believers toward maturity in Christ through teaching and discipline in genuine community
3. **Exaltation:** glorifying God through adoration and service.[6]

Any gathering that claims to be a church must have these biblical-historical marks and works. If any of these are intentionally missing for a prolonged period, that organization is not a legitimate local church in the biblical and historical sense. These marks and works not only place a church firmly on the foundation of the New Testament, but they also connect every true local church historically to the first church of the apostles. All true churches are united in glorifying God through building out and building up the body of Christ worldwide. True local churches know they are part of something bigger than themselves.

The Lone Ranger and Tonto Christians I met at that restaurant years ago were *not* a church. They had neither the marks nor the works of a church. They did not have the theological and historical depth, nor did they have the practical breadth of a true church. But sometimes we evangelicals can fall into the same kind of thinking. We can sometimes go to Sunday school class and think we did church. Or we can stay at home, do family devotions, pray, and sing songs and think we did church. Or we can just listen to a preacher on the radio and think we did church. Those may all be good things, contributing to our biblical knowledge and spiritual growth, but they are *not* a church.

The church is *not* just a gathering of a few believers, but a gathering of believers bearing necessary marks and works.

Myth 4: The Church Is Optional

Like me, you've probably heard the words "church is optional" said about (or by) a person who has confessed Christ but who has dropped out of the church scene. Individual stories vary. Some people were beat up by an abusive church. Others were forced into church by their parents and finally got out from under their thumb when they left home. Some slid into a sinful lifestyle, and church got too convicting. I don't know many Christians who would neglect local church involvement to such an extreme, but most people I know place a much lower value on the local church than the Bible does.

In the earliest church, believers met together at least every Sunday, the first day of the week (Acts 20:7; 1 Cor. 16:2). Many met more often than that (Acts 2:46). For Christians who were pursuing spiritual health and growth, local church involvement was not an option. Hebrews 10:24–25 says, "And let us consider how to stir up one another to love and good works, not neglecting to meet together, as is the habit of some, but encouraging one another." No Scripture is clearer on the necessity of sticking close to the church as an essential element in sanctification, the spiritual growth of believers.

Why do many Christians place their local churches far down on their list of priorities? Part of the problem is our mystical, individualistic view of the spiritual life. Many of us have been misled into thinking that our spiritual health depends *entirely* on a direct personal relationship with God—that the key to spiritual growth is a *private* quiet time that somehow summons the Holy Spirit and flushes away our sins. While I don't reject the importance of personal spiritual disciplines, they are only *part* of God's plan for spiritual health and growth. The truth is that God intends Christians to grow together as a community.[7]

For Christians seeking spiritual growth, the church is not optional. The Holy Spirit baptized each of us into the body of Christ so that all members could minister to each other, not so we could later amputate ourselves from the body and fight our spiritual battles on our own. The award-winning television series *Lost* chronicled the adventures of airplane survivors forced to live together on a bizarre island reminiscent of the *Twilight Zone*. In one episode a main character, Jack Sheppard, broke up a brawl and iterated a truth that became a major theme of the series: "If we can't live together, we're going to die alone." The same theme is true of Christians today. If we can't learn to grow together, we will wither alone.

To grow in Christ, believers *need* each other. In fact, when the apostles spoke of growing in Christ, they almost always referred to Christians growing *together* as a community.[8] Without denying a personal relationship with Christ, Scripture clearly emphasizes corporate spiritual growth. In fact, God gave us our individual spiritual gifts for the growth of the community: "To each is given the manifestation of the Spirit for the common good" (1 Cor. 12:7). As radical as this may

✳———— THE FOUR MYTHS DISPELLED ————✳	
MYTH ✳	TRUTH
The church is merely a human organization.	The church is the spiritual-physical body of Christ.
The church is a supermarket of spiritual groceries.	The church is a family with covenant commitments.
The church is just a gathering of a few believers.	The church is a gathering of believers bearing necessary marks and works.
The church is optional.	The church is essential for spiritual growth.

sound to those who have been brainwashed by an individualistic, me-theistic cultural evangelicalism, we must reject the idea that balanced spiritual growth can occur outside of a covenant commitment to an authentic local church.

But growing in community means more than just showing up on Sunday morning. It means submitting to the teaching and shepherd-ing of church leaders (Eph. 4:11–16; Heb. 13:17). It means going to church to minister to others, not simply to be ministered to (1 Cor. 12:7; Phil. 2:1–4). It means staying committed even when you feel put out or offended (Col. 3:12–23). Local church involvement isn't a game. It isn't a convenience. It isn't something you shoehorn into your schedule. God is serious about your involvement in the local church—dead serious (see 1 Cor. 3:12–17). In short, the church is *not* optional, but is essential for spiritual growth.

Going Retro

Leaving Church?

In our fast-food culture of leased cars and changing telephone companies, many local churches have not fared well. Church shopping, hopping, and dropping have become normal—so normal that many people reading this probably haven't thought very much about it. Certainly, this cavalier attitude toward local church membership is common among evan-gelicals today. But have we paused to consider whether it's *biblical*?

Some get bored and wander off to a more exciting church. Some get angry and stomp off, taking several members with them. Some change their minds about a particular doctrinal issue and realign themselves with a church that seems purer. Some people are just in a rut of discontent, staying for a few months or years and then straying on to something, well, *new*. But when we contrast this modern epidemic of forsaking our membership in a local church with the two positive and two negative biblical examples of leaving church and the long his-

tory of church commitment, we probably ought to rethink
this issue.

First, on the positive side, Christians in the Bible changed
churches because of *physical relocation.* In Acts 18 Aquila and
Priscilla changed from one local church to another when
they moved to a new city. Second, people left churches for
ministry opportunities. Ministers and missionaries departed
local churches to serve elsewhere—always with the blessing
of the sending churches (Acts 10:23; 15:40; 2 Cor. 8:16–18).
On the negative side, the New Testament presents examples
of people leaving the church because of *discipline* (Matt.
18:15–17; 1 Cor. 5:11–13), always with the hope that the disciplined believer would repent and return to fellowship. Also,
false teachers and heretics left in *apostasy,* departing in willful rebellion and often taking followers with them (1 John
2:18–19).[9]

Relocation . . . ministry . . . discipline . . . apostasy.

These four biblical examples—two positive, two negative—
are legitimate departures from local congregations and serve
not to weaken, but to strengthen, both the local church and
the universal body of Christ. And these examples make one
thing clear: the common reasons Christians give for forsaking
their covenant with a local church just don't measure up. If
believers take the Bible as the guide and love as the rule, they
should never simply stomp out of their churches in anger or
slip quietly out the back door.

Of course, we can't assume that the Bible covers every
legitimate reason for leaving a church. Sometimes churches
become so corrupt or doctrinally impure that the marks of
a true or healthy church are lost. Other times God may want
certain believers in certain places to accomplish certain
things. However, we must always remember that local church
commitment is necessary for spiritual growth (Heb. 10:24–25;
Eph. 4:4–16). And we must recall that we entered into church
membership as a covenant relationship—as serious as marriage. If we keep these facts in mind, we'll have the right heart
for considering a godly decision about whether or not to leave,
and how to do it appropriately.

Some practical principles can point us in the right direction as we consider God's mind about leaving church.

First, *communicate and seek counsel.* Discuss your options with the church leadership. Ask trusted Christian friends or mentors whether your reasons for leaving are legitimate. The issues leading you out of the church likely can be resolved—to the benefit of everyone. Perhaps your confidants will help you discover that the Lord is, in fact, leading you to another ministry elsewhere. However, simply stomping off in a huff is rude and immature. And keeping your real reasons for leaving a secret is usually a sign that your conscience isn't clear.

Second, *be prudent and discerning.* Don't make an emotional or quick decision. Just as in natural families, people hurt people in churches. You can count on it. But my reaction to a harsh word or other offense reveals as much about my own spiritual immaturity as it does about the immaturity of the offender. Don't make a decision based on anger, fear, resentment, or pain, but on the principles of God's Word. And don't turn everything into a "doctrinal issue." *Everybody* disagrees on some interpretations of Scripture, but not every doctrinal disagreement is worth rushing for the door. In fact, I can count the absolutely essential marks of orthodoxy on two hands; if your list of "fundamentals" is much longer, you may have slipped into exaggerated dogmatism. Keep your eye on the center—the gospel of Jesus Christ—and show grace in the dozens of disputable matters.

Finally, *seek God's will.* Even though God wants us to be faithful to our local churches and to contribute positively to its ministry, we can't limit God's direction in our lives. Though my tone may sound absolute, the truth is that occasionally God may want people elsewhere for his own purposes. However, we must still make transitions cautiously—communicating with leadership, exercising prudence, and seeking counsel. To hop from church to church without earnestly (and honestly) seeking the Lord's will in the matter shows contempt for the temple he loves and can even result in discipline from God (1 Cor. 3:16–17).

In light of God's high view of local church commitment and the clear teaching of Scripture (Heb. 10:24–25; Eph. 4:4–16), we should prayerfully consider each decision we make regarding our local churches—from membership and attendance to our level of involvement and decisions regarding departure. If we seek to honor him and demonstrate genuine love for our brothers and sisters in Christ, the Lord will guide us in wise, prudent, and godly decisions regarding our involvement in the local church.

So, are you thinking about leaving church? *Think again.*

Four Classic Marks of the Historical Body of Christ

They called them the Cola Wars—the epic showdown between Coke and Pepsi. As a young adult I remember taking the "Pepsi Challenge," in which taste tests demonstrated that more people preferred the taste of Pepsi to Coke. Other cola brands were driven into virtual obscurity by that grand clash of the cola titans. Then in the 1980s, Coca Cola changed. They reformulated the classic Coca Cola soft drink with a sweeter, more "Pepsi-ish" flavor, hoping to win the younger drinkers of Pepsi—that self-billed "choice of a new generation."

In its attempt to convince consumers that new Coke was better than both Pepsi and old Coke, the Coca Cola Company launched a fierce marketing campaign. They snared the popular Bill Cosby to push the new product. Then they harnessed the MTV energies of the computer-generated Max Headroom and his "C-c-c-catch the wave" campaign. Yes, new Coke had it all: flash, glitz, glamour, freshness, trendiness. *Yet it flopped*, creating so much controversy and outrage among a discerning and loyal consumer base that Coke was forced to bring back the original formula under the name "Coca Cola Classic."

As it turns out, the taste tests indicating that people liked sweeter cola misled Coke's decision-makers in two important ways. First, when consumers had to drink full cans of soda rather than tiny sips in the taste tests, the sweeter version was actually *less* preferred; thus, the reformulation was based on misleading data. Second, the marketers at Coca Cola failed to take seriously the place of their brand in the historical consciousness of American culture. In other words, people drank Coke not *merely* for the flavor. The *meaning* of Coke was just as important to many people as the *taste* of Coke. When Coca Cola acknowledged their miscalculation and undid their mistake, not only did they win back their customers, but they won that skirmish in the unending Cola Wars.[10]

You're probably wondering, "What do the Cola Wars have to do with the church?" Well, like the 1980s' New Coke with its jazzy Max Headroom campaign, modern evangelicals have been trying to update the church based on the ever-shifting standards of pop culture in order to market it more successfully. All too often the result has not been an *improvement* of the church, but an *abandonment* of the classic Christian formulation established by the apostles and handed down through church history. Today our ideas of what a church *is* and what a church *does* too often reflect flighty preferences and personal tastes. Like the market-driven savants responsible for too quickly reformulating Coca Cola in order to appeal to the superficial cravings of the masses, many well-meaning evangelical leaders have modified churches based not on classic Christian beliefs and practices, but on apparent popular appeal.

Having dispelled some common myths of the preference-driven church, we're ready to embark on an examination of the original formula of "Church Classic." In the remainder of this chapter, I'll briefly introduce what many call the four classic marks of the *historical body of Christ*; that is, the church as *one, holy, catholic,* and *apostolic*. Then in chapters 8 and 9 we will explore in greater depth the three marks and three works of legitimate *local* churches: the marks of orthodoxy, order, and ordinances and the works of evangelism, edification, and exaltation.

We Believe in One, Holy, Catholic, and Apostolic Church ... Don't We?

The second-century Apostles' Creed affirms belief in "the holy catholic church, the communion of saints." About two centuries later, after the church endured numerous trials and overcame several errors, the consensus on the doctrine of the church expanded the statement to include the following: "We believe . . . in one, holy, catholic, and apostolic Church." What do we mean when we confess the oneness, holiness, catholicity, and apostolicity of the church? More importantly, how does this belief about the church affect our practices? Let's treat each of these in turn, and then consider them together as an inseparable whole.

Oneness: The Unity of the Church

By confessing the unity of the church, we mean that the church is a new redeemed humanity called by the will of God the Father, united through the person and work of Jesus Christ, and incorporated into his body by the Holy Spirit (Eph. 2:14–16). Every generation should strive to bear out the oneness of the church by seeking unity between other orthodox believers and churches despite the ever-present reality of doctrinal and practical diversity.

Paul the apostle articulated the oneness of the church in Ephesians 4:4–6 when he wrote, "There is one body and one Spirit—just as you were called to the one hope that belongs to your call—one Lord, one faith, one baptism, one God and Father of all, who is over all and through all and in all." Christ himself expressed this unity of the body in his high priestly prayer just prior to his arrest:

> I do not ask for these only, but also for those who will believe in me through their word, that they may all be one, just as you, Father, are in me, and I in you, that they also may be in us, so that the world may believe that you have sent me. The glory that you have given me I have given to them, that they may be one even as we are one, I in them and you in me, that they may become perfectly one, so that the world may know that you sent me and loved them even as you loved me. (John 17:20–23)

The unity of the church is both a theological *reality* and a practical *ideal*. Theologically, we are truly one in Christ, spiritually united to him by the baptism of the Holy Spirit and destined to be gathered together into one complete and perfect kingdom when he returns. This hope is beautifully expressed in an early Christian prayer associated with the Lord's Supper: "Just as this broken bread was scattered upon the mountains and then was gathered together and became one, so may your church be gathered together from the ends of the earth into your kingdom."[11]

It must be emphasized, however, that to be "spiritually united" to Christ does not mean that our union with him and with other believers is merely invisible. Earlier in this chapter we argued that the church is not *merely* a human organization. Similarly, the church is not *merely* a spiritual organism. Though the physical and spiritual aspects of the church can be distinguished, they can never be separated. And though they must never be separated, they can never be confused. We must conceive of the church as having both a spiritual nature and a physical nature, without mixture, confusion, separation, or division.

Throughout history the unity of the church has been a hallmark of faith. The sixth-century church father Boethius wrote, "Therefore is that heavenly instruction spread throughout the world, the peoples are knit together, churches are founded, and, filling the broad earth, one body formed, whose Head, even Christ, ascended into heaven in order that the members might of necessity follow where the Head was gone."[12]

Likewise, the great Reformer, John Calvin, wrote, "All the elect of God are so joined together in Christ, that as they depend on one head, so they are as it were compacted together into one body, being knit together like its different members; made truly one by living together under the same Spirit of God."[13]

The doctrinal statement of the seminary where I teach expresses my own beliefs about the theological reality and practical ideal of unity: "We believe that by the same Spirit all believers in this age are baptized into, and thus become, one body that is Christ's, whether Jews or Gentiles, and having become members one of another, are under solemn duty to keep the unity of the Spirit in the bond of peace, rising above all sectarian differences, and loving one another with a pure heart fervently."[14]

When we confess the theological reality of the unity of the church, we must resist the temptation to regard this unity as purely theoretical, invisible, and spiritual. Yet we must not forget that a full realization of this physical unity has never been experienced in history. Practically the church has experienced internal conflict and factions from the New Testament times onward (see 1 Cor. 1:10). Nevertheless, the church must strive for the ideal, taking opportunities to exhibit unity of mind and purpose among other orthodox believers wherever possible.

Holiness: The Purity of the Church

When we confess the holiness of the church, we hold that the church's beliefs and practices are completely distinct from the beliefs and practices of the world. Why? Because the church was set apart by the election of God the Father, washed clean by the blood of Christ, and sanctified by the work of the Holy Spirit.[15] Practically speaking, every generation should strive to bear out the holiness of the church by confession of sin, conformity to God's standards, and commitment to right belief and practice.

In an exhortation for husbands to love their wives in the same way that Christ loves the church, the apostle Paul draws on the theological ideal of the holiness of the church: "Husbands, love your wives, as Christ loved the church and gave himself up for her, that he might sanctify her, having cleansed her by the washing of water with the word, so that he might present the church to himself in splendor, without spot or wrinkle or any such thing, that she might be holy and without blemish" (Eph. 5:25–27). As in the case of the unity of the church, the holiness is both a theological *reality* as well as a practical *ideal*. Theologically, the church of the elect is sanctified (set apart), reckoned holy by the decree of God in light of the cleansing work of Christ and in anticipation of the future purification in the resurrection and glorification of the church. However, in the present time, the church is characterized by both the *presence* of sin and the *process* of purification.

Irenaeus of Lyons emphasized the doctrinal purity of the whole church throughout the world when he wrote, "For the faith being ever one and the same, neither does one who is able at great length to discourse regarding it, make any addition to it, nor does one, who can say but little diminish it."[16] Likewise, Luther's larger catechism emphasizes the holy character of the church: "I believe that there is upon earth a little holy group and congregation of pure saints, under one head, even Christ, called together by the Holy Ghost in one faith, one mind, and understanding, with manifold gifts, yet agreeing in love, without sects or schisms."[17]

Thomas Oden sums up this doctrine of the holiness of the church:

> As body of Christ, the church is called to holiness. Yet its holiness is enmeshed in continuing human imperfection and finitude until the end of history. The church is holy while not ceasing to be subject to the infirmities of the flesh that accompany all historical existence. . . . The holiness of the church is best expressed in the imperfect or unfinished tense—that God is now sanctifying the church.[18]

Catholicity: The Whole(some)ness of the Church

When I was in grade school, a teacher explained that most people in America were Christians. Then she polled the class: "How many of you consider yourself to be a Christian?"

All the students raised their hands except one girl near the front of the room. She looked nervously around the class and spotted another girl raising her hand along with the rest of the class. Apparently expecting to have gotten some support from her friend, she rebuked her out loud: "Hey, Tina, put your hand down! We're not Christians, *we're Catholics*!"

For most evangelicals the word "catholic" brings to mind popes, statues, rosaries, crusades, and the Spanish Inquisition. But the term actually expresses an important biblical, historical, and theological truth. It comes from two Greek words: *kata*, meaning "according to" and *holos*, meaning "whole." Protestants have often tried to replace the uncomfortable word "catholic" with "Christian," as in the Apostles' Creed: "I believe in the holy ~~catholic~~ Christian church." However, the term "Christian" is too broad. It designates a world religion in all its diverse (and even perverse) forms. It doesn't catch the specific intention of "catholic." Others have attempted to replace "catholic" with the term "universal" or even "global," referring to the entire church spread throughout the world versus a local congregation. This comes closer to the original use of the term, but it also fails to capture important nuances of "catholic." Instead, I prefer to redeem the actual term for evangelicals, who represent the best expression of catholicity in keeping with the original meaning of the term.

So, what does it mean to be catholic? To define it, let me play off the original root of the word, meaning "whole." In the earliest appearances of the word "catholic," it was used to distinguish the church in its geographical *wholeness* (the catholic church throughout the world) as well as its theological *wholesomeness* (the catholic faith as opposed to heretical sects).[19] So, when we confess the catholicity of the church, we mean that the church as a whole shares in a confession and a commission that transcend time, place, culture, and language. These also rise above denominational differences and theological distinctives. Every generation of Christians should therefore strive to overcome their provincial and temporal concerns and readily align themselves with the "community of communities" of orthodox Christianity.

Around AD 110, Ignatius of Antioch first used the term "catholic" in reference to orthodox Christian churches. In order to strengthen the mark of orthodoxy and prevent heresy, Ignatius instructed the local church in Smyrna to trust the teachings of their bishop (or "head pastor"), who at that time was Polycarp, a personal student of the apostle John.[20] Ignatius wrote, "Wherever the bishop appears, there let the congregation be; just as wherever Jesus Christ is, there is the catholic church."[21] Ignatius drew a parallel between the headship of the bishop over the local congregation and the headship of Christ over the *wholeness* of the church throughout the world. The context of Ignatius also emphasized doctrinal purity by union with the ordained leadership in the local church, just as doctrinal *wholesomeness* was maintained when the body of Christ remained firmly united on the central teachings regarding Jesus Christ.[22]

A few decades later, around AD 155, the same church in Smyrna described the Lord Jesus as "the Savior of our souls and Helmsman of our bodies and Shepherd of the catholic church throughout the world."[23] According to the ancient church's use of the term "catholic," the modern Roman Catholic Church doesn't seem to fit the bill. If "catholic" means "according to the whole," then no single local church can be regarded as constituting the whole universal church. And to the degree that the catholic church must strive to hold what has been believed everywhere, always, and by all, the Roman Catholic Church also falls short, requiring its members to hold as saving dogma doctrines that were never part of the center of orthodoxy.[24]

The pope in Rome was originally simply the bishop of Rome—the head pastor of a local city church. Through the centuries, however, the Roman church expanded its political and ecclesiastical influence over the churches in the West and North Africa. Then it attempted to triumph over the entire universal church East and West—an attempted takeover rejected by the Eastern Orthodox as well as by the Protestant churches. Thus, the Roman Church is not "catholic" in the sense originally intended by Ignatius or the early church fathers. Rather, it must be regarded as a renegade local church that has transgressed its jurisdiction and claimed for itself powers never given to any single apostle or bishop. Christ alone, not the pope, is the "Shepherd of the catholic church throughout the world."[25]

The Protestant Reformation reemphasized the early sense of catholicity. For example, the *Westminster Confession* states, "The catholic or universal Church, which is invisible, consists of the whole number of the elect, that have been, are, or shall be gathered into one, under Christ the head thereof; and is the spouse, the body, the fulness of him that filleth all in all. The visible Church, which is also catholic or universal under the gospel (not confined to one nation, as before under the law), consists of all those throughout the world that profess the true religion."[26] In light of this biblical and historical understanding of catholicity, evangelicals can and should legitimately claim the title "catholic." With a proper emphasis on the essentials of orthodoxy, focused attention on the authenticating marks and works of the church, and a balanced perspective on diverse beliefs and practices, evangelical Christians can reflect the original sense of the ancient catholic church. Yes, we need to shore up areas of weakness, yet despite all of its shortcomings, I believe evangelicalism is the most authentic expression of "catholicity" in the world today.[27]

Apostolicity: The Stability of the Church

When we express our belief in the apostolicity of the church, we mean that the church stands under the authority of the apostolic teaching contained in Scripture, faithfully building on the foundation of the apostles and prophets, with Jesus Christ as the chief cornerstone (Eph. 2:20; 3:4–5). Every generation of Christians should strive to maintain fidelity to apostolic authority by constantly returning to the inspired Scriptures, taking care to build on that foundation with quality materials.

In short, the church is apostolic when its leaders profess, preserve, and promote the apostolic teaching in both word and works; this apostolic teaching is centered on the saving person and work of Christ within Trinitarian orthodoxy. Of course, the primary source of apostolic teaching is the New Testament. Thus, evangelicalism's emphasis on the supreme authority of Scripture marks it as a legitimate stream of the apostolic tradition.

Tertullian stated that the mark of apostolicity is not limited merely to those churches historically founded by apostles themselves, but to all subsequent churches that agree with apostolic doctrine, a test that heretical churches can never pass: "To this test [of apostolicity], therefore will they [the heretics] be submitted for proof by those churches, who, although they derive not their founder from apostles or apostolic men (as being of much later date, for they are in fact being founded daily), yet, since they agree in the same faith, they are accounted as not less apostolic because they are akin in doctrine."[28]

Apostolicity also refers to faithfully carrying on the apostolic traditions handed to the early church, including properly ordained church leadership (discussed more fully in the next chapter) and properly administered rites of the church (baptism and the Lord's Supper). Paul the apostle wrote, "Stand firm and hold to the traditions that you were taught by us, either by our spoken word or by our letter" (2 Thess. 2:15). The duty of the church in every generation is to hold firmly to the traditions set forth by the apostles as the foundation of the church—those things clearly contained in Scripture and faithfully preserved in the church's early and enduring practice.

Pursuing Unity, Holiness, Catholicity, and Apostolicity

Thomas Oden sums up the four classic marks of the historical body of Christ in a comprehensive harmony when he writes:

> The church is one, finding its oneness in Christ. The church is holy, set apart from the world to mediate life to the world and bring forth the fruits of the Spirit amid the life of the world. The church is catholic in that it is whole, for all, and embracing all times and places. The church is apostolic in that it is grounded in the testimony of the first witnesses to Jesus' life and resurrection, and depends upon and continues their ministry.[29]

As I have already mentioned, the global and historical church has always fallen short of fully realizing these four classic marks of oneness, holiness, catholicity, and apostolicity. As we confess these as theological realities and practical ideals, we must constantly strive to achieve these in day-to-day life.

In certain periods of the church's history, the four marks have suffered immensely, leading to attempts at retrieving these marks and healing the church. For example, regarding the condition of the church at the eve of the Protestant Reformation, Christian historian Euan Cameron writes, "Every traditional epithet applied to the Church, 'one, holy, catholic, and apostolic', had been somehow put in doubt in the fifteenth century: unity by schisms, holiness by moral failings,

AVOID THE COMMON MYTHS	&	PURSUE THE CLASSIC MARKS
The church is merely a human organization, not the spiritual-physical body of Christ.		The church is *one*, united in Christ by the Holy Spirit and called to mutual love.
The church is a supermarket of spiritual groceries, not a family with covenant commitments.		The church is *holy*, purified by Christ's blood and exhorted to live in moral and doctrinal purity
The church is just a gathering of a few believers, not a gathering of believers bearing necessary marks and works.		The church is *catholic*, its local assemblies sharing a common confession and commission.
The church is optional, not essential for spiritual growth.		The church is *apostolic*, submitting to the authority of apostolic doctrine and practice.

catholicity by lack of general agreement, apostolicity by doubts about individual popes."[30] The same can be said of every generation of the church to varying degrees. Even today, the evangelical church suffers from schism and conflict, moral compromise and failure to remain distinct from the world, the claims of denominational exclusivity or local church superiority rather than catholicity, and a failure to submit to the final authority of Scripture and to maintain the marks and works of the church established by the apostles.

As we consider our own church's health, we must consciously avoid being duped by the four common myths about the church that have spread like viruses within our evangelical subculture. At the same time, we must embrace as theological realities and pursue as practical goals the four classic marks of the global and historical church.

The Essential Marks
of a Local Church

During the sixteenth century Reformation, Protestant leaders like Luther and Calvin sought to define what it meant for any particular congregation to be counted as an authentic Christian church. They knew they couldn't define themselves by medieval Roman Catholic standards under the pope, with his seven saving sacraments and rigid rituals. But amidst a growing diversity of Protestant practices, what could they identify as the essential marks of a true local church? The Lutheran *Augsburg Confession* put it this way: "The Church is the congregation of saints, in which the Gospel is rightly taught and the Sacraments rightly administered."[1] Later the *Westminster Confession* expressed a common Protestant perspective on what it meant to be truly "catholic" in the Protestant sense: "This catholic Church hath been sometimes more, sometimes less visible. And particular churches, which are members thereof, are more or less pure, according as the doctrine of the gospel is taught and embraced, ordinances administered, and public worship performed more or less purely in them."[2]

As the evangelical heirs of the Reformation tradition, we should be just as careful as the Reformers were about answering the question, "What makes a congregation of believers a true and faithful church of Jesus Christ?" In struggling with this question over the years, I have found it helpful to think in terms of essential "marks" and "works" of a true church, incorporating biblical and historical emphases that have stood the test of time and can be said of every generation of Christians. Though my terms are different, these marks and works fit the classic early church and Reformation "marks of the church" as the one, holy, catholic, and apostolic church (described in the last chapter) manifesting itself in various local congregations.[3]

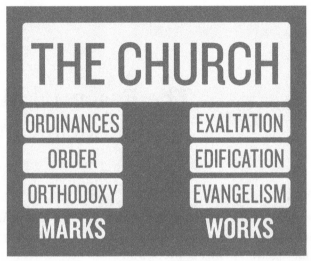

An authentic local church is supported by two pillars: the essential marks (orthodoxy, order, and ordinances) and the essential works (evangelism, edification, and exaltation).

The pillar of essential marks includes *orthodoxy, order,* and *ordinances.* *Orthodox* believers are those who hold to the essential truths of the Christian faith—those fundamentals of the faith that have been believed everywhere, always, and by all. This mark corresponds with the Protestant emphasis on the Word of God purely preached and heard. *Order* emphasizes the necessity of properly trained, trusted, and tested pastors, teachers, and leaders of the church, to whom the orthodox faith has been entrusted to pass on to the next generation. The term *ordinances* refers to the sacraments of the church—baptism and the Lord's Supper—as they are closely associated with the growth, discipline, and purity of the church's members.

The pillar of essential works, discussed in the next chapter, includes *evangelism, edification,* and *exaltation. Evangelism* focuses on the unsaved world, balancing both local and global missions. *Edification* describes the church's role in building up believers in love and good works. Finally, *exaltation* refers to the purpose, goal, and focus of the church—to glorify God the Father, through the Son, by the power of the Spirit.

If a local church does not consciously and continually revisit and strengthen these pillars of essential marks and works of the church, they will eventually erode, crack, and crumble. It doesn't take a structural engineer to predict what will happen when the foundational piers of this structure collapse.

Orthodoxy stands as the first stone in the pillar of the essential marks of an authentic local church.

The First Mark: Orthodoxy

After our detailed discussion of orthodoxy in part 2, you should be familiar with the first stone in the pillar of a local church's essential marks. I argued that a conscious awareness of orthodoxy prevents us from gross distortions, overreactions, or dangerous distractions from the foundational truths of the Christian faith. Orthodoxy refers to the core essential truths of Christianity—those classic fundamentals that have been believed everywhere, always, and by all.[4] We explored seven simple, easy-to-remember, essentials of the classic Christian faith that generally describe the content of orthodox belief:

1. The triune God as Creator and Redeemer
2. The fall and resulting depravity
3. The person and work of Christ
4. Salvation by grace through faith
5. Inspiration and authority of Scripture
6. Redeemed humanity incorporated into Christ
7. The restoration of humanity and creation.

Without orthodox doctrinal content, local churches are neither catholic nor apostolic. They are neither holy nor united with true Christianity past or present. In fact, they are not Christian. Evangelical churches must strive to keep the *center* of Jesus Christ, the *story* of the triune God's creation and redemption, and the *markers* of classic orthodox doctrine at the forefront of their preaching, teaching, education, and discipleship. Sadly, this does not always happen.

Sometimes we so emphasize the distinctive doctrines over which we differ that we lose sight of the foundational mark of orthodoxy. In fact, we can get so wrapped up in our detailed doctrinal statements that we fall into the error of thinking *everything* we believe is of utmost importance. Or, toward the other extreme, we might de-emphasize doctrine and conclude that *nothing* is worth fighting for. In both cases the truly orthodox doctrines are neglected . . . then forgotten . . . then eventually forsaken.

In response to these nondoctrinal or hyperdogmatic extremes, we need to reclaim the evangelical mark of orthodoxy. It's not enough to bury the essential truths deep down in a dense doctrinal statement so they appear to be at the same level as the origin of angels and the order of the end times. More than anything else in our postmodern, post-Christian world, evangelical churches must clearly, unambiguously, and intentionally identify themselves with the biblical and theological core of the ancient and enduring Christian faith.

How can local churches strengthen the mark of orthodoxy? An official statement of essential truths that focuses attention on the content of classic orthodoxy would be a good place to start. And, as in the apostolic and ancient church, these orthodox essentials should be constantly used as explicit standards for baptismal instruction, membership, discipleship, and discipline. In this way orthodoxy would play a real role in establishing and maintaining Christian identity. Also, keeping our own personal theological distinctives *out* of that ancient and unchanging center would go a long way to promote humility and unity.

The Second Mark: Order

The term *order* points to properly trained, trusted, and tested pastors, teachers, and leaders, to whom the orthodox faith has been entrusted for defending and passing on to the next generation.[5] The primary

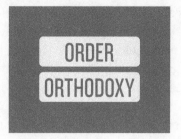

Order, the second stone in the
pillar of essential marks of a local
church, rests upon the foundation
of orthodoxy.

responsibility of church leadership is to safeguard the essential marks
and works of a local church. Paul sought to prevent the danger of heresy when he told Timothy, his handpicked pastor in Ephesus, "What
you have heard from me in the presence of many witnesses entrust
to faithful men who will be able to teach others also" (2 Tim. 2:2).
Earlier Paul described the leadership in Ephesus as apostles, prophets,
evangelists, pastors, and teachers, who were given to the church "to
equip the saints for the work of ministry, for building up the body of
Christ" (Eph. 4:12).

Though the offices of apostles and prophets ceased in the first
century, the other offices of evangelists, pastors, and teachers were to
endure until the church arrives at unity, maturity, and doctrinal stability (4:13–14)—that is, in every generation since the first century.[6]
So, the idea of gifted leaders doing local church work of proclamation
(evangelists), shepherding (pastors), and instruction (teachers) is not
a man-made concept. The Holy Spirit called such men to specially-
ordained offices in the church for the purpose of protecting and promoting orthodox beliefs and practices.

In fact, Clement of Rome—a contemporary of the apostles and
later known as a pastor of Rome around AD 96—recalled the establishment of this order by the apostles that continued to his own day:
"Our apostles also knew . . . that there would be strife on account of
the office of the overseer. For this reason . . . they appointed those
ministers already mentioned, and afterwards gave instructions, that
when these should fall asleep, other approved men should succeed
them in their ministry."[7]

Just a dozen years after Clement (AD 110), the aged pastor Ignatius of Antioch, who had also been a personal acquaintance of the apostles, said of the ordained pastor, elders, and deacons in a local congregation: "Without these no group can be called a church."[8] This is what we mean by the essential mark of order—that the leadership offices in the church established by the apostles must continue in our own day.

The Protestant Reformers viewed ordained leadership as an essential mark of a true church, indispensible for the orthodox teaching of the Word of God and the right administration of the ordinances of the church. The Lutheran *Augsburg Confession* of 1530 pronounced that "no man should publicly in the Church teach or administer the Sacraments, except he be rightly called."[9]

John Calvin also wrote regarding the necessity of ordained leadership for proper order:

> But as our ignorance and sloth . . . stand in need of external helps, by which faith may be begotten in us, and may increase and make progress until its consummation, God, in accommodation to our infirmity has added much helps, and secured the effectual preaching of the gospel, by depositing this treasure with the Church. He has appointed pastors and teachers, by whose lips he might edify his people, (Eph. iv.11); he has invested them with authority, and, in short, omitted nothing that might conduce to holy consent in the faith, and to right order.[10]

Having set the basic building block of church order as a necessary mark of an authentic local church, we are now in a position to work out some details of the nature of church order as established by the apostles, received by their successors, and passed on in the early church. Though the discussion may be somewhat technical, a firm grasp the biblical-historical model of church order is an essential starting point for any discussion of qualified leadership in our contemporary local churches.

I will first show that the New Testament apostles and prophets intended that local Christian churches reflect a threefold office later identified with the terms *episkopos* (overseer), *presbyteroi* (elders), and *diakonoi* (ministers). Though the names and titles of these three offices changed and developed over the first hundred years of church history, eventually the early church fathers settled on these particular terms to describe the offices necessary for administering the works of the church. Today we might call these same three offices "senior/lead pastor," "elders," and "deacons."[11]

How Was the Church Ordered During the Time of the Apostles? (AD 40–90)

During the widespread missionary activities of the apostles and their delegates, a simple twofold church order emerged, established by the apostles and based on the order of the original church in Jerusalem.[12] In the Jerusalem church the original twelve disciples, themselves the "elders" of the church, established the order of men to assist them in carrying out the work of the ministry (Acts 6:1–7). These "ministers" or "deacons" as they came to be called, were taken from the congregation and were ordained to their ministry by the apostles through the laying on of hands and prayer (Acts 6:6).

Acts 20:17, 28, clearly describes the ministry of the elders in a local church. Near the end of his third missionary journey around AD 58, Paul stopped in Miletus on the western coast of Asia Minor. From there "he sent to Ephesus and called the elders (*presbyteroi*) of the church to come to him" (Acts 20:17). Then he gave them the following charge: "Pay careful attention to yourselves and to all the flock, in which the Holy Spirit has made you overseers [*episkopoi*], to care for [*poimaino*] the church of God, which he obtained with his own blood" (Acts 20:28). From Acts 20 we see the convergence of three key terms used to identify the same group of leaders in each local church: *presbyteroi* ("elders"), *episkopoi* ("overseers"), and *poimaino* (a verb that means "to pastor" or "to shepherd"). At this stage in the development of local church order, "elder" and "overseer" were interchangeable terms, and these officers of the church were responsible for pastoral work. Also, there was no distinction between pastors and elders; these terms described the same group of leaders.

A few years later (AD 61), Paul wrote his letter to the Philippians, in which he addressed "all the saints in Christ Jesus who are at Philippi, with the overseers [*episkopoi*] and deacons [*diakonoi*]" (1:1). Thus, the local church in Philippi had a leadership structure of overseers (synonymous with "elders" and "pastors") and deacons (synonymous with "ministers"), distinct from the general congregation of "saints." Both overseers and deacons were under the direct authority of the apostles and their delegates.

At about the same time, Paul wrote to the church in Ephesus and revealed the offices current in the apostolic period. In Ephesians 4:11–12, he wrote, "And he gave the apostles, the prophets, the evangelists [*euangelistai*], the shepherds [pastors, *poimenai*] and teachers [*didas-kaloi*], to equip the saints for the work of ministry." Here we see the foundational ministries of the apostles and prophets listed first (see Eph. 2:20). "Evangelists" may refer to apostolic delegates or, perhaps, to a type of leader in the local church responsible for proclamation of the Word (see 2 Tim. 4:5). It is apparent, though, that "pastors and teachers" refers to those who were elders or overseers in the local church.[13] Therefore, among the general group of "elders/overseers" we see a diversity of distinct responsibilities: pastoring, teaching, and proclaiming. All of these offices were under direct authority of the apostles and prophets in the first-century church.

Near the end of Paul's earthly ministry, he wrote his letters to Timothy, who was at that time the apostolic delegate in charge of the local church in Ephesus.[14] In this context, Paul wrote to Timothy, "If anyone aspires to the office of overseer [*episkopos*], he desires a noble task. Therefore an overseer [*episkopos*] must be above reproach" (1 Tim. 3:1–2). Here we see the general qualifications for the "overseer" or, as it is called in other texts, the "elder." The qualifications include teaching, managing, and shepherding (1 Tim. 3:2, 4–5). Following this description, Paul deals with the other office in the local church, the "deacons" (1 Tim. 3:8–10). He also gives qualifications for "women," which I understand as a reference to a distinct office of "deaconess."[15]

Paul then explains to Timothy why he wrote these instructions: "If I delay, you may know how one ought to behave in the household of God, which is the church of the living God, a pillar and buttress of the truth." (3:15). That is, Paul was both *describing* and *prescribing* how leadership in the local church should be ordered under the oversight of Timothy, Paul's personal apostolic delegate. Here we see emerging, with the absence of the apostle himself, a threefold ministry—the appointed leader (Timothy, called the "evangelist" [2 Tim. 4:5]), the elders/overseers/pastors/teachers/managers (the *episkopoi* and *presbyteroi*) and the deacons/ministers (*diakonoi*).[16]

It is important to point out that at this time some elders in the church of Ephesus were financially compensated for their labors. First Timothy 5:17–18 states, "Let the elders [*presbyteroi*] who rule well be considered worthy of double honor, especially those who labor in preaching and teaching. For the Scripture says, 'You shall not muzzle an ox when it treads out the grain,' and, 'The laborer deserves his wages.'"The church at this time was undoubtedly compensating those who devoted their lives to full-time proclamation and teaching. The modern distinction between "elders" as unpaid lay leaders and professional "pastors" as paid staff was unheard of in the New Testament and early church. All pastors were elders.

Paul wrote a similar epistle to Titus, whom he left in Crete: "This is why I left you in Crete, so that you might put what remained into order, and appoint elders [*presbyteroi*] in every town as I directed you" (Titus 1:5). Paul then used the alternate term, *episkopos*, in reference to the office of elder (1:7). The responsibilities of the elders/overseers include moral qualities, but also the ability to "hold firm to the trustworthy word as taught, so that he may be able to give instruction in sound doctrine and also to rebuke those who contradict it" (1:9). That is, the elders/overseers were primarily responsible for doctrine, teaching, and correction.

Around the same time (AD 63–64), the apostle Peter also mentioned the kind of church order established under the authority of the apostles and prophets:

> I exhort the elders [*presbyteroi*] among you, as a fellow elder [*presbyteros*] and a witness of the sufferings of Christ, as well as a partaker in the glory that is going to be revealed: shepherd [*poimaino*] the flock of God that is among you, exercising oversight [*episkopeo*], not under compulsion, but willingly, as God would have you; not for shameful gain, but eagerly; not domineering over those in your charge, but being examples to the flock. (1 Pet. 5:1–3)

In this passage, Peter used the same trio of descriptions for leadership—elder/overseer/pastor—indicating that these various responsibilities rested within the same group of leaders in the churches. In fact, Peter counted himself among the "elders," even though he exercised direct authority over them as an apostle.

This apostolic church order prevailed only as long as the apostles, prophets, and their delegates were present among the churches to exercise oversight and leadership. The apostles and prophets, such as Peter and Paul, appointed and instructed elders, ordaining them to their offices, and serving as advisors and supervisors (Acts 14:23). Also, it was typical for each elder/overseer, in conjunction with the deacons, to be responsible for individual "home churches" within the larger city church. We see this described in detail in Paul's letter to the Romans (AD 57–58), where he mentions several names and those congregations that met in their homes (Rom. 16:3–15). That is, in Rome we see a single local city church composed of smaller groups, with each group under the care of an elder/overseer/pastor working with one (or more) deacons/ministers. Thus, in some places each local city church was composed of smaller identifiable groups each under the care of an elder and deacon.

However, this kind of "home group" model was not the only one. Other small first-century churches or large churches with access to adequate facilities would have been able to meet with a plurality of elders attending each meeting.[17] In this case, each elder would have likely carried different responsibilities within the single congregation—some shepherding, some teaching, some administrating.[18] In other words, though we see a clear establishment of a plurality of elders and plurality of deacons during the apostolic period, there seems to have been some diversity with regard to how these offices actually functioned in each local church.

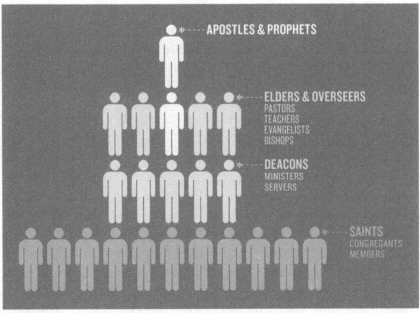

The temporary order of the local church during the ministry of the apostles and prophets (AD 40–90) consisted of a plurality of elders and deacons serving under the direct authority of apostles and prophets or their appointed delegates.

Going Retro

Neither Anarchy nor Democracy

The biblical-historical church order makes it clear that *the church is not an anarchy*, an assembly without clearly defined leadership. In fact, God never established any secular or sacred institution that lacked clear order. From human government (Rom. 13:1) to the family (Eph. 5:22), from Israel (Ex. 22:28) to the church (Titus 1:5)—God's institutions reflect order. Even within triune equality, God the Father functions as the head, sending the Son and the Spirit into the world (John 14:16–17; Gal. 4:4, 6; 1 Cor. 11:3). A group of Christians without ordained leadership is not a church.

Neither is the church a democracy, in which final authority over the shepherds is distributed among the flock. Unfortunately, many Christians believe God leads the church by majority rule. *But not if the Bible has the final say!* God intends that the local church have ordained leadership. The elders—a term synonymous with pastors and overseers and including the presiding elder—were to be the leaders of the church, to shepherd the flock gently and with compassion, but as *leaders* nonetheless.

Some of you may be thinking, "Doesn't this kind of elder authority rest decision-making in a select few—the pastors and teachers of the church?" Yes. This is the countercultural teaching of Scripture and the order established by the apostles. To be sure, the covenanted members are to be involved in ministry as the Lord has gifted each one (see Rom. 12:4–8; 1 Corinthians 12–14). However, their primary relationship to the appointed elders is to *submit* (Heb. 13:7, 17).

Now that's a word many of us hate: *submit*. In a world were political rebels are heroes, the suggestion of submission to our human leaders sends chills up our spines. Yet Scripture is clear. The congregation was to pray for, support, and follow the leadership of the ordained pastors (Heb. 13:7, 17). When we read the Bible in its historical context, letting it say what it says (and not what we want it to say), then there's nothing ambiguous, nuanced, or complex about this. Submit. Obey.

Anticipating objections, though, the writer of Hebrews adds the fact that elders will "give account" for their work to God. We often forget that since God is sovereign and Christ is the head of the church, every elder is under the headship of God and Christ. Instead, we think they are under *our* headship and try to turn God's order upside down. We treat elders like our representatives, as if they are supposed to be moved and molded by the whims of the masses or champion the agendas of their "constituents."

In other words, both the ordained elders (pastors and teachers) and the covenanted members (congregation) have their biblical roles and responsibilities. Leaders shouldn't abdicate, and members shouldn't usurp. Leaders should pastor, and members should submit.

- - - - - - - - - - - - - - -

How Was the Church Organized after the Time of the Apostles? (AD 70–)

After AD 70, when many original apostles had been martyred or began to pass away, the need arose for the dwindling number of itinerant apostles and prophets to establish a more permanent form of church leadership structure that would survive them. Such a postapostolic church order would not only have to be in continuity with what was already established in the middle of the first century, but it would also need to be reproducible from generation to generation.

As would be expected, this postapostolic church order already begins to emerge in later New Testament books as well as in the earliest noncanonical Christian writings.[19] The *Didache* (or *Teaching of the Twelve Apostles*) was written between AD 50 and 100 as a basic manual of church instruction.[20] In this early text we see a transition occurring from the itinerant leadership of apostles and prophets to a more stable local ministry. In this document we read, "And concerning the apostles and prophets, act thus according to the ordinance of the Gospel," indicating that when *Didache* was written, the churches were still under the leadership of first-century apostles and prophets.[21] However, anticipating that these foundational ministries would soon be passing off the scene, the *Didache* also says, "Therefore appoint for yourselves bishops [*episkopoi*, "overseers"] and deacons [*diako-noi*, "ministers"] worthy of the Lord, men who are humble and not avaricious and true and approved, for they too carry out for you the ministry of the prophets and teachers. You must not, therefore, despise them, for they are your honored men, along with the prophets and teachers."[22] What we observe in this earliest historical document is a necessary transition from the temporary apostolic/prophetic pattern of ministry described in the last section to the permanent and localized offices. Elsewhere in the *Didache* we find among these offices untitled individuals responsible for proclaiming God's Word: "My child, remember night and day the one who preaches God's word to you, and honor him as though he were the Lord. For wherever the Lord's nature is preached, there the Lord is."[23] Is there any evidence that the early church already had an individual leader in each church with the unique responsibility of proclamation distinct from the other elders?

In fact, we see evidence of this kind of individual leader among the elders in the book of Revelation (around AD 95).[24] In the messages to the seven churches of Asia Minor, Jesus repeatedly addressed the "messenger" (*angelos*) of each church. Though some have taken this to refer to an angelic being, the word *angelos* in Greek is a general term that simply means "messenger," either human or heavenly.[25] In Revelation 2–3, though, we can be confident that a *human* messenger is meant by *angelos*.[26] In the Greek text of the messages in chapters 2–3, Jesus addressed the *angelos* in the second person singular, commending the "messenger" for what he had done well as well as condemning the "messenger" for his failings. Jesus is not addressing the whole church directly in the second person plural, but the singular messenger (*angelos*) of each church, who is held responsible for the welfare of the local church body.[27] Angelic beings could never be condemned for sin and urged to repent, nor does it make sense to address, commend, condemn, *and call to repentance* the symbolic personification of the "prevailing spirit of the church."[28] So *angelos* most likely refers to a human leader in the local church who exercised distinct oversight among the elders.[29] (However, Christ's words to the pastor simultaneously apply to anyone "who has an ear"—you and me—and indirectly address "the churches" through their individual "messengers"; see Rev. 2:7, 11, 17, 29; 3:6, 13, 22.) This identification is further strengthened by the correlation of historical evidence outside the New Testament from literature composed about the same time as the book of Revelation, an aspect of the historical context almost always ignored by commentators.[30]

About the same time as the book of Revelation addressed the single "messenger" in each of the seven churches in Asia Minor, a similar messenger in Rome, Clement, wrote a lengthy letter on behalf of the Roman elders to the church in Corinth in order to admonish them to unity.[31] In this letter, Clement indicates that the apostles did, in fact, establish a permanent church order intended to endure beyond their death. Clement wrote: "So, preaching both in the country and in the towns, they appointed their first fruits, when they had tested them by the Spirit, to be bishops [*episkopoi*, "overseers"] and deacons [*diakonoi*, "ministers"] for the future believers."[32] Clement, who is early enough to have received his teaching directly from several of the apostles themselves, explains that this church order included the overseers (elders) and deacons (ministers). However, we also see that Clement himself was functioning as a presiding representative elder, with distinct responsibilities of oversight in the congregation.[33]

Within a few years, this threefold order of (1) presiding elder, (2) elders, and (3) deacons would be widespread throughout the entire Christian world, a situation we would expect to see if the apostles did, in fact, establish this order in their own generation. By the early second century the three offices in a local church began to develop distinctive titles.[34] Whereas the book of Revelation called the presiding elder the "messenger" (*angelos*), and *Didache* simply called him "the one who speaks the word of God to you," the need developed to give this particular leader a consistent technical label. The name "overseer" (*episkopos*), which had previously been synonymous with "elder" (*presbyteros*), came to be exclusively used to describe this individual leader among the elders. Traditionally, the word *episkopos* is translated "bishop." The "bishop" (*episkopos*) in each local church served among the company of elders (*presbyteroi*) with the assistance of the deacons (*diakonoi*), and the "bishop" was himself one of the elders.[35]

A little later, around AD 110, Ignatius, bishop of Antioch, had been arrested, tried, and sentenced to death by the Roman governor. While being transported by Roman soldiers from Antioch in Syria to Rome to be fed to the wild animals for his faith in Christ, he was able to stop in several cities in Asia Minor and receive visitors from nearby villages. Through the letters of Ignatius we see quite clearly that the threefold order of bishop, elders, and deacons was widespread throughout Asia Minor. We know, for example, that a certain Onesimus was bishop of the church in Ephesus.[36] We also know that Ignatius had been visited in Smyrna by leadership from the church in Magnesia: "I was found worthy to see you in the persons of Damas, your godly bishop [*episkopos*], and your worthy presbyters [*presbyteroi*] Bassus and Apollonius, and my fellow servant, the deacon [*diakonon*] Zotion."[37] Also, the famous Polycarp, who had himself been a disciple of the apostle John, spent considerable time with Ignatius while the latter was in Smyrna. At one point Ignatius referred to the need for unity and submission to the established leadership in the church in Smyrna:

> Pay attention to the bishop [*episkopos*], in order that God may pay attention to you. I am a ransom on behalf of those who are obedient to the bishop [*episkopos*], presbyters [*presbyteroi*], and deacons [*diakonoi*]; may it be granted to me to have a place among them in the presence of God! Train together with one another: compete together, run together, suffer together, rest together, get up together, as God's managers, assistants, and servants.[38]

Through numerous early church writings and historians, we know that Polycarp was the bishop of Smyrna, having been appointed by the apostles themselves. We also know that Onesimus was the bishop of the church in Ephesus. Many of these bishops, or "presiding elders," had been students of the apostles and had been appointed to their positions of local church leadership by apostles, prophets, or their delegates.[39]

What we see when the apostles and prophets pass off the scene is a distinct order: (1) the single overseer (*episkopos*), who was the presiding elder, or, in our modern idiom, the "senior pastor"; (2) the elders (functioning as pastors, teachers, evangelists, etc.), who led individual home groups or, when the whole local church could meet in one place, carried on distinct responsibilities in the church; and (3) the deacons and, perhaps, deaconesses (ministers, servants, administrators), who assisted the elders in the work of the ministry.[40] There were no pastors who were not elders. The senior pastor was also an elder and accountable to the other elders, but he was uniquely responsible for overseeing the leadership, shepherding, and teaching work of the elders and deacons.

Though we don't have a lot of details about how these offices functioned from day to day, we can assume that the various tasks differed from church to church. Again, diversity within a basic structure seems to be the rule in the early church. Nevertheless, we can discern this basic postapostolic order of bishop (head pastor), elders (pastoral team), and deacons (pastoral assistants). This appears as the order established by the apostles, who intended it to continue after their departure.

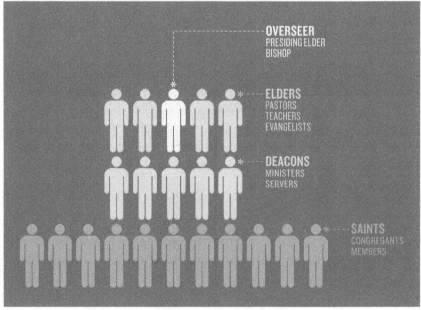

The permanent order of the local church established near the end of the ministry of the apostles and prophets consisted of a plurality of elders and a plurality of deacons led by a presiding elder.

How Did the Church's Order Develop throughout History?

As the centuries progressed, especially when the church first became a legal religion and then the favored religion in the Roman Empire, the office of bishop became a position of great honor and power. The church no longer regarded the bishop as a fellow elder and prime among equals, but his office was treated as higher than the elders. In this developed system the bishop had broad independent powers over large regions. The elders (later called "priests") were responsible for carrying out the bishop's work in their local church parishes. Deacons were the ministers who assisted the priests in the local ministry. As the churches developed greater complexity of relationships among bishops, additional levels of oversight developed, including archbishops. By the sixth century, the bishop of Rome maintained that he held a place of primacy over all other bishops and archbishops in the universal ("Catholic") church.[41]

We therefore can discern a development of church order that started with a relatively low local episcopal form established by the apostles and their delegates, then grew to a moderate local episcopal form after the apostles, and ultimately gave way to a hierarchical episcopal form in the medieval period. The low episcopal form seems to have functioned at a time when local churches had some degree of governmental autonomy, though they always had a consciousness of belonging to a greater universal community of churches and bishops, and often corresponded, fellowshipped, and shared in ministry together.[42] These were not what we would call independent churches, but interdependent churches, each with its own local church structure and headship, but actively engaged in a

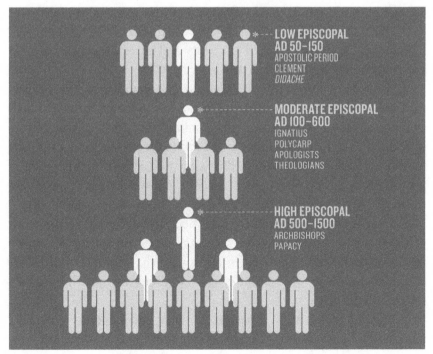

LOW EPISCOPAL
AD 50–150
APOSTOLIC PERIOD
CLEMENT
DIDACHE

MODERATE EPISCOPAL
AD 100–600
IGNATIUS
POLYCARP
APOLOGISTS
THEOLOGIANS

HIGH EPISCOPAL
AD 500–1500
ARCHBISHOPS
PAPACY

Through the centuries, church order developed in complexity and hierarchy far beyond that established by the apostles.

metacommunity of churches both near and far. To draw on a modern analogy, these local city churches functioned as a loose association similar to the Evangelical Free Church or, perhaps, the Southern Baptist Convention.

However, as history progressed, the original low to moderate episcopal structure became more and more complex and bureaucratic, resulting in a hierarchical system seen in the Episcopal, Anglican, Catholic, Orthodox, and, to some degree, Methodist traditions today. Though this episcopal model reflects the postapostolic office of the "bishop," it takes the office beyond the "prime among equals" status we see in the early church to an almost monarchical and independent status.

In reaction to this system many Protestants of the Reformed tradition, relying almost entirely on the temporary apostolic model of elders and deacons seen in the Bible, as well as addressing their own State-sponsored church needs, developed a Presbyterian or synod form of governance in which authority rested in levels of presbyteries—local, regional, and national. Though this "Presbyterian" system reflects the biblical and historical emphasis on the authority of the council of elders, it fails to take into account the apostles' appointment of the bishop as head elder and responsible leader of the local church. It also adds concentric rings of authority and bureaucracy that are not apparent in the Bible or the early church.

In reaction to both episcopal and Presbyterian forms, the congregationalists, drawing primarily on political concepts of constitutionalism, democracy, and independence, established a form of governance in which final authority rested in the local congregation of voting members. Such a church order does not at all reflect the apostolic or postapostolic order, which repeatedly emphasized the authority and responsibility resting on the shoulders of the presiding elder, elders, and deacons, who were trained, qualified, and ordained to the work of the ministry. Although congregations were the source of leadership and were often involved in approving the ordination of elders and deacons, the congregation of lay members was not the primary center of authority.[43]

It is typical for evangelical pastors, teachers, and scholars—especially independent church evangelicals—to say that the Bible does not have a prescriptive local church order, and that it is therefore up to us to determine what kind of governance works best in our own cultures.[44]

However, the statement that the Bible does not present a church order can only be maintained if we fail to read the Bible in its actual historical context, being insensitive to the transition from the apostolic to postapostolic ministry, and not allowing early Christian writings to help paint a fuller picture of what this postapostolic structure actually looked like. Sadly, while evangelicals have been great at studying the Bible, they have not been great at studying church history—especially the earliest church history that would help them actually read the Bible in its historical context in order to interpret it more accurately.[45]

As I have mentioned earlier, many evangelicals today insist that the threefold offices—in particular that of the presiding elder—were not authoritative apostolic developments, but illegitimate changes made in the second century. These changes, they believe, deviate from a simpler form of plurality of leadership and congregational self-rule. However, it is vital for conservative Bible-believing Christians to understand that this common perspective is *not* the result of an objective study of Scripture by Bible-believing scholars. Rather, this view entered evangelicalism when pastors and teachers uncritically adopted the views of liberal scholars such as F. C. Baur, Albrecht Ritschl, and Adolf Harnack.[46] Burtchaell writes:

> The beginnings of biblical criticism had made it possible—though not in sophisticated enough fashion to justify the confident reliance scholars would put upon it—to discern earlier from later New Testament publications, and hence to reconstruct a chronology of events and of theological development in the first (and, as many thought, early second) century. In addition, textual criticism of the Patristic literature now enabled scholars to date texts and to verify their authenticity better than before. This led the partisans of the consensus to hypothesize that in the most primitive period there were no officers or church organization, but that they had become solidly established in the course of the second century.[47]

Many evangelicals are unwittingly buying into the conclusions of liberal scholars who formed their historical reconstructions dependent on a late dating of New Testament documents.

But in the last twenty-five years, an explosion of interest in second-century studies among evangelicals has led many scholars to question the old, worn-out answer that the Bible does not prescribe a church order. Many scholars have come to critique many historical and contemporary forms of church governance, comparing them to the local church order the apostles established near the end of their ministries.[48] Though we Patristic scholars may disagree on various details of how these offices functioned, the general contours of a biblical-historical model of postapostolic church order are discernible.[49]

To conclude, a biblical-historical model of local church order includes trained, qualified, and ordained *deacons* (who function variously as ministers, servants, assistants, etc.); trained, qualified, and ordained *elders* (who function variously as pastors, teachers, evangelists, administrators, etc.); and a single trained, qualified, tried, and tested *overseer* (also known as bishop, presiding elder, senior pastor, etc.). Such a model incorporates the strengths of episcopal, Presbyterian, and even congregational church models, while remaining faithful to the order established by the apostles.[50]

Retrofitting

Restoring the Biblical-Historical Church Order

Though I have presented the contours of the biblical-historical local church order as established by the apostles to outlive their first-century ministries, the practical question becomes, is this early church order *descriptive* or *prescriptive*? That is, though the apostles and prophets established a particular church order in the late first century, are we Christians in the twenty-first century bound to this apostolic church order?

To this question we may see three kinds of responses. Those suffering from the Benjamin Button Syndrome (extreme primitivism) might seek a radical return to the most ancient model possible, even claiming to have new apostles and prophets.[51] Those infected with the Émile Coué Syndrome (extreme progressivism) couldn't care less what the apostles established for the early church, because times have changed and we know how to do things much better in our own culture. Those with an acute case of the Fuddy-Duddy Syndrome (extreme stagnation) are more or less stuck in their traditional way of organizing church leadership; even if the apostles themselves showed up in their churches and tried to change things, they'd beat them over the head with a copy of their church bylaws!

RetroChristianity seeks to *adapt* the apostolic teaching for the unique twenty-first-century context. Generally, this mediating position is compelled to *begin* with the apostolic model described in this chapter as its starting point, applying it to our twenty-first-century context in a way that acknowledges the cultural differences between the world of the apostles and our own. This position acknowledges that some things simply do not fit in our current cultures, but thinking through these issues is a difficult process that requires time, deliberation, and constant reevaluation.

In light of Paul's admonition to "stand firm and hold to the traditions that you were taught by us, either by our spoken word or by our letter" (2 Thess. 2:15), are we not obligated to pay close attention to the biblical-historical model as we think about our own twenty-first-century church order? It should not necessarily *radically transform* our current models, but as we seek to adjust our models of church order, the postapostolic model should at least *inform* our decisions. As we make adjustments, they must be thoughtful and prudent, not merely pragmatic and convenient.

However, we must never forget that the apostolic age was very different from our own, and simply *adopting* the biblical-historical model without *adapting* it can be disastrous. For example, the earliest bishops and elders were handpicked by the apostles and their delegates. Today we do not have apostles to appoint our pastor and elders. Also, the early churches enjoyed much more intimate interchurch community, so that each bishop and church was accountable to other bishops and churches in the region. Today our independent churches and many denominations do not have this kind of mutual accountability.

Another difference is that the early church did not have a complete canon of New Testament Scripture, and therefore the bishop and elders had to be relied upon to preserve and defend the oral teaching of the apostles. Today we have a full canon of Scripture, and final authority rests in the inspired, inerrant Word of God, to which all pastors and elders must submit. Similarly, the early church faced great challenges from false teachers with no stable creedal statements like the ones we have had since the fourth and fifth centuries. These threats demanded a strong leadership structure to provide doctrinal guidance in the midst of a hurricane of heresies. But today we have two thousand years of theological development and reflection, including the markers of orthodoxy, so that some of the issues that caused such concern in the early church are unquestioned by most believers. Differences like these must be considered as we approach the issue of how the biblical-historical model of church governance ought to inform our own approach. In short, we must *proceed with caution.*

I believe the biblical-historical model of church order should inform us as we think through questions of church governance, especially in constitutionally established independent churches and new church plants. As I reflect on "typical" (if I can use this term safely) tendencies in independent churches with regard to church governance, I suggest considering the following, all of which require careful, wise, and prayerful thought.

1. Consider unifying the pastoral staff and elders into a single leadership team of elders. It's impossible to justify biblically or historically a separation of elders and pastors into two separate groups. Biblically, all pastors must be elders. Certain elders may be ordained to full-time paid work in preaching, teaching, and evangelism, but being thus appointed does not mean these "employees" cease to be elders.[52] In the biblical-historical model, elders did not merely oversee the work of pastors, teachers, and evangelists, but they *were* the pastors, teachers, and evangelists.

2. Consider identifying the lead pastor as chairman of the elder board. If our senior pastor is to function in a way similar to the overseeing elder (*episkopos*) of the postapostolic model, then he should also function as the head of the team of elders. This would mean, of course, that we must consider restoring the senior pastor to his biblical place as the primary shepherd of the local church—not in a dictatorial sense, but always being accountable to his fellow elders while providing the personal point of leadership. This would make a separate

chairman of the elder board redundant, as the pastor himself would be the chairman.

3. Consider revising elder and deacon term limits. Many independent churches have elder and deacon term limits, like elected politicians. Nothing in the biblical-historical model suggests that elders and deacons in a local church served for a short time on a rotating basis. In fact, according to Clement of Rome's recollection, the apostles had appointed presbyters to serve until death. Without doubt, permanent or at least long-term elders would better fit the biblical-historical model.

4. Consider revisiting qualifications for elders and deacons. In light of the above suggestions, especially the return to the biblical identification of pastors as elders, the question of qualifications for eldership needs to be revisited. Because elders were the teaching, pastoring, and preaching leaders of the early church, we drift from the biblical model if our elders are not functioning in these roles. Those who are currently teaching, pastoring, and preaching should therefore be the elders. Since there is no biblical distinction between elders and pastors, our local church's elders should be sufficiently trained, ordained men, meeting the same qualifications as our pastors. Here are a couple rules of thumb: (1) if you wouldn't call a person to be a pastor at your church, don't make him an elder; (2) if a person couldn't pass a real ordination exam, he is not qualified to be an elder.

Of course, this final consideration challenges the concept of the "lay elder," which has become extremely popular in independent evangelical churches. Biblically, there is no such thing as a "lay elder." It's true that elders were identified, trained, approved, and ordained from among the congregation. It's also true that many elders in the early church carried on other professions besides preaching, teaching, and leading. And it's true that most elders were probably not full-time, compensated "clergy." However, it's simply not true that elders were drawn from untrained laypeople perceived as wise, mature saints who have good management skills and who represent a particularly important constituency in the church, but who have little or no actual ministry experience or training in Bible, theology, and history.

Again, if you couldn't ordain the person as a pastor, he has no
business being an elder. Any church member appointed to be an
elder must be functioning in a pastoral or teaching capacity. He
should be trained (though not necessarily formally at a Bible
college or seminary) in the essential elements of biblical, theological, and historical studies. And he should be able to pass an
ordination exam expected of any pastor.

The Third Mark: Ordinances

To maintain a balanced *orthodoxy*, we must focus on the fundamental
doctrines of the Christian faith in our preaching and teaching, which
will exclude destructive heresy and allow for diverse views on nonessentials. To uphold a proper biblical church *order*, church leaders
(presiding elder, elders, and deacons) must lead with wisdom and
humility, and the congregation must obey and submit to the ordained
leadership. But before we move on to the essential works of a church,
we must introduce the third mark—*ordinances* of baptism as the rite
of initiation into the covenant community and the Lord's Supper as
the rite of ongoing covenant renewal.

Not long ago a young man contacted me with concerns over his
church's apparent teaching and practice of Communion. He reported
that the pastor of the church taught that the biblical Lord's Supper
was never intended to hold a special place in church worship. Rather,
the Lord's Supper, he said, was identical to the love feast mentioned
once in Jude 1:12, and was therefore *any* meal that believers enjoyed
together. In fact, that Bible Church pastor boldly asserted that the
traditional in-church observance of the Lord's Supper was a "bas-
tardization" of its original intent (these are *his* words, not mine!).
And he added that he partook of the Lord's Supper three times a
day—whenever he "broke bread" with fellow believers at breakfast,
lunch, or dinner![53]

This radical teaching sounded strange to my friend. And rightly so!
All his life he had been taught that the Lord's Supper was a special
solemn rite of the covenanted church community—an integral and
special part of Christian worship. So, unsure of how to handle the
situation at his church, he called me for advice. My response to him

was simple: confirm that this was really what the pastor taught, then leave that "church," and bring as many people with him as he could.

I can count on one hand the times in my life I've recommended that people actually leave their local churches. But when a church's leadership intentionally tampers with a foundational mark of the local church, that organization ceases to be a biblical church. It may be a parachurch preaching or teaching ministry, it may be a worship experience, and it may contribute in its own way to the spiritual nourishment and growth of believers. But without the essential biblical mark of the ordinances, that organization is not an authentic local body of Christ.

Some of you may be scratching your heads, wondering, "What's the big deal? It's just the Lord's Supper. A piece of cracker and a sip of juice—barely a crumb and hardly a swallow!" My response? If you wouldn't leave your church over a failure to rightly observe the Lord's Table, you don't quite understand the essential mark of the ordinances and the role they play in the sanctification of the church. While most nontraditional evangelical churches say very little about the "ordinances" or "sacraments" of the church, every one of them mentions the observance of baptism and the Lord's Supper—the two sacraments that have always been held as central rites of the Christian church.

Much more will be said about the proper observance of the ordinances in part 4. Here we simply introduce the importance of baptism and the Lord's Supper as marks of the church. They transition us well into the next chapter on the works of the church, as these ordinances dovetail with the church's God-given tasks of evangelism, edification, and exaltation.

The first pillar of an authentic local church: the marks of orthodoxy, order, and ordinances

Conclusion

We have labored hard in this chapter constructing the first pillar of an authentic local church, which comprises the three marks of *ortho-doxy*, *order*, and *ordinances*. Orthodoxy refers to those fundamentals of the Christian faith that have been believed everywhere, always, and by all and corresponds with the Protestant emphasis on the Word of God purely preached and heard. Order emphasizes the necessity of properly trained and ordained elders and deacons of the church, to whom the ministry of the church has been entrusted. The ordinances of a local church are baptism as the rite of covenant initiation and the Lord's Supper as the rite of covenant renewal, both of which are closely associated with discipleship, discipline, and purity of the church.

In the next chapter we will construct the parallel pillar of the local church, which comprises the three essential works of *evangelism*, *edification*, and *exaltation*. Assuming the marks are firmly in place as the heart and soul of the church, that local body of believers will be poised to carry out its mission of glorifying God by making disciples of all nations.

The Essential Works
of a Local Church

He started out as a wandering soul. Born in Samaria near Jacob's well around AD 110, Justin spent the energy of his youth seeking ultimate meaning in the various competing philosophical schools of his day. He started with the Stoics, then moved to the Peripatetics, then to the Pythagoreans, and finally landed in the school of the Platonists, the followers of Socrates and Plato.[1] There he found what seemed to be a sublime depth of learning, a system that promised to finally lead his thoughts toward the true perception of God.

Yet at this time Justin had a "chance" encounter with a man near the city of Ephesus, a meeting that would alter the course of his life. While wandering in reflective solitude through a remote field far from the bustle of the city, Justin noticed an old man following him from a distance. Turning toward the man, who appeared to him "meek and venerable," Justin stared intently, surprised at his presence in such a secluded place.

After a few brief pleasantries, the old man engaged Justin in a deep discussion about whether Justin's budding philosophical inquiries were able to give him any certain and reliable knowledge about God. After wrangling about the limits of philosophy and convincing poor Justin that his studies in Platonism would lead to no sure knowledge of the divine, Justin asked the old man, in essence, "Then should any one even hire a teacher of philosophy? Or how could anyone be helped, if there isn't even truth in the philosophers?"[2]

With this open door, the old man helped Justin find the source of truth for which he had been searching:

> There existed, long before this time, certain men more ancient than all those who are esteemed philosophers, both righteous and beloved by God, who spoke by the Divine Spirit, and foretold events which would take place, and which are now taking place. They are called prophets. . . . Their writings are still extant, and he who has read them is very much helped in his knowledge of the beginning and end of things, and of those matters which the philosopher ought to know, provided he has believed them. . . . They both glorified the Creator, the God and Father of all things, and proclaimed His Son, the Christ [sent] by Him: which, indeed, the false prophets, who are filled with the lying unclean spirit, neither have done nor do, but venture to work certain wonderful deeds for the purpose of astonishing men, and glorify the spirits and demons of error. But pray that, above all things, the gates of light may be opened to you; for these things cannot be perceived or understood by all, but only by the man to whom God and His Christ have imparted wisdom.[3]

A few years later, Justin reflected on this first divine appointment with the gospel of Jesus Christ: "Straightway a flame was kindled in my soul; and a love of the prophets, and of those men who are friends of Christ, possessed me; and whilst revolving his words in my mind, I found this philosophy alone to be safe and profitable."[4]

Thus Justin's life as a Christian began. He continued to don the philosopher's distinct apparel, but when asked about his philosophical convictions, Justin pointed his hearers to the "true philosophy"—faith in Jesus Christ. About fifty-five years later, while serving as a renowned Christian teacher in the city of Rome, Justin Martyr was arrested, tried, and beheaded for his unwavering faith in Jesus Christ.

Prior to his martyrdom, Justin wrote two defenses of the Christian faith addressed to the Roman emperor, the Imperial family, the Roman Senate, and all the people of Rome. Besides responding to false charges against Christians, Justin described Christian worship in some detail in order to clear up any rumors regarding the practices of the church. His words give us a unique insight into the inner workings of the churches in the first fifty years after the apostles.[5]

> The wealthy among us help the needy; and we always keep together; and for all things wherewith we are supplied, we bless the Maker of all through His Son Jesus Christ, and through the Holy Ghost. And on the day called Sunday, all who live in cities or in the country gather together to one place, and the memoirs of the apostles or the writings of the prophets are read, as long as time permits; then, when the reader has ceased, the president verbally instructs, and exhorts to the imitation of these good things.
>
> Then we all rise together and pray, and, as we before said, when our prayer is ended, bread and wine and water are brought, and the president in like manner offers prayers and thanksgivings, according to his ability, and the people assent, saying Amen; and there is a distribution to each, and a participation of that over which thanks have been given, and to those who are absent a portion is sent by the deacons.
>
> And they who are well to do, and willing, give what each thinks fit; and what is collected is deposited with the president, who succours the orphans and widows and those who, through sickness or any other cause, are in want, and those who are in bonds and the strangers sojourning among us, and in a word takes care of all who are in need.
>
> But Sunday is the day on which we all hold our common assembly, because it is the first day on which God, having wrought a change in the darkness and matter, made the world; and Jesus Christ our Saviour on the same day rose from the dead. For He was crucified on the day before that of Saturn (Saturday); and on the day after that of Saturn, which is the day of the Sun, having appeared to His apostles and disciples, He taught them these things, which we have submitted to you also for your consideration.[6]

This was the common Christian experience according to Justin Martyr. Having been converted through the personal evangelism of an elderly Christian wandering in search of lost souls, Justin was instructed, baptized, and welcomed into fellowship with a local community covenanted to keep Christ and his commands at the center of their lives. His description of early Christian worship demonstrates that both edification of the body of Christ and exaltation of the triune God were essential features of the church's life.

In the last chapter we constructed the first pillar of a faithful and true local church—the marks of *orthodoxy, order,* and *ordinances.*

Returning to our incomplete structure, I want to focus on the three stones of the second pillar, which are exemplified in the writings of Justin Martyr and continually emphasized throughout church history: the essential works of a true local church, *evangelism, edification*, and *exaltation*. *Evangelism* focuses on the unsaved world, balancing both local and global missions. It includes invitation and initiation into the church through the gospel of salvation by grace through faith in the person and work of Christ (Matt. 28:18; Luke 24:46–49; John 20:30–31; Acts 1:8; Eph. 2:8–9). *Edification* describes the church's role of building up believers in love and good works through the participation of its various members in their Spirit-gifted ministries, resulting in unity and maturity (Matt. 28:19–20; Rom. 12:4–8; 1 Cor. 3:10–17; Eph. 2:19–22; 4:11–13; Heb. 5:12–14; 10:23–25). Finally, *exaltation* refers to the purpose, goal, and focus of the church—to glorify God the Father, through the Son, and by the power of the Spirit. The church must exalt God through corporate worship and prayer as well as by a God-glorifying presence in the world (Matt. 5:16; 25:34–40; Rom. 11:33–12:2; Gal. 1:3–5; 1 Pet. 4:8–11).

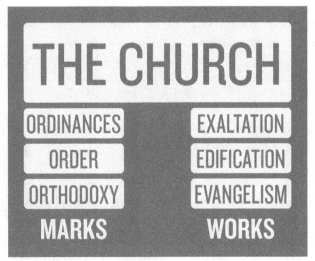

An authentic local church is supported by two pillars: the essential marks (orthodoxy, order, and ordinances) and the essential works (evangelism, edification, exaltation).

Let's take a closer look at the three essential works of a true local church.

Evangelism stands as the first stone in the pillar of the essential works of an authentic local church.

The First Work: Evangelism

When Justin Martyr asked the old man why he was wandering the remote fields around Ephesus, the man responded coyly, "I am concerned about some of my household. These are gone away from me; and therefore have I come to make personal search for them, if, perhaps, they shall make their appearance somewhere."[7] This response reminds us of Jesus's own parable of the lamb that had gone astray in Luke 15:3–7, an illustration of the compassion Christ has for lost souls and the need for evangelism. In Justin's case, the old man had likely been praying and searching for an opportunity to personally engage in a discussion of spiritual things with unbelievers in order to bring a lost lamb into the sheepfold.

The Greek word *euangelizo*, from which we get our English word "evangelize," means "to proclaim a good message." Evangelism involves reaching out to unbelievers with the good news ("gospel") that Jesus Christ died for their sins and rose from the dead to bring forgiveness and new life. As such, evangelism is not directed toward the church, but toward the lost world. Thus, the normal venue for evangelism is not in the worship service (though it *may* occur here, as in 1 Cor. 14:24–25). Rather, the most effective evangelism takes place in the world through both passive and active *intentionality*.

Passively, as believers live their everyday lives, they exhibit the person of Christ and make the most of every opportunity to give a response to anyone who inquires about the hope they have (1 Pet. 3:15). At the same time, every believer must *actively* engage in planned evangelistic activities, either individually or corporately, designed to harvest those unbelievers whom God has prepared for faith in Jesus

Christ (Luke 10:2; John 6:44; Acts 2:39; 13:48). All believers must simultaneously prepare for opportunities for evangelism that may come their way and deliberately engage in active evangelism.

The church's essential work of evangelism is most clearly prescribed in Matthew 28:19. In the Great Commission Jesus ordered his disciples, "Go therefore and make disciples of all nations, baptizing them in the name of the Father and of the Son and of the Holy Spirit." Notice what Jesus doesn't say here. He doesn't say, "Donate to a global mission society," or, "Pay some seminary graduate a salary to run an outreach program," or, "Leave a tract for the waitress instead of a decent tip." He says, "Go!" He doesn't say, "Go to other churches and steal their sheep," or, "Place ads and hang flyers for a low-key, high-budget, nonoffensive outreach event," or, "Let your next-door neighbors see your bland, upper-middle-class, moralistic lifestyles and hope they somehow become curious enough about how you spend your Sunday mornings that they ask about how they, too, can be upstanding, right-leaning, well-to-do citizens." No, he tells his disciples to "go and make disciples of all nations."

Clearly, evangelism—with the goal of converting unbelievers to Christ and initiating them into the Christian faith—is an essential work of the local church. We should never replace it with either *ineffective* activity or *in*activity.

Evangelism and the Marks of the Church

The essential work of evangelism is dependent on the biblical marks of the local church. First, evangelism depends on the mark of orthodoxy with regard to the content of its message about Christ's person and work, that is, *the gospel* (Rom. 1:1–4; 1 Cor. 15:1–5). If a person engaged in evangelism doesn't have an orthodox view of the fundamentals of the gospel, that person may be involved in proselytizing, persuading, or even storytelling, but not in evangelism. A clear understanding of the essential truths of the historic Christian faith will help clarify our message and keep us from programmed distractions symptomatic of church leaders who don't have a grasp of the nature and purpose of the church's basic proclamation.

Second, the church's work of evangelism is dependent on proper order in the church. The pastoral elders are to equip the congregation for the work of evangelism (Eph. 4:11–17). They are to lead by example and to train the members of the church in both orthodox teaching concerning the gospel and how to share it with others. The teaching elders of the church should serve as excellent resources when believers encounter non-Christian religions, false-Christian sects, or difficult questions or challenges by unbelievers. Being able to turn to church leaders who have training and experience in such areas has great value for the church's work of evangelism. Thus, the leaders of the church play a major role in preparing, motivating, and mobilizing the church for the work of evangelism.

Finally, the work of evangelism is related to the mark of ordinances. Matthew 28:19 says we are to make disciples from among the nations by "baptizing them in the name of the Father and of the Son and of the Holy Spirit." Baptism is the act that signifies the end of the evangelism for the new believer and the beginning of the work of edification, or growing as a disciple of Christ. Many churches have too long deemphasized this profound and powerful moment when a person's inward conviction of faith is expressed through a public act of confession and pledge of commitment. Fearful that a new believer might confuse the rite of baptism for a work that brings salvation, many have downplayed its biblical role as *the exclusive response to the gospel.*

In the early church people who were convinced of the truth of the gospel and who committed to live the Christian life did not "come forward," "pray the sinner's prayer," "ask Jesus into their hearts," "raise their hands with their heads bowed," or confess their new faith by any other man-made external sign. Rather, following the clear and consistent example of the apostles themselves (Acts 2:41), they submitted to water baptism as the outward sign of their faith, without which the church did not officially accept their conversion. Justin Martyr recounts how Christians, having been convinced of the truth of the gospel through evangelism, responded by baptism:

> I will also relate the manner in which we dedicated ourselves to God when we had been made new through Christ. . . . As many as are persuaded and believe that what we teach and say is true, and undertake to be able to live accordingly, are instructed to pray and to entreat God with fasting, for the remission of their sins that are past, we praying and fasting with them. Then they are brought by us where there is water, and are regenerated in the same manner in which we were ourselves regenerated.[8] For, in the name of God, the Father and Lord of the

universe, and of our Saviour Jesus Christ, and of the Holy Spirit, they
then receive the washing with water.[9]

Everybody's an Evangelist

I sometimes hear Christians say things like, "The church needs to do
more outreach," or, "The church needs to focus more on evangelism,"
or, "The church doesn't baptize enough new believers." But if *we* are
the church, the responsibility lies with *us*, not with some undefined
invisible entity called "the church." If we wait around for our hyperbusy,
overburdened, time-taxed pastors and staff members to do everything
we're supposed to be doing, our churches will die. We sit back and
complain that this or that ministry isn't drawing people to our church.
Or we worry that visitors won't come back if we don't offer them
such and such amenities. But the problem isn't with the ministry, the
music, or the media. The problem is with *us*—the *messengers*!

Evangelism is not only the work of the gifted and trained evangelist
or the elders of the church. Evangelism is the work of every believer.
Each of us has a sphere of influence among unsaved family members,
friends, coworkers, and acquaintances we meet regularly. In fact, church
members have more contact with unsaved people than full-time church
workers! Remember, the role of the leadership of the church is not to
do the work of the ministry, but to equip the *saints* for the work of
service (Eph. 4:12). If you're a believer, you're an evangelist.

The sad reality about church growth in America is that few churches
grow because of evangelism. Most church growth comes from old-
fashioned saint-rustling. We think that if they aren't branded, they're
free for the taking! Why is it that when numbers decline and people
don't come, we scratch our heads and try to decide what piece of
furniture to plant in the lobby, what gimmick to add to the worship
service, or what PR stunt to pull to get people "out there" to notice us?
Let's set the gimmicks aside and go back to the ancient, time-tested,
foolproof method of authentic church growth: *evangelism*.

Cosmetic changes to our buildings, our programs, or our ministry
staff won't bring the change of heart needed with regard to rescuing
the perishing and initiating them into a living, growing community
of faith. Until we redirect our time, efforts, and funds to the essential
work of evangelism, we'll continue to have a tough time overcoming
the diminishing effectiveness of the preference-driven church.

Edification, the second stone in the pillar of essential works of a local church, flows practically from the work of evangelism.

The Second Work: Edification

Edification logically follows evangelism. Edification is best defined as "building up" believers in the faith and is synonymous with "discipleship" or "growing in Christ." Unlike the work of evangelism, edification is directed toward the church, not the world. It follows and flows from the rite of baptism. That is, only those who have been converted to Christ can grow in him. Edification is suggested in the second part of Jesus's command in the Great Commission of Matthew 28:19. The Savior charged the apostles to "go and make disciples, baptizing them [the end of evangelism] . . . teaching them to observe all that I have commanded you [the process of edification]." In edification, the disciple-maker's role is to teach and model. The disciple's role is to learn and follow.

In Justin Martyr's description of the life of the local church, we saw several body-building activities that occurred regularly, all of which find biblical precedence.

- The wealthy aided the needy through free will offerings (Gal. 2:10; 1 Cor. 16:2; 1 Tim. 6:18).
- The church gathered on Sundays to commemorate Christ's resurrection (John 20:1, 19; Acts 20:7; 1 Cor. 16:2; Rev. 1:10).
- The Old and New Testament Scriptures were read (Col. 4:16; 1 Thess. 5:27; 1 Tim. 4:13).
- The presiding elder taught and preached (1 Tim. 5:17; 2 Tim. 4:2).
- The church observed the Lord's Supper (1 Cor. 10:16–17, 21; 11:20–21; 23–26).

Many of these same practices continue today in our churches, perhaps taking on different forms. In the early church we see a healthy balance of providing for both physical and spiritual needs in the church. The primary purpose of the free will offering was to provide physical nourishment for the widows, orphans, sick, and destitute. However, most of the time spent during the weekly service involved instruction (teaching) and exhortation (preaching), culminating in a time of response through participation in the Lord's Supper.

Edification Requires Trustworthy Teaching

As a child I once tried putting my schoolbooks under my pillow at night, somehow believing that by mystical osmosis the information from the books would pass into my brain and I wouldn't have to actually study. The result? I ended up with a stiff neck and a bad grade! Sadly, this is how some Christians live their spiritual lives. They believe that by some mystical, supernatural miracle, the Holy Spirit will simply grow them toward maturity apart from any actual teaching, instruction, or active participation on their part. They just show up, soak in spirituality for an hour or so a week, then spend the rest of their week wondering why they're living a defeated Christian life instead of the victorious Christian life described in Scripture.

The truth is that we all need to develop an "Ezra" mentality. When the Old Testament figure Ezra discovered the treasure of God's Word, he "set his heart to study the Law of the LORD, and to do it and to teach his statutes and rules in Israel" (Ezra 7:10). However, as you work hard at studying the Scriptures, don't forget Peter's warning against the "untaught" who "distort" the Scriptures to their own destruction (2 Pet. 3:16 NASB). Learning God's Word was never meant to be an independent study or correspondence course. Rather, God gave teachers to the churches to equip the saints and to build them up toward maturity (Eph. 4:11–13).

Thus, a major emphasis in a healthy local church must be the unapologetic preaching and teaching of God's inspired Word by teachers who have been trained to handle it faithfully in its historical and theological context. Clearly this aspect of edification requires a robust order of qualified leaders and a clear sense of biblical orthodoxy.

Tertullian of Carthage, around the year AD 200, gave this fascinating snapshot of the teaching and preaching ministry in the church of his day: "We assemble to read our sacred writings, if any peculiarity of the times makes either forewarning or reminiscence needful. However it be in that respect, with the sacred words we nourish our faith, we animate our hope, we make our confidence more steadfast; and no less by inculcations of God's precepts we confirm good habits."[10]

Note that the teaching of Scripture focused on what was needful for the moment, providing practical exhortation sensitive to the congregation's needs. This requires teaching and preaching elders who *know* their congregations, live among them, endure the same trials, and face the same challenges. Sadly, many methods of modern preaching and teaching in the church prevent pastors and teachers from knowing their congregations intimately enough to apply the Scriptures to their lives. Massive meetings in which the pulpit is a stage and the congregation is an audience can make this difficult. Satellite campuses in which messages from the mother ship are piped in to little-known audiences create too much relational distance for pastors and teachers to minister the Scriptures effectively. And "virtual churches" with contact via the Internet is utterly unacceptable from this perspective. The church must emphasize smaller meetings, on-the-ground ministry leaders, and a truly *incarnational* ministry philosophy in which elders and deacons lead by serving *in the midst* of their congregations. This involves actually training and equipping others to assist in carrying out the work of the ministry.

Edification Requires Persistent Prayer

If teaching is the mind of the local body, prayer is the heart. Without prayer, edification is impossible. Paul wrote, "And it is my prayer that your love may abound more and more, with knowledge and all discernment, so that you may approve what is excellent, and so be pure and blameless for the day of Christ, filled with the fruit of righteousness that comes through Jesus Christ, to the glory and praise of God" (Phil. 1:9–11). When was the last time you prayed like Paul for the edification of your fellow believers in the church? In Ephesians 6:18 Paul urged his readers to pray "at all times in the Spirit" as the essential key to perseverance in the midst of spiritual warfare. In fact, just a brief survey of the book of Acts will reveal how vital prayer was for the growth of the infant church (e.g., Acts 1:14; 2:42; 3:1; 4:31; 6:4; 10:2; 12:5).

But Jude most explicitly ties prayer to edification when he writes, "But you, beloved, building yourselves up in your most holy faith *[that's edification!]* and praying in the Holy Spirit, keep yourselves in the love of God, waiting for the mercy of our Lord Jesus Christ that leads to eternal life" (Jude 1:20–21). Clearly, prayer is both the heart and the lifeblood of the local church.

Tertullian describes the early church's practice of prayer this way: "We meet together as an assembly and congregation, that, offering up prayer to God as with united force, we may wrestle with Him in our supplications."[11] Prayer indeed is a fundamental means of promoting unity and nurturing spiritual growth.

Edification Requires Church Discipline

Edification also includes corporate discipline, which we might call the "negative" aspect of applying God's Word. Sometimes when believers have hardened their hearts against the truths of Scripture, discipline is required, just as a child requires discipline from his parents to learn and grow. Jesus describes in Matthew 18:15–17 how this discipline is to be formally applied in a local church: "If your brother sins against you, go and tell him his fault, between you and him alone. If he listens to you, you have gained your brother. But if he does not listen, take one or two others along with you, that every charge may be established by the evidence of two or three witnesses. If he refuses to listen to them, tell it to the church. And if he refuses to listen even to the church, let him be to you as a Gentile and a tax collector" (Matt. 18:15–17).

The notion of "excommunication" comes from the biblical concept of church discipline. God has charged mature members—and ultimately the leadership—of a local church with the task of maintaining proper discipline in the church. This includes protecting the sanctity of the ordinances, which means preventing wayward saints from participating in the Lord's Table as the rite of continued fellowship and covenant renewal (see 1 Cor. 5:9–13). This may seem harsh, judgmental, and even unloving in our anything-goes culture, but anything less than proper discipline not only threatens the work of edification in the local body, but also damages the marks of order and the ordinances. In short, it leads to the destruction of the church.

It has become a common practice among our evangelical churches to neglect this aspect of edification, and the consequences have been disastrous. The individuals or groups who need to be confronted about their continued sin never receive discipline, and the entire church suffers from this failure to lead the sinners to repentance and restoration or to remove them from the fellowship. This major problem can be resolved by returning to a set of more historical practices with regard to our church communities.

First, churches must strengthen their approach to church membership, requiring better training and preparation for membership, maintaining accurate membership rolls, and presenting membership as a "covenant relationship" between the body and its members. Thus, when discipline becomes necessary, the church leadership will have consistent guidelines—made clear to members when they joined—for carrying out this difficult responsibility. The early church viewed baptism as part of a solemn "oath," in which the new believer was swearing to live as a Christian within the community, accepting both the rights and responsibilities of church membership. This included the expectation that if he or she were to stray, discipline was expected.[12]

Second, churches must restore a means of interchurch accountability through what former generations called "letters missive." It has become far too easy for unruly and rebellious believers or Christians under church discipline to simply leave their church and flee to another to make a fresh, undisciplined start. However, not many decades ago it was the common practice for churches of various denominations to provide "letters of dismissal" for covenanted church members in good standing who wanted to leave their current church and join a different one. Though Christians needed to fulfill the requirements for church membership at the receiving church, the "letter of dismissal" confirmed that the new candidate for membership was not currently under disciplinary action at his or her previous church. Restoring this practice to our local church life would help strengthen interchurch fellowship and accountability and return our churches to a more historically authentic and biblically faithful approach to church membership, discipline, and order.

Going Retro

The Axe and the Hose

Max DePree, author of *Leadership Is an Art,* relays a story about a fireman's response to a child locked in a bathroom. After several people failed to open the door, the fire department arrived and rescued the girl by smashing through with an axe. When the child's father complained to a friend about the damage, his friend replied, "A fireman has two tools, an axe and a hose. If you call him, you're going to get one."[13]

The answer to the dilemma of the child locked in the bathroom wasn't to ask the fireman to trade his sharp axe for a locksmith's precision tools. The answer was to call a locksmith.

I believe the "axe and hose" principle also holds true for the biblical principle of spiritual gifts in the body of Christ—the operations of which are necessary for carrying out the essential works of the church: evangelism, edification, and exaltation.

Many believers today understand spiritual gifts this way: at salvation the Spirit endows individuals with particular gifts. One may have the gift of teaching, another the gift of administrations, another helps, another faith, and so forth. In this model, the responsibility of the believer is to discover his or her gifts and then fulfill his or her purpose by exercising these gifts in ministry. This is the *violin soloist* model, in which you alone are responsible to play your part with excellence when the time arrives. Fail to show up or keep up, and the concert gets fouled up!

Years ago a friend of mine toyed with a different interpretation of spiritual gifts. He suggested that the Spirit actually gives all of the biblical gifts to a single individual Christian at different times in his or her ministry, depending on that person's needs. For example, if a believer needs to evangelize, the Spirit will give her the gift of evangelism. If a Christian needs to serve as a pastor, God would endow him with shepherding. If believers need to teach, the Lord will gift them as teachers. In other words, the Spirit will empower an individual with various gifts whenever that individual needs them for different aspects of ministry. I call this the *one-man-band* model, in which you play all the parts, by yourself, as the Spirit enables you. Oh, what a lovely quartet: me, myself, I, and the Holy Spirit!

I see flaws in both of these approaches. Though on the surface they may seem like complete opposites, in fact they have one thing in common: *they both focus on the individual.* But when I read Paul's passages on spiritual gifts, I discover that the focus always moves from individuals and their gifts to the family of God and their edification. First Corinthians 12:7 puts it clearly: "To each is given the manifestation of the Spirit for the common good."

God has gifted individual believers in such a way that we *need* each other for accomplishing the tasks of evangelism, edification, and exaltation. To put it bluntly: *God never intended for one person to do it all.* As far as spiritual gifts go, we're not called to be either a *violin soloist* or a *one-man-band.* Paul said, "God arranged the members in the body, each one of them, as he chose" (1 Cor. 12:18). This means God has placed you into his church for specific purposes. But those purposes are inseparably linked to the gifts and purposes of all other believers. We must depend on each other—*really depend on each other.* We're not just a single performer standing in the spotlight or an individual soloist dutifully playing an important part. By his sovereign design, God purposed that our unique spiritual gifts complement each other, like members of a jazz quartet or a chamber orchestra.

In fact, let me take this in a direction you may not have considered before. Instead of taking spiritual gift inventories simply to determine our personal giftedness, maybe we should also take note of our *un*-giftedness—those areas of weakness for which we desperately need others. As we survey our ministry goals, build our ministry teams, and then begin to minister, we need to be sensitive not only to our strengths, but also to our weaknesses.

But this demands the most difficult part of the equation: *humility.*

It takes humility to say, "I'm a teacher, but I'm a lousy administrator." Who wants to be a lousy *anything*? It takes a humble spirit to say, "I'm good at hospitality, but I have trouble discerning people's needs." And it takes an extra portion of meekness to turn this admission into a plea for help from those who are strong in those areas.

Ideally, church leaders try to match spiritual gifts to ministry needs. This doesn't always happen, of course. Sometimes, to fit urgent needs, administrators are asked to teach or teachers are asked to administrate. Let's admit it. The fireman comes a lot quicker than the locksmith. However, this arrangement often ends with Max De Pree's principle of the "axe and hose." The job might get done, but it will often leave a mess that requires a lot of cleanup.

But matching a person's gifts to a particular ministry is only a first step. We must also match believers' gifts with other believers' ungiftedness. This leads to three practical actions we can take.

First, have you matched your gifts with the right ministry needs for edification of the body? If not, do it. There's a gap that needs to be filled even as you read these words. Or, perhaps worse, a frustrated saint is dutifully holding your place until the right fit comes along. It's time for you to report for duty.

Second, if you've already matched your gifts with the right ministry, have you unwittingly adopted the "axe and hose" principle? Are you trying to do it all, forgetting that God intentionally un-gifted you in certain areas so other believers can complement your ministry? What are your weaknesses? Who can you ask to fill that need and free you to do what God meant for you to do?

Finally, if you've made your match and humbly built your team, are there others who need your help making their own matches? Gently encourage people to step up to the plate. Ask how they're fitting into the essential works of the church. Find out if they're frustrated in their roles. Playing "matchmaker" will not only help gifted saints, but it will also minister to the entire body of Christ.

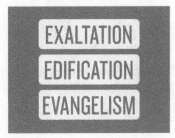

The complete second pillar of an authentic local church: the works of evangelism, edification, and exaltation

The Third Work: Exaltation

The Reformed *Westminster Shorter Catechism* of 1647 opens with this question: "What is the chief end of man?" The answer: "Man's chief end is to glorify God, and to enjoy him forever."[14] The chief end of man must of necessity be the chief end of the church, so the third essential work of every local church must be *exaltation*, that is, "giving praise and glory to God." Ultimately, everything we do should be to the praise of his glory (Eph. 1:12, 14). In fact, even the mundane things of this life should be done "to the glory of God" (1 Cor. 10:31). Thus, we glorify God through both our words and our works, in corporate as well as individual worship. We will examine the elements of personal worship in part 4; in this section we focus primarily on the elements of the church's corporate worship.

Returning to Justin Martyr's second-century description of Christian worship, we see that the church's worship focused on the triune God: "For all things wherewith we are supplied, we bless the Maker of all through His Son Jesus Christ, and through the Holy Ghost." Gathering every Sunday to commemorate and celebrate Christ's day of resurrection, these early believers engaged in corporate prayer, often led by the presiding elder and assented to by the church's "amen." At the climax of this worship, they offered prayers and thanksgivings in conjunction with the corporate observance of the Lord's Supper on a weekly basis: "When our prayer is ended, bread and wine and water are brought, . . . and there is a distribution to each, and a participation of that over which thanks have been given, and to those who are absent a portion is sent by the deacons."[15]

With just this brief glimpse at early Christian worship, we see that the three marks of the church—orthodoxy, order, and ordinances—are already put to work in the church's exaltation. By coming together on Sunday to celebrate the Lord's Supper and to offer praise and prayer to the triune God, the church is rehearsing their christocentric theology and Trinitarian creation and redemption narrative.[16] Similarly, proper church order is necessary, as the presiding elder and other ministers of the church are to be actively involved in prayer and distribution of the Lord's Supper. Finally, it was the original and universal practice of all of the churches to observe the ordinance of the Lord's Supper at the climax of their worship, the table open only to those who had been baptized in the name of the Father, Son, and Holy Spirit. The work of exaltation also involved the edification of believers, as those who participated in the church's worship were themselves nourished in their faith. Thus, the vital mark of exaltation becomes the crowning work of the local church—the foundation and capstone, ground and goal of its existence.

In light of these biblical and historical emphases, we must recognize that the vital mark of exaltation involves more than just lending our physical presence to a Sunday morning worship service. Exaltation involves adoration and service and represents our *response* to the proclamation of the Word. This will be described in greater detail in part 4, when we examine details of corporate spiritual disciplines and worship.

There is no limit to the varieties, means, and manner of corporate worship if the clear and uncompromising purpose is to declare the glory and majesty of our Creator and Redeemer, the triune God. The Bible, especially the book of Psalms, gives a stunning example of the variety of ways in which believers adore God and attribute all glory and honor and worth to him. The worship style is not the main issue. The direction of worship is primary. We are to worship God-ward, not man-ward. Means of worship that don't turn our hearts and minds and whole beings to God can't be properly regarded as biblical exaltation.

But we must never reduce exaltation merely to what goes on during Sunday worship. Rather, a life of worship is a life of continual consecration to God, involving not only how we respond personally and corporately to the triune God, but how we respond to others. Christ tells us that the service we perform for others is actually service to him (Matt. 25:34–40).

Similarly, 1 John 3:23 says, "And this is his commandment, that we believe in the name of his Son Jesus Christ and love one another, just as he has commanded us." This love for others reflected in our good works is meant to bring glory to God. Jesus said, "In the same way, let your light shine before others, so that they may see your good works and give glory to your Father who is in heaven" (Matt. 5:16).

Christians shouldn't stop glorifying God with the final worship chorus, closing hymn, or benediction on Sunday morning. We are to live lives of worship by loving others, serving them, and meeting their needs. God is glorified when his people, who are made in his image, fulfill the purpose for which they were created. Love fulfills that purpose. Therefore, the local church must be in the business of organized adoration of God as well as genuine love and service for one another. Both adoration and service are meant for exaltation of the Almighty.

In fact, in the early second century the Greek apologist Aristides of Athens was able to point to the good works of the Christians as a mark of their authentic faith. In this way Christian charity became a means of accomplishing *all three works of the church*—evangelism, edification, and exaltation. Aristides wrote:

Now the Christians, O king, . . . do good to those who are their neighbors, and when they are judges they judge uprightly . . . and whatever they do not wish that others should do to them, they do not practice toward any one . . . and those who grieve them they comfort, and make them their friends; and they do good to their enemies. . . . And from the widows they do not turn away their countenance, and they rescue the orphan from him who does him violence, and he who has gives to him who has not, without grudging; and when they see a stranger they bring him to their dwellings. . . . But when one of their poor passes away from the world, and any of them sees him, then he provides for his burial according to his ability; and if they hear that any of their number is imprisoned or oppressed for the name of their Messiah, all of them provide for his needs, and if it is possible that he may be delivered, they deliver him.[17]

For too long evangelicals have neglected the poor, the sick, the homeless, and the outcasts. With few exceptions, church growth strategies of the last several decades have focused on the upwardly mobile, the healthy, the affluent, and the culturally refined—those who could immediately invest their time and money into the church, bring their middle-class friends and families, and project a desirable image for the growing church. The time has come for the church to fully embrace her mission to the world, opening wide her doors to those who can give nothing in return for her benevolence, and thereby glorifying God alone through her acts of unconditional, Christ-like love.

Conclusion

In this chapter we have completed the second pillar of an authentic local church: the three works of *evangelism, edification,* and *exaltation.* Assuming the marks of *orthodoxy, order,* and *ordinances* are firmly in place as the heart and soul of the church, the works of the church direct its mission, vision, and daily activities toward the proclamation of the person and work of God the Son (*evangelism*), through the building up of the body of Christ for the work of ministry through God the Holy Spirit (*edification*), ultimately directing us to the glorification of God the Father (*exaltation*). Having constructed this basic framework of the marks and works of a local church, we are ready to approach the topic of growing in Christ in the final section of this book, "RetroSpirituality."

Part 4

RetroSpirituality:
Living the Forgotten Faith Today

Like newborn infants, long for the pure spiritual milk, that by it you may grow up into salvation. —1 Peter 2:2

Speaking the truth in love, we are to grow up in every way into him who is the head, into Christ, from whom the whole body, joined and held together by every joint with which it is equipped, when each part is working properly, makes the body grow so that it builds itself up in love. —Ephesians 4:15–16

In the 1997 film *As Good as It Gets*, Jack Nicholson played an author named Melvin Udall with severe obsessive-compulsive disorder struggling to cope with the real world. In one scene Nicholson's character, after unsuccessfully attempting to barge in on his psychiatrist for an emergency meeting, stares into the waiting room filled with nervous, troubled clients and blurts out, "What if this is as good as it gets?"

After many years studying the forefathers of our faith, I've learned that a common experience among the vast majority of Christians is *struggle*. Just when our struggle brings victory, it opens up a whole new (or even *old*) conflict with sin. And in the midst of the conflict, with no end in sight, we can easily grow disillusioned, wondering, "Is this as good as it gets? Does God even *want* my life to be better? Why doesn't he help?"

We've all been there. Slowly climbing the narrow road of the Christian life, we suddenly take a bad step and end up blowing it . . . *again*. The progress we had made along that precarious path becomes pointless as we slide down that craggy ledge and find ourselves once again brushing the dirt off our white robes and bandaging bruises that mark us as defeated saints. As we ponder whether it's even worth pressing on, Satan taunts us from the nearby outcroppings, urging us to just give up. Even worse, our more "saintly" brothers and sisters in Christ shake their heads and cluck their tongues as they peer at us accusingly from farther up the slope.

The life of spiritual growth, impressively called "sanctification," can often feel like an exercise in absolute and utter futility. Frustration, exasperation, exhaustion, disillusionment, depression—sadly, these are some of the feelings that accompany the failures of struggling saints as they desperately try to live the Christian life, putting to death the desires of the flesh and living out the fruit of the Spirit. The seemingly endless cycle of *sin—repentance—sin—repentance—sin—repentance* can nauseate us, making us wonder whether real sanctification is even possible in this life—convincing many that it's not.

Let's face it, in many of our approaches to the Christian life, it's easy to get burned out, wiped out, worn out . . . *sancti-fried*.

One cause of our frustration with sanctification is our unrealistic expectation. We've heard so many stories about people being "delivered" from alcoholism, drug addiction, or sexual immorality. Testimonies shine brilliantly with flashy conversions in which a person's life alters dramatically, in which a new birth seems to have completely killed the old man. The struggling Christian who endures the painfully slow process of sanctification might be able to handle hearing about these miraculous transformations if it weren't for those few who try to force their amazing experiences on everybody else. "God saved me and delivered me instantly from such-and-such, and he'll do the same for you!" But when my instant deliverance doesn't come, whose fault is it? God's? Surely not! It must, of course, be *my* fault because I'm just too weak, too faithless, too immature, too carnal. Or maybe I'm just not really saved. If the Spirit of God did it for *her*, why won't he do it for *me*?

I'll never forget the answer an older Bible college professor of mine, Dr. Charles Ryrie, gave, when a student asked about how to win in his struggle against sin. I paraphrase: "Young Christians are always coming to me saying, 'I'm struggling with this sin, or I keep struggling with that sin,' as if there's something wrong with struggling with sin. That's good! Struggle! It's when you give up struggling that something's wrong."

Those words are golden. Not only do they reflect the thoughts of a mature saint with many decades of Christian living behind him, but they represent the totality of the Christian tradition as it relates to the spiritual life: *the struggle is normal*. Put another way, *the daily struggle against sin has been the normal Christian experience everywhere, always, and by all*. And by "all" I mean all believers of *every* age—

- from Paul's deeply moving transparency in Romans 7,
- to Augustine's soul-wrenching conflict with his sinful lifestyle,
- to Martin Luther's constant warfare against the world, the flesh, and the devil,
- to John Bunyan's allegory of Christian's journey in *The Pilgrim's Progress*,
- to my own up-and-down life of temptation, sin, repentance, and victory.

Being a Christian connected to the historical Christian faith means standing in a long line of dirty, ragged, beaten-up pilgrims struggling with daily sin, putting up a brutal fight against temptation, and hoping for deliverance with a seemingly unreasonable faith. The frustrating, unending, wearisome struggle between the flesh and the Spirit is, in most cases, as good as it gets.

Already in our journey through the basics of RetroChristianity, we've touched on several topics addressing the issue of spiritual growth or "sanctification." In part 4 of our exploration, we focus directly on a number of biblical, historical, theological, and practical issues related to spiritual growth. In chapter 10, I discuss the church's role in spiritual growth—the work of the Spirit in the community that leads to sanctification. This includes a discussion of corporate worship, the sacraments, and the priesthood of believers. In chapter 11, I examine the need for personal spiritual discipline, balancing the individual approach to the spiritual life with biblical and historical insight. Finally, in chapter 12, I conclude with a discussion of how the concepts of RetroChristianity can be implemented immediately and constructively in the Christian life, with suggestions for moving forward to reform evangelicalism by reclaiming the forgotten faith.

From "Me" to "We"

Growing Together in Christ

f you've ever had a vehicle got stuck in the mud or snow—I mean really *stuck*—you know the feeling of absolute frustration and hopelessness. You try everything: shifting into low gear, jerking the steering wheel to the right or left, spinning the wheels in reverse, pushing the gas pedal to the floor, even emptying extra weight to lighten your load. Finally, with mud or slush covering every square inch of your vehicle, you admit defeat. You accept the fact that the only solution to your inextricable dilemma is to call for help.

Whether we like it or not, that's the Christian life. Each of us, *left to ourselves*, is hopelessly stuck in the mire of our own depravity. We've already seen in chapter 4 that classic orthodoxy holds that apart from God's sovereign acts of grace, we're helpless. In light of the biblical and historical view of depravity, even the analogy of being stuck in the mud breaks down. The truth is that apart from God's illuminating grace, we're ignorant of our condition and thus unwilling and unable to do anything about it. Instead, without God pulling us free from the muck and washing us clean, we would willingly wallow in the slime of our own filth like hogs rolling in the mud.

But thankfully God didn't leave us to ourselves. He provided the death and resurrection of Christ to pay the penalty for our sin and to grant us new life. He sent his Spirit to regenerate us—not merely on our spiritual birthday, but *constantly*. We have an eternal relationship with the Spirit of Life, who continues his regenerating work in us. Yes, God has *declared* us righteous once and for all in Christ Jesus ("justification"). But he is also *making* us righteous by his Spirit ("sanctification"). But if Christianity teaches that God is responsible for the work of sanctification, what part do we play in our spiritual growth? Is there nothing we can *do* to effect our sanctification?

Methods of nullifying the old habits and nurturing the new are almost as plentiful as the people who peddle them. Whole systems of sanctification—even entire denominations, traditions, and theologies—have grown up over the centuries, each promising *the* most effective way to holiness. The victorious Christian life, exchanged life, Methodism, holiness, second blessing, sacramentalism, personal disciplines, corporate disciplines, mysticism, asceticism, monasticism, contemplation . . . the list goes on.

The problem I have with these various historical approaches is not that they're wrong, but that they often claim to be too right. Most of them have something true to contribute to a diverse tradition of Christian spirituality, and I have personally found some of them helpful.[1] But none of them can claim to be the *sole* path to spiritual maturity. Most of the models of sanctification came on the scene when individual Christians (or small communities) experienced remarkable spiritual blessing while engaged in a particular approach to the Christian life. But instead of viewing their method as one means among many God uses to work his sanctifying grace, their gaze became fixated on the method itself.

This presents us with a quandary. If there is no single, clearly prescribed Christian *method* of sanctification, what should we *do*? Is the solution to be passive, to "wait on the Lord" for an instant change of heart? The idea of passive sanctification reminds me of a student at my Bible college who would return to his dorm after a weekend of shameless fornication. When I confronted him about it, he responded, "God's in control. When he wants me to stop living this way, he'll take the desires away."

Yes, God is in control. And in his sovereignty he eventually cast that student out of Bible college.

The answer is obviously *not* to passively wait for God to spontaneously and miraculously change our hearts, minds, and carnal instincts. Though that kind of deliverance may happen to a few, it probably won't happen to you and me. Instead, the answer to the question of what we should do in response to God's sovereignty over our sanctification is quite simple, perhaps unexpected. *Do whatever it takes! And do it now!*

The guiding text for this view is Philippians 2:12: "Therefore, my beloved, as you have always obeyed, so now, not only as in my presence but much more in my absence, work out your own salvation with fear and trembling." I can't think of a clearer text regarding our responsibility to obey in the process of sanctification. The verb "work out" in Greek is a simple imperative, a straightforward command. As the Philippians responded well to God in past obedience, Paul said they should continue to express their salvation with obedience and good works. This text means working, not waiting; being productive, not passive. Paul left no room for the misguided theology of my immoral Bible college acquaintance who justified his sin by passive *dis*obedience. According to Paul, our responsibility for sanctification is to simply *obey.*

Paul could have stopped at verse 12, and his practical intentions would have been perfectly clear. But instead, he removed the service panel from the Christian life and revealed the inner workings of sanctification. In just a few powerful words we see that our work of willing, active obedience in salvation is not the *cause* of sanctification, but the *effect.* Paul said, "Work out your own salvation with fear and trembling, *for it is God who works in you, both to will and to work for his good pleasure*" (Phil. 2:12–13).

In the remainder of this chapter and in the next we will dig more deeply into the issue of spiritual growth, or "sanctification"—first corporate spirituality, then personal devotion. However, in keeping with the overarching thesis of *RetroChristianity*, let's start with a historical perspective on the topic of sanctification.

A Biblical, Historical, and Theological Perspective on Sanctification

In the early catholic period (100–1000), the Christian tradition emphasized God's work of *making* us righteous (sanctification) by grace. In the early fifth century Augustine championed the doctrine of total depravity—that all human beings after the fall of Adam are spiritually dead, resulting in the absolute necessity of total grace. He argued vigorously that God's grace alone produces both faith and good works, resulting in the real improvement of the elect, who then merit salvation. However, this in no way implies that humans work for or earn their salvation on their own. Rather, "when God crowns our merits, He crowns nothing but His own gifts."[2] In an Augustinian framework, from first to last, salvation and sanctification are by grace through both faith and good works, neither of which is the result of innate human ability. However, Augustine did not clearly distinguish sanctification (being *made* more righteous, resulting in good works) from justification (being *declared* righteous in spite of our actual unrighteous acts).

EARLY CATHOLIC MODEL (AUGUSTINIAN)

GRACE ➡ FAITH + WORKS ➡ SALVATION
(SANCTIFICATION = JUSTIFICATION)

Gracious Enablement:
Grace Necessary and Sufficient,
Producing Faith and Works unto Salvation

Some of Augustine's contemporaries and many more of the later medieval period (1000–1500) backed away from his clear and decisive emphasis on God's sovereign grace, preferring a model that included much more human responsibility. Aquinas, one of the more Augustinian teachers of the Middle Ages, clearly taught that no one can merit initial grace,[3] but he also taught that "by every meritorious act a man merits the increase of grace."[4] Though Aquinas himself was still within the sphere of Augustine's view of sin and grace, eventually the medieval church drifted farther from an emphasis on unmerited grace toward a virtual abandonment of total depravity and unconditional grace. Humans were not viewed as totally depraved, but as "deprived"—not spiritually *dead*, but spiritually *sick*. An extreme form of this idea that God boosts our efforts with grace is seen in the late medieval dictum, "God does not deny grace to the person who does what is in him."[5] In the minds of many people living in this period, salvation was the result of a mixture of grace, faith, and good works. Thus, sanctification (being more righteous in character) led to and resulted in justification (being declared righteous by God).

LATER CATHOLIC MODEL (MEDIEVAL)
GRACE + FAITH + WORKS ➡ SALVATION
(SANCTIFICATION ➡ JUSTIFICATION)

Cooperation with Grace:
Grace Necessary but Not Sufficient,
Enabling Cooperation with God's Work unto Salvation

This medieval model of justification by means of progressive sanctification wouldn't have been so bad if those clever theologians hadn't also lost sight of the fact that God was the one who worked in believers both to will and to work (Phil. 2:13). Instead, medieval theology degenerated into a twofold error: it neglected Paul's teaching of justification by grace through faith alone, and it embraced the doctrine of meriting God's grace by human will and effort.[6]

In response to the medieval doctrine of justification *as a result of* sanctification, Protestant Reformers (1500–1700) like Martin Luther, Ulrich Zwingli, and John Calvin returned to Augustine's earlier formulation and adjusted it based on their understanding of Paul's teaching on justification. The result was a more developed expression of justification and sanctification, which, having gone through a long history of trial and error, was made clearer. The Reformers recognized that God declares the believer eternally righteous at the moment of saving faith, regardless of his or her actual experience of righteous living. A Christian is, as Luther said, simultaneously a sinner and a saint.[7] In the perspective of the major Reformers, justification meant being declared righteous; sanctification meant being made righteous. Both were distinct but inseparable aspects of salvation by grace through faith, and justification came first, followed by sanctification.

REFORMATION MODEL (PROTESTANT)

GRACE ➡ FAITH ➡ SALVATION ➡ WORKS
(JUSTIFICATION ➡ SANCTIFICATION)

Salvation by Grace Alone:
Grace Necessary and Sufficient,
Producing Saving Faith and Enabling Works

As the theological prowess of the Reformation wound down, two errors began to emerge among the Protestants' evangelical heirs (1700–present day). First, many evangelicals began to strictly *separate* justification and sanctification, overemphasizing the former to the neglect of the latter. That is, they insisted that God had *declared* them righteous by Christ's death and resurrection, but they forgot that God was also *making* them righteous by the Spirit's continual work of putting the old ways to death and bringing the new to life. Today this kind of sharp division between justification and sanctification leads to a false view of the Christian life. We must remember that justification and sanctification are *distinct, but integrally related*, and that God effects both by grace through faith on the basis of the death and resurrection of Jesus Christ and by the power of the Holy Spirit. Just as God's regenerating Spirit acts on the depraved sinner both to will and to actively respond to the gospel, that same regenerating Spirit, now abiding with the believer, works in him or her both to will and to work out godly obedience (Eph. 2:8–10; Phil. 2:12–13). So, the first error among evangelicals took the Protestant development too far, *separating* justification and sanctification so much that there was no relationship between them.

The second error is the opposite of the first. After the Reformation many Protestants abandoned the Reformers' teaching that the grace of God meant absolute unmerited favor, believing instead that humans had to contribute *something* to their salvation, whether it was a willing heart, a freewill decision, their own meager faith, a token first act of devotion, or some other kind of cooperation with God. In fact, in many respects those new "my will and my works" approaches to salvation and sanctification were even more aberrant than those nuanced views of Augustine and the early catholic Christians, forgetting the words of Paul that "it is God who works in you, both to will and to work for his good pleasure" (Phil. 2:13).

All too often I meet Christians who want to soften this language, to read into it some foreign concept of salvation as a team effort, of God's response to our willing hearts, of the Spirit's work of lending a helping hand to our honest efforts. Too many believers want to live the Christian life as if God were simply waiting for them to be willing before he will provide supernatural strength—or as if God were holding back his provision of power until they take the first step. This team effort approach to sanctification is contrary to what Paul said in Philippians 2 about our obedience in salvation. God is at work in us, *not only to work, but also to will.* At the same time, God works all things in this world together for our good (Rom. 8:28). And he himself has prepared the good works beforehand as part of the entire salvation package (Eph. 2:10). So, by both inward and outward means, God effects our sanctification. Simply put, God's unmerited grace enables our hearts to yield to his commands and strengthens us to cooperate with his Spirit.

However, rather than instantly zapping us into mature saints, God gradually effects our spiritual growth through numerous "means of sanctification," traditionally called "means of grace."[8] The eighteenth-century Methodist preacher John Wesley defined these means as "outward signs, words, or actions, ordained of God, and appointed for this end, to be the ordinary channels whereby he might convey to men, preventing, justifying, or sanctifying grace."[9] These include practices such as prayer, reading or hearing Scripture, and even faith—*any* means by which God chooses to communicate his saving or sanctifying power to the recipients of his mercy and grace.

The nineteenth-century Presbyterian theologian B. B. Warfield described the Protestant doctrine of sanctification through means this way:

> The sanctifying operations of the Spirit are supernatural, and yet effected in connection with and through the instrumentality of means: the means of sanctification being either internal, such as faith and the co-operation

of the regenerated will with grace, or external, such as the word of God, sacraments, prayer, Christian fellowship, and the providential discipline of our heavenly Father.[10]

Just as the external proclamation of the gospel meets our internal response of faith, these means of sanctification are external things that stir our faith, and that faith then manifests itself through the fruit of the Spirit, resulting in obedience. Note that sanctification is not *caused by* works, but *results in* works. The agent of our sanctification is always the Holy Spirit, working in us and through us, so that we both will to do and do what pleases him (Phil. 2:12–13). We will see that God's means of sanctification include both *personal* and *community* disciplines. Chapter 11 will focus on *personal* discipline for the purpose of godliness; the remainder of this present chapter focuses on several important *community* means of spiritual formation—those activities that lead to spiritual growth such as the reading and preaching of the Word, observance of the sacraments, and ministry in the body of Christ.

But first we need to better define what we mean by "community."

What Is True Community?

Community groups . . . community centers . . . building community . . . promoting community . . . community life . . . community churches . . . faith communities . . . the Christian community . . .

Community has become a buzzword in twenty-first-century evangelicalism. Today's churches have reacted decisively against the unhealthy and unbiblical obsession with the personal preference, private spirituality, and individualistic Christianity so prevalent in the nineteenth and twentieth centuries. In its stead, many have been drawn to a community-oriented Christianity that more accurately reflects the *koinonia* emphasis of the New Testament and the early church—the corporate disciplines of worship, fellowship, and ministry.

But what does true Christian community look like?

Imagine this kind of community: an uncomfortable hodgepodge of people we barely know, or, what's worse, maybe we know some of them far too well and wish we didn't. They come from different backgrounds, different walks of life, different pay grades, different generations. They're just plain *different*. But we've been artificially mashed together in some kind of church program—a Bible study, a

Sunday school class, a small group, a ministry team. We grudgingly do our duties but keep our guards up and our masks on. We just can't wait until this excruciating, forced community is over so we can get back to the people we're comfortable with, the people we know, the people we love.

But then there's a different model of community: comfort, familiarity, friends whose names we know and whose faces we're actually happy to see. People we spend time with outside the church, people we'd actually *want* to invite for dinner. That kind of community usually means developing warm relationships with those of our own age group, our own stage of life. We love that kind of community. It feels more natural. This is the ideal kind of community we strive for. Clearly, the uncomfortable and awkward community can't possibly result in a healthy church; spiritual growth is much more likely in a community of comfort and ease rather than personality conflict and politics.

Or is it?

One day a student wandered into my office to chat. After a few minutes, the conversation moved to the pervasive politics and personality conflicts involved in Christian communities. Our brief exchange went something like this:

"It's everywhere," I said. "Every church or ministry deals with this."

"But we're Christians. It's not supposed to be this way. Doesn't it bother you?"

I hesitated, then grabbed a thick book from one end of my desk and placed it in front of him. Pointing at the volume on the history of Christianity, I said, "But this is how it's always been. This is how it will always be." Then I placed my Bible on top of the history book: "And if you look in there, it's exactly the same. Until Christ returns, this is the best we can hope for. But God's Spirit works out his perfect plan in spite of us."

It's normal for Christians to be disappointed in other Christians. Sometimes we can be downright mean to each other. Even if we avoid outright conflict, there will still be frustration, inconvenience, discomfort—*all the necessary ingredients and effects of true community*.

Let me suggest that the more comfortable you feel in your Christian community, the less authentic your community is. In 1 Corinthians 12:13 Paul writes, "For in one Spirit we were all baptized into one body—Jews or Greeks, slaves or free—and all were made to drink of one Spirit."

Sometimes we read a passage like that and fail to think through its practical implications. Jews and Greeks didn't get along in the ancient world. They came from completely different religious and cultural backgrounds, lived in separate communities, and had different customs and languages. Slaves and free were from opposite social and economic communities. They didn't mix well together. Division was the order of the day.

When these groups of men and women, slaves and masters, Jews and Greeks became one community, awkward discomfort—even outright conflict—ensued. Read 1 Corinthians to see for yourself. That's the natural result of mixing these diverse minicommunities into one metacommunity. It was like mixing oil and water. Church growth experts opt for affinity groups. Common sense tells us not to even try this kind of mixing. Our emotions tell us to run in the other direction.

But shouldn't Christian community transcend the natural? Shouldn't it defy common sense? Shouldn't it seek to overcome the desire to fellowship only with people who make us comfortable?

Confusion. Discomfort. Frustration. Uneasiness. Conflict. These are the effects of *true* community. These conditions promote real spiritual growth. It's easy to fake the fruit of the Spirit among people we pick as fellowship partners. It's far more difficult to pretend love, joy, peace, patience, kindness, goodness, faithfulness, gentleness, and self-control among those who irritate us. And putting our *natural* human inclinations to the test of real life gives God an opportunity to work among us in *supernatural* ways.

Let me make myself very clear. From a balanced biblical, historical, and theological perspective, *true community is an essential part of sanctification*. In *true community* the Spirit manifests the diversity of his gifts and provides the means necessary for spiritual growth. Apart from *true community* there can be no authentic and lasting progress in the Christian life.

Going Retro

Living in True Community

In a moving description of authentic Christian community, the third-century church father Dionysius of Alexandria described the self-sacrificial work of Christians in the face of a disastrous plague:

> The most of our brethren were unsparing in their exceeding love and brotherly kindness. They held fast to each other and visited the sick fearlessly, and ministered to them continually, serving them in Christ. And they died with them most joyfully, taking the affliction of others, and drawing the sickness from their neighbors to themselves and willingly receiving their pains. And many who cared for the sick and gave strength to others died themselves having transferred to themselves their death. And the popular saying which always seems a mere expression of courtesy, they then made real in action, taking their departure as the others' "offscouring."[11]

When I read this description of true community in the ancient church, I wonder whether similar conditions today would mark us as Christians or heathens. Would we stick around only until the risk became too great—or until we had expended our last energies taking care of our own? Having observed the way so many Christians utterly disregard their brothers and sisters today, I think I know the answer.

It doesn't need to be this way. We can begin living in true community today by starting right where we are. Perhaps you're feeling uncomfortable in your church, Bible study, Sunday school class, or fellowship group. Maybe it's just a lingering sense that you'd fit in better somewhere else. You're probably right! But fitting in isn't the goal of Christian community. The Spirit of God has been sent to create unity out of diversity, peace out of conflict, and healing out of wounded hearts. The greatest spiritual growth will come from overcoming differences, persevering through conflict, and dealing with difficulties. And the greatest testimony of God's supernatural work in a Christian community will be the love and unity that results from taking the long, hard road of true community (John 13:35).

Don't try to get out from under the sometimes excruciating conflict that comes through true community. Don't try to seek only those who share your opinions, your lifestyles, or your careers. Rather, living in true community means caring for and fellowshipping with those who share nothing with us but the common bond of Christ. It may take time. It will certainly take faith, hope, and love. But the end result will be authentic relationships with real people based not on worldly reason or on fleeting feelings, but on the unifying work of the Spirit of God.

The Sanctifying Work of the Sacraments

It is an indisputable fact of church history that the two sacraments of baptism and the Lord's Supper have always functioned as the primary marks of Christian identity and the primary works of Christian initiation and renewal. Consider these facts regarding the practices of baptism and the Lord's Supper in the first and second centuries:

1. After examination and instruction in basic beliefs and the expected lifestyle of Christianity, all believers who confessed their faith in Christ were baptized as a mark of covenant initiation into a local church community and thereby also into the visible universal church.[12]
2. Believers in Christ who had not received the seal of baptism were not admitted into church membership, and they were not invited to the Lord's Supper.[13]
3. Though the most attested form of baptism in the early church was that of believers by immersion, sometime in the course of the second century many churches began admitting the children of Christians into the covenant community by administering baptism to infants.[14]
4. Only those who had been baptized and were members in good standing in their local Christian churches were invited to partake of the Lord's Supper; unbelievers and unbaptized believers were strictly excluded from the bread and wine.[15]
5. The Lord's Supper was observed every Sunday as the climax of the church's worship. It was administered by the pastor or elders of each local church, associated with the proclamation of the incarnation, death, and resurrection of Jesus Christ, and

accompanied by prayers of thanksgiving, confession of sins, and offerings of material goods for those in need.[16]

6. Though the bread and wine used in the Lord's Supper were universally regarded as representative, the early Christians also universally regarded Christ as somehow truly present in the observance of the Lord's Supper, actively bestowing spiritual blessings as well as practically bestowing physical blessings through the physical gathering of the body of Christ, the church. Baptism and the Lord's Supper were both understood to actually affect participants, confirming, strengthening, and nourishing faith and *thus communicating sanctifying grace*. They were not viewed as *mere* symbols, but symbols that stirred faith, hope, and love.[17]

So early, geographically widespread, fundamental, and enduring were these six facts that we are compelled to regard them as immovable elements of Christian practice. However, many of these practices have been tampered with, exaggerated, distorted, rejected, or changed over the centuries. The Roman Catholic Church has added several more sacraments to these two original ordinances, regarding them as means of *saving grace* rather than means of *sanctifying grace*. Protestants have often reduced the frequency of the Lord's Supper from weekly Sunday observances to monthly, quarterly, or annual events, thus removing these prescribed means of corporate spiritual growth from the midst of their congregations. Some free evangelical churches have so deviated from the biblical and historical pattern of the sacraments that they admit unbaptized believers into church membership and admit unbaptized believers to the Lord's Supper. Some have even invited unbelievers to the Lord's Table as an evangelistic strategy!

In short, many evangelical churches—especially free churches—must rethink and reform their beliefs and practices related to baptism and the Lord's Supper. Let's begin by examining a few key passages and concepts related to these essential corporate means of sanctification.

Yes, "Baptism Now Saves You"

In the New Testament, baptism is closely related to believing and being saved (Mark 16:16; Acts 18:8). Its practice is associated with receiving the Word, repentance, forgiveness, the washing away of sins, calling on Christ, and receiving the Holy Spirit (Acts 2:37–41; 22:16). It also pictures a new lifestyle free from the bondage of sin (Rom. 6:3–4). However, before we jump to the mistaken conclusion that these associations indicate that water baptism itself saves us or brings forgiveness or washes away sins, we must note that water baptism and baptism by the Holy Spirit are clearly distinguished in Scripture (Acts 1:4–5). In fact, in some cases water baptism preceded baptism by the Spirit (Acts 8:14–16). Other times Spirit baptism—received by simple faith—preceded baptism in water (Acts 10:44–48). In this way God demonstrated that water baptism and Spirit baptism, though related, are not equated.

How do we reconcile the close connection—but clear distinction—between water baptism (the outward sign) and Spirit baptism (the inward reality)? First Peter 3:21 helps. Peter wrote that "Baptism . . . now saves you," clarifying the kind of rite he had in mind—"not a cleansing of dirt from the flesh"—that is, the physical rite itself—"but a pledge to God from a good conscience" (AT).[18] That is, the rite of water baptism is itself the public pledge or confession that results from a conscience cleansed by the Holy Spirit (see Heb. 9:14; 10:22). Baptism must be closely *associated* with our conversion to Christ by grace through faith alone—but it should never be *equated* with it.

In this view, the language of 1 Peter 3:21 is best understood as indicating a covenant "oath," "vow," or "pledge," in which the recipient of baptism not only publically confesses faith in Christ but also swears to live the Christian life by the help of the Spirit working through the covenanted community.[19] We see this dual function in Justin Martyr's description of water baptism in the early second century, as it was administered to those who "are persuaded and believe that what we teach and say is true, and undertake to be able to live accordingly."[20]

In the earlier first-century document of church order, the *Didache*, baptism was administered after basic instruction on the Christian faith and life. In typical Jewish fashion, the instructor placed before the new believer the option of two very different lifestyles—a path associated with sinfulness (death) and a path associated with righteousness (life). By submitting to water baptism, the new Christian was publically confessing his or her faith and promising to walk "by the Spirit," the lifestyle associated with "the way of life." The *Didache* says, "Now concerning baptism, baptize as follows: after you have reviewed all these things [concerning the new way of life versus the old way of death], baptize in the name of the Father and of the Son and of the Holy Spirit."[21]

Similarly, the fourth-century church father, Basil of Caesarea, regarded faith and baptism as "kindred and inseparable," though he distinguished them this way: "Faith is perfected through baptism, baptism is established through faith, and both are completed by the same names. For as we believe in the Father and the Son and the Holy Ghost, so are we also baptized in the name of the Father and of the Son and of the Holy Ghost; first comes the confession, introducing us to salvation, and baptism follows, setting the seal upon our assent."[22]

In short, in both the Bible and the church of the first few centuries, water baptism was the outward, visible testimony of our conversion to Christ. Church historian J. N. D. Kelly writes, "From the beginning baptism was the universally accepted rite of admission to the Church."[23] Just as a wedding ceremony functions as a public demonstration and pledge of an engaged couple to lifelong marriage, water baptism is the public celebration of our genuine devotion and commitment to Christ and his church. It's the rite of initiation into the community of other baptized believers, and therefore it *must* precede church membership, discipleship, leadership, and observance of the Lord's Supper. As such, it's a mark of covenant commitment, rendering us accountable to the church community. Just as Spirit baptism unites us spiritually to Christ and makes us members of his mystical body (1 Cor. 12:13; Eph. 2:6), so water baptism unites us physically to the body of Christ, the visible church, making us members of his covenant community.[24]

Let me make one final note regarding baptism in order to clarify a common misunderstanding. Although the idea of "baptismal regeneration" is universal among the early church fathers, it should not be confused with the notion of "baptismal salvation" common in later church history. In the early church, the term "regeneration" or being "born again" originally referred to a *practical change in lifestyle*. The candidates for baptism had resolved to live new lives, abandoning their lives of unbelief, idolatry, and sin. The early Jewish Christian communities regarded baptism as the conscious decision to abandon the "way of death" characterized by sin and to begin a journey on the "way of life" characterized by righteousness (see *Didache* 1–6). Even in the New Testament baptism is associated with being "made alive" (Col. 2:12–13) and setting a believer on the path of "newness of life" (Rom. 6:4).

Given this background of instruction that contrasted death and life, the language of "regeneration" in the earliest church fathers likely derived from the notion that baptism was the point of one's conversion from the *lifestyle* characterized by death to a *lifestyle* characterized by life. Similarly, the early church also referred to baptism as "illumination" or "enlightenment," as baptism marked the new believer's change of course from the "path of darkness" to the "path of light."[25]

How, then, did the idea develop that says the water of baptism saves a person from damnation, not merely from a sinful lifestyle? While the early church used regeneration and illumination to refer to the practical change of lifestyle, later Christians began to interpret these metaphorical terms more literally and metaphysically, resulting in the notion that the water itself supernaturally mediates saving (life-giving) grace to the recipient.[26] From that point on until the Reformation, the idea that water baptism was a gracious means of *salvation* rather than a gracious means of *sanctification* became common.

I believe the Protestant *Westminster Confession of Faith* represents the apostolic and early church's balanced attitude toward water baptism: "Although it be a great sin to contemn or neglect this ordinance [of baptism], yet grace and salvation are not so inseparably annexed unto it, as that no person can be regenerated or saved, without it; or, that all that are baptized are undoubtedly regenerated."[27] In this light, it seems most proper to regard baptism as intended to be the first means of *sanctifying grace*, the moment when a new believer commits to live the Christian life by God's grace, to walk in newness of life, forsaking sin and covenanting with a local church community.

Retrofitting

Baptism in the Local Church

The biblical, historical, and theological perspective on baptism views it as (1) the exclusive outward response to the gospel message, (2) the exclusive public sign of a believer's saving faith, (3) the exclusive means of initial dedication to living the Christian life, and (4) the exclusive rite of covenant initiation into membership of a local, visible church. In light of this, those of us who have the ability to influence our church's practice of baptism might consider some of the following:

1. Restore baptism as the sign, seal, and symbol of a person's conversion and commitment to Christ. Over the centuries we have replaced baptism with other outward responses to the gospel—coming forward at a gospel invitation, reciting a prayer, raising our hands, even shaking the hand of the evangelist. In all these things we clarify that "this act doesn't save you, but it's a way of letting God and others know of your saving faith." Do we really have the right to replace baptism as the exclusive biblical and historical faith response to the gospel message with some man-made tradition?

2. Evangelicals are probably far too eager to extend the rights and responsibilities of Christians to unbaptized believers. In the apostolic church Jews and God-fearing Gentiles with some knowledge of the Old Testament were baptized immediately upon their confession, and then they were regarded as true converts. As the gospel reached pagan, idolatrous Gentiles, the church saw the need to train new believers in the basics of the Christian faith and lifestyle, a process called "catechesis." Only after this training were they baptized by water. Perhaps in our increasingly post-Christian culture the practice of catechesis (basic Christian instruction) should be restored for new baptismal candidates. In this way baptism can be seen as the moment of a believer's one-time commitment that sets him or her apart for a lifestyle of godly living.

3. Finally, we ought to cease the all-too-common practice of admitting into membership believers in Christ who have not been baptized and trained in the basics of the Christian faith and life. We especially ought to stop inviting the unbaptized to the Lord's Supper. We must strive to return baptism to its rightful place as the exclusive means of initiation into the visible covenant community of the church, which admits a person to both the rights and responsibilities of church membership.[28]

Yes, Christ Is Present in the Eucharist

At the outset of our discussion of the Lord's Supper, let's define two terms. First, the term "eucharist" comes from the Greek word *eucharistia*, which means "thanksgiving." When we use this term, we're not referring primarily to the broken bread or the poured wine, *but to the observance itself*—the celebration, the commemoration, the participation as a community. "Eucharist" at the time of the apostles meant the time of prayer, confession, benevolence toward the needy, and the spiritual fellowship that centered on reproclaiming Christ's incarnation, death, and resurrection—*the gospel* confessed and lived in true community. It included the believers' responses of reflection, repentance, reconciliation, and renewal in light of their mark of baptism and their ongoing fellowship with God and with one another. It often involved acts of charity, as Christians with means would bring offerings to provide for those in need. (This was the original observance of the "love feast.") The Eucharist also involved confession of sins to one another and thus mending broken relationships. It always included prayer and proclamation of the truths of Christ's person and work.

So, when we say "Christ is present in the Eucharist," we mean that Christ is uniquely present in the proper observance of the Lord's Supper in our worship service. But what do we mean by the presence of Christ? Well, we don't mean that Christ has somehow physically merged with the bread and wine. We don't mean his spirit has left his body and descended from heaven and attached itself mysteriously with the wafer and the juice.[29]

What I *do* mean by Christ's presence in our right observance of the Lord's Supper is that he has made good on his promise that "where two or three are gathered" together in his name, according to his will, by his standards, and centered on him, then he is there in their midst (Matt. 18:20). If this is true for prayer and worship, it must also be true when the unified church comes together in obedience and submission to Christ to partake of the sacred meal he himself ordained! This understanding of the bread and wine as reflecting the unity of the church is seen explicitly in Cyprian of Carthage:

> For when the Lord calls bread, which is combined by the union of many grains, His body, He indicates our people whom He bore as being united; and when He calls the wine, which is pressed from many grapes and

clusters and collected together, His blood, He also signifies our flock linked together by the mingling of a united multitude.[30]

Because I understand "eucharist" to include the *observance* and not merely to refer to the *elements*, I take it by faith that Christ is present in a way in which he is not present in any other church observance. In a very *real, physical, fleshly* sense, when the physical and spiritual *body of Christ*—his church—joins together in unity and submission to Christ, Christ is physically present, having associated himself mystically—but truly—with the gathered church.[31]

What, practically, is the significance of Christ's presence? When we pray that God will be "with" somebody or draw near to us, we are really asking God to *do* something. We're seeking real, tangible *effects*. In fact, where God *is*, God *does*. Where God is *present*, God is *active*. When we think of Christ present in the Eucharist, we should think less about how he is or isn't lingering in the bread and wine, but more of *what* he is doing in the midst of the people. God has chosen to work his sanctifying power through the proper observance of the Lord's Supper in a way that's different from any other church practice.

One effect of Christ's active presence is the unity and purity that result from self-examination, proclamation, and participation. In this sense, the Lord's Supper is an essential means of sanctification. God has chosen to bring about sanctification of the whole church through the Lord's Supper in a way that no other individual or corporate discipline can. When we properly observe the ordinance, we will grow together spiritually as a family of God. However, there's another side of his promise of participation in the "cup of blessing" (1 Cor. 10:16). Failure to partake properly brings judgment in the form of weakness, sickness, and even death (1 Cor. 11:29–30)!

Going Retro

Our Personal Response to the Ordinances

Regardless of how or how often a particular church observes baptism or the Lord's Supper, each of us has a biblical responsibility to participate faithfully in these holy practices. Let me suggest three personal responses to the ordinances you can apply right away.

First, many evangelical church traditions have overreacted against the Roman Catholic dogma that understands baptism and the Eucharist as means of salvation rather than as means God uses in his work of sanctification. As a result, we have spent much of our time emphasizing what baptism and the Lord's Supper *don't* do, all the while neglecting the biblical teaching on what the ordinances *do*. It's time we move on from telling what baptism and the Lord's Supper *aren't* and get back to explaining what they *are*. We need to return to the biblical and historical centrality of baptism as the ceremony of initiation into the community of faith and to the Eucharist as the celebration of continued fellowship. We need to recall the indispensable role these ordinances play in our spiritual growth as individuals and as churches.

Second, if you or your children are unbaptized believers, what's keeping you from taking that initial step of baptism as the God-ordained public act of initiation and commitment to the Christian community? As you arrange for this act of obedience to Christ, let me urge you to follow the biblical order of the ordinances, holding off on participation in the Lord's Supper until you've been baptized. This isn't a light matter. Proper order is a vital part of proper observance. Just as a wedding ceremony frees a man and woman to participate in the intimate act of marriage, baptism publicly confirms a believer's devotion to Christ, allowing the believer to participate in the intimate fellowship of the Lord's Supper. From the biblical perspective, participation in the Lord's Supper without baptism is like shacking up before the wedding!

Finally, if you harbor unresolved conflict with a fellow member of the church or hide unrepentant sin, stop participating in the Lord's Supper. On the authority of the Bible, if you don't repent you will become weak, sick, and die. And as long as we as a church continue to practice the Lord's Supper while tolerating unrepentant members, the entire body will continue to suffer as it fails to experience the full blessing that comes from the presence of Christ in the right observance of the ordinances.

- - - - - - - - - - - - - - -

Pulpit/Altar-Centered Worship

If you were to step into a Swiss parish church in the year 1200, chances are you'd first pass a small baptismal font placed near the entrance of the sanctuary as a reminder that people are to enter the church through baptism. Then you would pass into an open space for worshipers to stand and kneel, facing toward the front of the sanctuary. At the front, the congregation focused their attention on the altar, where the priest prepared the elements of the Eucharist—the bread and the cup. At this table the priest would conduct the liturgy of the mass in Latin. In the middle of the Sunday worship a qualified layperson would read prescribed sections of Scripture from a raised lectern off to the side of the altar. The priest would read from the Gospels and deliver a homily from a raised pulpit on the other side. Both the lectern and the pulpit flank that church's true center of worship—the altar. After the short exhortation, the priest would continue the liturgy, climaxing when the parishioners approached the altar to receive what they believed to be the real body and blood of Christ.

Fast forward to the year 1600: same Swiss village, same church building. But now the furniture has been rearranged. The Protestant Reformation has swept through and this once Roman Catholic Church has adopted the reforms of Geneva under John Calvin. The open space has been filled with pews, indicating that once the service began you were likely to be there for a while. The baptismal font may or may not have been moved to the front of the church, but one thing has changed—the altar is no longer the main focus of worship. Instead, the pulpit stands at the center of the platform with a large Bible open for both reading and proclamation. Now the homily is called a sermon, Scripture reading involves preaching and teaching, and hymns, prayers, and lessons are heard in common Swiss French. Clearly the new center of worship is the proclamation of the Word in the pastor's lengthy sermon, a fact that's reinforced by the placement of a large pulpit where the altar had stood from time immemorial. In fact, in this particular church, Communion is only observed monthly, breaking from the biblical and ancient Christian practice of weekly observance of the Lord's Supper.

Leap forward to the year 2000. Several generations ago the abandoned church building was purchased by an evangelical missionary team planting an independent church in this growing new Swiss village, now a bustling suburb of a nearby metropolitan city. The church plant attracts mostly English-speaking Christians with some kind of connection to Canada, the United States, the UK, or Australia, but several Swiss nationals show up to improve their English and see what's going on in that ancient building. The baptismal font is gone, replaced by a rack of multilingual Christian literature. That's okay, though, because baptism isn't something this particular church focuses on. Instead, it emphasizes evangelism and conversion. There's no altar, either. A table is set up every few months during a Sunday evening service, when a small group of church attendees observe the Lord's Supper as part of a potluck meal. The main Sunday worship service first centers on singing praise and worship songs with a guitar, keyboard, bass, and drums; then the second half of the service focuses on the preacher. The pulpit is also gone, and a minister in jeans delivers a practical message from a stool with a small Bible in his left hand and a remote control in his right. Attention shifts from the speaker to the PowerPoint slides projected on the screen up front.

A lot can change in eight hundred years—from altar, to pulpit, to projector. Many Protestants took pride in the fact that they had gotten rid of the altar and its "idolatry of the Mass," replacing it with the pulpit. And many evangelicals flaunt the fact that they have gotten rid of the pulpit with its stifling dogma and overly intellectual teaching, replacing it with a hip, young, life coach "sharing a few thoughts" from a four-legged stool. From ordained priest, to compelling preacher, to magnetic personality—that has been the transformation of the church's corporate worship in the last thousand years.

However, as evangelical churches today struggle to come to terms with just what they're supposed to be doing during Sunday morning worship, very few are considering the simplicity and sensibility of the early church's approach to worship. We have already seen that the earliest Christians from the apostolic period onward observed the Lord's Supper as a vital part of their weekly Sunday worship. One might be tempted to conclude, then, that the church of AD 1200 had it right—the altar should stand at the center of authentic corporate worship.

However, this would be inaccurate. We might describe a full-bodied eucharistic worship as involving both the pulpit and the altar, proclamation and consecration, sermon and sacrament, word and worship. Let's return to that poor Swiss church building once more and arrange it in a way that would reflect what can be called a "pulpit/altar-centered worship." The pulpit would stand at the front of the sanctuary with an altar before it. The ordained pastor-elder would preside over the service, in which fellow elders, deacons, and laypeople participate in reading the Word and leading the congregation in singing, special music, and whatever else contributes positively to the edification of the church and to the glory of God the Father, through the Son, and by the power of the Spirit.

At some point in the service an elder would lead the congregation in corporate prayer, to which the whole church would assent by an "amen." After appropriate Scripture readings, the presiding elder would preach the sermon, exhorting his congregation to faith, hope, and love, exalting the Father through Jesus Christ by the power of the Holy Spirit. The message would be biblically accurate, expositing the text with theological, historical, and practical faithfulness. The pastor will have prayed, studied, written, and prepared his message with a view toward addressing the specific needs of his flock and speaking to Christ's church with their spiritual health in mind.

Yet the sermon would not end with a few practical pointers or moral platitudes that can be written on a 3 x 5 card or jotted in the margins of the parishioners' Bibles. Rather, the message would call the people to repentance, to consecration, and to action (2 Tim. 4:1–2).[32] The sermon would be followed by an invitation for the baptized believers to respond to the message by coming forward to receive the Lord's Supper as from the hand of the Lord himself. This act would mark the church's renewal of its covenant commitment to live the Christian life together in the bond of peace and by the power of the Spirit.

In the several minutes leading up to the observance of the Lord's Supper, the pastor or elders would exhort the congregation to reflect on their relationships in the church and to make amends with any brothers or sisters with whom they may have conflicts. They would be encouraged to confess their sins to God and to one another, coming to the table having their consciences cleansed by the mercy of forgiveness. Finally, the congregants' approach to the table and reception of the Lord's Supper would be a sign of renewed commitment and consecration to abide in their new Christian life. In short, the proper observance of this intimate fellowship of the body of Christ around his table would provide an opportunity for cleansing, reconciliation, spiritual nourishment, and blessing.

Ideally we should envision the primary purpose of the church's worship as twofold—proclamation and response . . . pulpit and altar . . . word and worship. Together this inseparable unity focuses the church's entire worship in a specifically Godward direction. It transforms the gathered local body of Christ from a passive audience to active participants, calling believers weekly to live up to the covenant commitment of their baptism through covenant renewal at the table of the Lord. In this sense, the "sacrifice" offered at the altar is not the flesh and blood of Jesus *per se*, but the gathered community themselves— the "body of Christ," the church, his flesh and blood on earth—as they offer themselves as living sacrifices to God (Rom. 12:1), just as St. Augustine declared: "This is the sacrifice of Christians: we, being many, are one body in Christ. And this also is the sacrifice which the Church continually celebrates in the sacrament of the altar, known to the faithful, in which she teaches that *she herself is offered in the offering she makes to God.*"[33]

This picture of worship intentionally avoids any discussion of music, worship style, or the ongoing tensions between traditional and contemporary forms. As I study Christian worship from a biblical, historical, and theological perspective, the issues that have led to numerous "worship wars" concern me less and less. As we saw in chapter 6, *everything we do in our church is a development*. Every ancient liturgy was once new, every classic hymn was once unknown, and every common order of worship was once unfamiliar. The church has constantly contextualized its order of worship, style, music, and architecture to best communicate in the variety of cultures it has encountered. Nothing said so far specifically rejects or advocates any particular music or preaching style. Rather, if our churches would return to a basic pulpit/altar-centered approach to worship, many of the conflicts leading to the "worship wars" would diminish. When

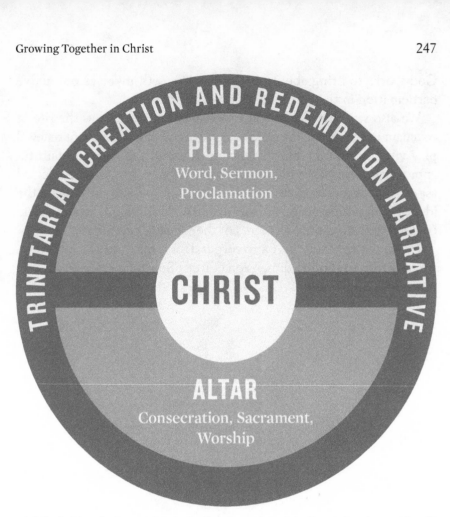

A biblically, historically, and theologically informed model of local church worship will strive to be pulpit/altar-centered, with every aspect of the worship service bounded by the proclamation of the Trinitarian creation and redemption narrative, centered on an encounter with the person and work of Christ, and culminating in a response of the congregation toward covenant renewal.

churches don't really know *what* the center of the worship service ought to be, they will make things like instruments and music style the central concern.

Conclusion

In this chapter we have seen that the Christian doctrine of sanctification has gone through a long history of trial and error, resulting in an evangelical Protestant view that distinguishes but does not separate justification from sanctification, both of which are the work of God's Spirit (Phil. 2:12–13). The primary means of sanctification by which

God works to bring about our spiritual growth involves our active participation in the community life of the church.

We also saw that the proper observances of baptism as the rite of covenant initiation and the Lord's Supper as the rite of covenant renewal play vital roles in a biblically, historically, and theologically faithful approach to Christian spirituality. In connection with this long-neglected aspect of classic Christian corporate worship, we also introduced the idea of "pulpit/altar-centered worship," in which both proclamation and consecration are central elements of the worship experience.

Having established this basic corporate approach to sanctification, we now turn to another dimension of RetroSpirituality: the individual means of sanctification.

From "We" to "Me"

Nurturing Personal Christian Identity

*W*hile serving as the head of a famous Christian school in north Egypt during the late second century, Clement of Alexandria composed three major works addressing three distinct groups of people. His *Exhortation to the Heathen*, written around AD 190, targeted unbelievers, explaining the Christian faith in a way that would dispel rumors and promote the truth of Christianity. A second work, *The Instructor*, provided a guide to the Christian life for everyday baptized Christians to grow in their faith at the feet of the one true Instructor, Jesus Christ. Finally, *The Miscellanies* addressed "knowledge-able" Christians, those more advanced in theoretical and speculative knowledge who could handle discussions of the Christian faith and philosophy at a higher intellectual and spiritual level. In *Miscellanies*, Clement wrote:

His sacrifices are prayers, and praises, and readings in the Scriptures before meals, and psalms and hymns during meals and before bed, and prayers also again during night. By these he unites himself to the divine choir, from continual recollection, engaged in contemplation which has everlasting remembrance. And what? Does he not also know the other kind of sacrifice, which consists in the giving both of doctrines and of money to those who need? Assuredly.[1]

Clement of Alexandria's words reflect an essential aspect of sanctification: personal spiritual discipline. And this reminds us of an important truth: the individual devotional life of each believer is a valid and vital part of a life of living sacrifice.

Avoiding Two Extremes in Sanctification

History and experience teach us that both the corporate and the individual dimensions of sanctification can be pushed to an extreme. Corporate spirituality was exaggerated to a great degree in the medieval Catholic period, in which the corporate disciplines of the sacramental system—inextricably linked to the life of the institutional Church under a strict hierarchy—made the notion of a personal relationship with God seem strange. In reaction to the extreme position that only those means of grace officially connected to the Church were trustworthy and valid, early attempts at reform emphasized the other side of the Christian life—the direct, personal, unmediated relationship with God through the Holy Spirit. This became a major emphasis of the Protestant Reformers in the sixteenth century.

However, during the modern era, from about 1600 onward, when education, religion, philosophy, and politics increasingly emphasized individualism over community, many Christians uncritically adopted an excessively individualistic approach to spirituality. The church started to be viewed as an optional voluntary gathering of individual believers, and congregational forms of church government began to take shape. With it, the idea of corporate spirituality was replaced increasingly by individual spirituality. The proverbial pendulum swung to the opposite extreme from the medieval Catholic imbalance.

Today, most evangelicals are heirs of the extreme individualistic approach to the spiritual life. For example, many of you reading these words were not converted to Christianity or admitted into the church, but "accepted Jesus Christ as your personal Savior." Then, as a follow-up, you may have been taught that the key to the spiritual life was to "read your Bible and pray every day" or to "have your quiet time" or to "practice in the spiritual disciplines," or to "nurture your personal relationship with God."

The balanced Christian life cannot stay in the extreme of corporate spirituality, nor retreat into a radically individual spirituality. Rather, a balanced, stable approach to spirituality must simultaneously embrace both corporate and individual means of sanctification. Augustine of Hippo described the individual and corporate aspects of worship leading to spiritual union with God this way: "To Him we owe the service which is called in Greek latreia, whether we render it outwardly or inwardly; for we are all His temple, each of us severally and all of us together, because He condescends to inhabit each individually and the whole harmonious body, being no greater in all than in each, since He is neither expanded nor divided."[2]

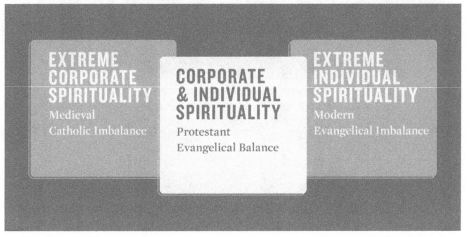

EXTREME
CORPORATE
SPIRITUALITY
Medieval
Catholic Imbalance

CORPORATE
& INDIVIDUAL
SPIRITUALITY
Protestant
Evangelical Balance

EXTREME
INDIVIDUAL
SPIRITUALITY
Modern
Evangelical Imbalance

The Christian life must maintain a balance between extreme corporate spirituality and extreme individual spirituality.

Scripture presents a balanced view of both corporate and individual aspects of the spiritual life. Paul illustrates this balanced approach in Galatians 6:1–5. Verses 1–2 stress the need for all of us to work together to bear each other's burdens; but verses 3–5 remind us that each individual is personally accountable before God for how we have carried out the tasks God has given to each of us. Similarly, in a passage directly related to building the church on the foundation of Jesus Christ, Paul writes, "Let each one take care how he builds upon it," warning that God's judgment "will test what sort of work each one has done" (1 Cor. 3:10, 13). Finally, Romans 12:1–8 proves to be a key passage on personal consecration and its corporate implications as each committed believer, having offered himself or herself to God's service, contributes to the building up of the body of Christ.

In these passages (and many more) the spiritual growth of a believer involves an inseparable and dynamic interplay between both individual and community means of sanctification. To neglect either the personal or the corporate in the process of sanctification will inevitably result in an unbalanced Christian life.

Spiritual growth involves an inseparable relationship between both personal and corporate means of sanctification. The neglect of either the individual or the community results in an imbalance in the Christian life.

The Need for Personal Means of Sanctification

In 1 Thessalonians 4:1–3, Paul wrote, "We ask and urge you in the Lord Jesus, that as you received from us how you ought to walk and to please God, just as you are doing, that you do so more and more. For you know what instructions we gave you through the Lord Jesus. For this is the will of God, your sanctification." The life of sanctification involves a walk that pleases God, which increases as we obey the teachings of Christ according to God's will (see 2 Pet. 1:5–8). It results in moral purity, avoiding all kinds of sexual temptation (Rom. 6:19; 1 Thess. 4:3–4, 7). It includes a conscious presentation of ourselves to God (Rom. 6:19; 12:1), something to be strived after (Heb. 12:14). Yet the fruit of sanctification comes to believers solely by grace, just as eternal life is a gift unearned (Rom. 6:22–23). In fact, Jesus Christ himself is our source of sanctification, as he is also our source of wisdom, justification, and redemption (1 Cor. 1:30). Furthermore, the Holy Spirit is the direct agent of God's sanctifying work (2 Thess. 2:13; 1 Pet. 1:2). The New Testament's discussion of the sanctification of the individual believer portrays the process as both a gracious work of the sovereign God as well as something we cooperate with through personal devotion and action (1 Thess. 5:23; 2 Tim. 2:21).

By what means do we engage in the process of sanctification? Scripture points to several things related to being made more holy in this life.

Christ links sanctification with the truth of the Word of God (John 17:17, 19). Paul tells Timothy that sanctification comes through repentance—fleeing our fleshly passions and pursuing righteousness, faith, love, and peace (2 Tim. 2:21–22; see 1 Pet. 1:14–16). And Romans 12 describes our transformation into people who are "holy and acceptable" as a presentation of our whole selves as living sacrifices, which includes the renewal of the mind (Rom. 12:1–2). Paul told his disciple, Timothy, "train yourself for godliness; for while bodily training is of some value, godliness is of value in every way, as it holds promise for the present life and also for the life to come" (1 Tim. 4:7–8). Thus, spiritual training toward godliness includes positive activities like reading Scripture, prayer, and fasting. Yet training also includes things you might do to protect yourself from temptation or to break a pattern of sin.

Individual spiritual disciplines are perhaps the most personal aspect of sanctification, for no two believers' struggles are precisely the same, and not all individuals respond the same way to the same means. The key is to keep hard at it, engaging in spiritual disciplines that move you closer to God and to his people, not wallowing in stale rituals that push you farther from a joyful Christian life. You want to be sanctified? Discover a fruitful pattern of spiritual disciplines that works for you.

Any of the numerous spiritual disciplines may work well for many people. But it's not ultimately the method itself that does the work. Through these means *God* works in you and for you. Instead of fixing your gaze on the method that seems to work (that's methodolatry), fix your gaze on "the founder and perfecter of our faith" (Heb. 12:2), for it is God at work in us to conform us to the image of Christ by the power of his Spirit.

Personal Prayer as the Persistent Presence of God

Prayer has always figured prominently in any approach to the spiritual life. Paul says in 1 Thessalonians 5:17, "Pray without ceasing," indicating that the life of faith is to be a life of constant prayer. As we pray, we constantly commune with God, reminding ourselves of his unbroken presence with us and expressing our confidence in his abiding power. I can't imagine anything more sanctifying than an unending experience of the presence of God through personal and continual devotion to him.

The fourth-century church father, Lactantius, described this kind of prayerful life this way:

> For we ought to sacrifice to God in word; inasmuch as God is the Word, as He Himself confessed. Therefore the chief ceremonial in the worship of God is praise from the mouth of a just man directed towards God. That this, however, may be accepted by God, there is need of humility, and fear, and devotion in the greatest degree, lest anyone should chance to place confidence in his integrity and innocence, and thus incur the charge of pride and arrogance. . . . And let him not suppose that this is to be done by him only in the temple, but at home, and even in his very bed. In short, let him always have God with himself, consecrated in his heart, inasmuch as he himself is a temple of God.[3]

The discipline of constantly practicing the personal presence of God didn't die with Lactantius. This idea of a "personal relationship with God" through prayer, praise, devotion, and thanksgiving has always been part of the Christian faith. It appears in its most pronounced and obvious forms among the monastic orders and especially the hermits. The fourteenth-century classic devotional, *The Imitation of Christ*, reflects on the prayerful lives of the early church fathers, contrasting their devotional zeal with the lukewarm spirituality of the late medieval church:

> What frequent and ardent prayers they offered to God! What rigorous fasts they observed! How great their zeal and their love for spiritual perfection! How brave the fight they waged to master their evil habits! What pure and straightforward purpose they showed toward God! By day they labored and by night they spent themselves in long prayers. Even at work they did not cease from mental prayer. . . . Today, he who is not a transgressor and who can bear patiently the duties which he has taken upon himself is considered great. How lukewarm and negligent we are! We lose our original fervor very quickly and we even become weary of life from laziness! Do not you, who have seen so many examples of the devout, fall asleep in the pursuit of virtue![4]

Though spontaneous prayer should be part of every believer's life, throughout history Christians have often found it helpful to schedule prayers at set times throughout the day. The Protestant Reformer, John Calvin, describes the need for such structure this way:

> Although . . . we ought always to raise our minds upwards towards God, and pray without ceasing, yet such is our weakness, which requires to be supported, such our torpor, which requires to be stimulated, that it is requisite for us to appoint special hours for this exercise, hours which are not to pass away without prayer, and during which the whole affections of our minds are to be completely occupied; namely, when we rise in the morning, before we commence our daily work, when we sit down to food, when by the blessing of God we have taken it, and when we retire to rest. This, however, must not be a superstitious observance of hours, by which, as it were, performing a task to God, we think we are discharged as to other hours; it should rather be considered as a discipline by which our weakness is exercised, and ever and anon stimulated.[5]

Another method that has also helped Christians remain disciplined and focused in prayer has been to read, write, recite, or even sing prayers. From the first century onward, the prayer Jesus taught his disciples, commonly called "The Lord's Prayer," has been recited not only during corporate worship, but also in private devotion. The *Didache* instructs readers to pray the words of the Lord's Prayer "three times a day."[6] Though many evangelicals today regard this kind of recitation of prayer as "dead traditionalism," we should listen rather to the words of the great Reformer, Martin Luther, who pointed out the value of the Lord's Prayer for constant personal devotion:

> [The Lord's Prayer] is a great advantage indeed over all other prayers that we might compose ourselves. For in them the conscience would ever be in doubt and say: I have prayed, but who knows how it pleases Him, or whether I have hit upon the right proportions and form? Hence there is no nobler prayer to be found upon earth than the Lord's Prayer which we daily pray because it has this excellent testimony, that God loves to hear it, which we ought not to surrender for all the riches of the world.[7]

Over the years I have personally come to find the practice of praying the words of the Lord's Prayer to be extremely beneficial. Sometimes I rephrase the prayer or expand it by adding details to its petitions, and I always follow it with my own thanksgivings, petitions, and intercessions. However, I find Luther's remarks quite accurate: in the Lord's Prayer I never doubt that I have prayed according to God's will.

Nevertheless, whether we choose to pray the Lord's Prayer, utilize the countless prayer books available from the history of the church, or pray strictly in our own words, God's instruction for us to pray without ceasing still stands as a primary means of personal worship. This constant state of prayerful worship throughout the day is, at an experiential level, to be closely associated with worshiping "in spirit" (John 4:23, 24), walking "by the Spirit" (Gal. 5:16, 25), and praying "in the Spirit" (Eph. 6:18; Jude 1:20). Though not equated, they all point to a continual practice of the presence of God as worshipful, prayerful, and intentional Christian living.

The seventeenth-century French Carmelite, Nicholas Herman, better known simply as "Brother Lawrence," describes worshiping the Father "in the spirit and in truth" this way:

> To worship GOD in truth is to acknowledge Him to be what He is, and ourselves as what in very fact we are. To worship Him in truth is to acknowledge with heart-felt sincerity what GOD in truth is,—that is to say, infinitely perfect, worthy of infinite adoration, infinitely removed from sin, and so of all the Divine attributes. That man is little guided by reason, who does not employ all his powers to render to this great GOD the worship that is His due.
>
> Furthermore, to worship GOD in truth is to confess that we live our lives entirely contrary to His will, and contrary to our knowledge that, were we but willing, He would fain make us conformable to Him. Who will be guilty of such folly as to withhold even for a moment the reverence and the love, the service and the unceasing worship that we owe to Him?[8]

Whether you pray the Lord's Prayer, pray and fast for particular people and needs, work through a daily prayer list of petitions and requests, sing your praises to God throughout the day, or pray at set times with written prayers, the practice of the presence of God through personal prayer is a primary means of sanctification for the growing Christian.

Sanctification by the Word and the Spirit

If asked to identify a Christian's primary means of sanctification, many evangelicals wouldn't hesitate to answer, "Read your Bible and pray every day." Personal Bible reading and prayer are the two most common practices during a person's "quiet time with the Lord." Praying has often been described as "me talking to God," while reading Scripture is "God talking to me."

However, as ironic as it may sound, personal Bible study can produce both the most humble and encouraging saint as well as the most prideful and damaging heretic. Because every heretic in history has pointed at the Bible and claimed to have come to their teachings based on the Bible alone, we need to address how we sometimes read the Bible wrongly as well as how to read it rightly. As you might expect, proper reading, interpretation, and application of Scripture maintains the same balance as other means of sanctification—avoiding the errors of extreme individual autonomy as well as the error of extreme corporate uniformity.

Basic Theology for Biblical Literacy

Since the Reformation evangelicalism has suffered from a false view of how to read the Bible. The healthy emphasis on *personal* Bible study has sometimes led to the unhealthy view that with an open Bible, a fresh cup of coffee, and a quick prayer to conjure the Holy Spirit like a genie, reading the Bible is as easy as 1-2-3, or at least "observation," "interpretation," and "application." While this is partly true, another ancient and vitally important principle of biblical interpretation and application has often been forgotten and sometimes been forsaken by naïve and overconfident individualistic Bible readers—both laypeople and scholars.[9] What is this vital principle?

We must read the Bible the way it was meant to be read.[10]

The Bible was originally read by believing communities who already had a basic understanding of doctrine and practice. That is, not only did they come to the text with basic theological presuppositions, but they were fully expected to do so![11] Let me give you an example. The original recipients of Paul's letters were already believers with some fundamental teachings under their belts. They had a conscious sense of the center—the person and work of Jesus Christ, the perfect God-man who died for their sins and rose from the dead. They had been baptized in the name of the Father, Son, and Holy Spirit and knew the basic story of creation, redemption, and restoration through the triune God. And they were already aware of basic boundaries of authentic Christian beliefs and drew distinct lines between Judaism, Paganism, and false forms of Christianity. Thus, the postholes for later creedal markers had already been dug.

Where did these first Christians receive their basic theology? They learned it from Paul and the other apostles and prophets of the early church, who preached, planted churches, and taught them essential Christian truths. So when these young churches received Paul's letters, they read them in light of the doctrines they had already received from their teachers. This is why Paul could say in 2 Thessalonians 2:15, "So then, brothers, stand firm and hold to the traditions that you were taught by us, either by our spoken word or by our letter." The original in-person teachings of the apostles established the new converts in the fundamentals of the Christian faith. Paul and the other apostles expected these new Christians to read the Old Testament Scriptures as well as the growing collection of New Testament books in light of this basic theology.

You may recall that in chapter 2 we examined seven reasons for looking back at the history of the church to help us reclaim the forgotten faith. The seventh reason was, "It will clarify our interpretation of Scripture." This final reason for studying church history directly addresses a safeguard against an overly individualistic reading of Scripture. We introduced the concept of "early tradition" and "enduring tradition" as tools to help us identify the core doctrines of the Christian faith. These core doctrines are what we call the essential truths of Christian orthodoxy. In fact, we explored in some detail the contours and content of basic orthodox theology in chapter 4, identifying seven areas of doctrinal continuity that can be discerned throughout the history of the church:

1. The triune God as Creator and Redeemer
2. The fall and resulting depravity
3. The person and work of Christ
4. Salvation by grace through faith

5. Inspiration and authority of Scripture
6. Redeemed humanity incorporated into Christ
7. The restoration of humanity and creation.

Because we are expected to read the Bible in light of basic Christian truth, a clear understanding of orthodox Christian theology is essential if we are to read the Bible rightly, think better doctrinally, and live our lives faithfully. So, to avoid reading, interpreting, and applying Scripture wrongly, we must keep the basic plotline of the Bible's message in view, recognizing that Christ stands at the center of God's revelation.

What about Sola Scriptura?

At this point you may be thinking, "But what about *sola Scriptura?*" Isn't *the Bible alone* the infallible guide for faith and life? This question almost always comes up among those who imagine that any attempt at theological guidelines, doctrinal boundaries, or organizing centers for interpreting and applying the Bible is a retreat toward Roman Catholic dogmatism and an abandonment of the Reformation. In reaction to the idea of any kind of doctrinal norms informing our reading of Scripture, some pick up the sword of *"sola Scriptura"* and start swinging in self-defense. This is because few principles have been more misunderstood by modern evangelicals than the Reformation principle of *sola Scriptura.* Many—perhaps most—Christians know the translation of these two Latin words: "Scripture alone"; but it seems that only a precious few actually know its original meaning for Protestantism.[12]

The short phrase is one of a family of battle cries of the Reformation that served to set it apart from the gross distortions of medieval Roman Catholic theology. Other members of the family included *solus Christus,* "Christ alone," *sola gratia,* "by grace alone," and *sola fidei,* "by faith alone." These emphases created Protestant identity in response to Catholic doctrinal corruption. *Christ alone:* not Christ, the Church, the pope, the saints, and the Virgin Mary. *Grace alone:* not grace in cooperation with meritorious works dispensed by the sacramental system of Mother Church. *Faith alone:* not faith, good works, and papal indulgences. And *Scripture alone:* not Scripture, papal decrees, Roman Catholic Canon Law, and ecclesiastical tradition.

Today many have forgotten the original meaning of *sola Scriptura.* Historical ignorance has overtaken them.[13] Five centuries after Martin

Luther, the Reformers' sword of *sola Scriptura* has been picked up by those who have never learned how to wield it. And just like any weapon in the hands of a novice, a misunderstood *sola Scriptura* can be a dangerous thing.

If I were to ask a random believer at my own church what Luther meant by "Scripture alone," he or she would probably answer something like: "Luther rejected tradition and replaced it with Scripture," or, "Luther got his theology only from the Bible," or, "The Bible—not creeds, popes, or councils—is the only source of truth," or, "The Bible is the only authority for faith and practice." After all, 2 Timothy 3:16 says, "All Scripture is inspired by God and profitable for teaching, for reproof, for correction, for training in righteousness" (NASB). Surely, this means the Bible alone is all that's needed . . . right? Although this is a common understanding, it's a distortion of what Luther and the Reformers meant by *sola Scriptura*. What, then, does it mean?

Simply put, *sola Scriptura* means that Scripture alone is the final authority and inerrant source of truth. It is the *norma normans non normata*—the "norming norm which cannot be normed." That is, if Scripture and church tradition clash, tradition has to go. If the Bible bumps our experience, our experience must be rejected. If God's written Word contradicts science, philosophy, or reason, all those things must bow to the authority of God's Word. Nothing can correct the plain teachings of Scripture.

However, this does not mean that all these things—tradition, experience, science, philosophy, and reason—cannot contribute to a better understanding of Scripture. The Reformers valued tradition, experience, philosophy, reason, the contribution of scholarship, science, history, and other fields to help our feeble, limited minds better understand God's revelation. But none of these things were permitted to correct the Bible. Scripture is not our *only* source of knowledge; nor is it our *only* source of true knowledge. But *Scripture alone* is the only source of true knowledge that cannot be corrected by other sources of knowledge.

Many people mistakenly believe Luther arrived at his earth-shaking Protestant theology by simply reading the Bible. This is another half-truth. In fact, Luther's criticisms of the Roman Catholic Church of his day came from reading the Bible *better*. His eyes were opened to the Catholic theologians' false reading of Scripture when he began reading the much earlier works of Saint Augustine (who died around AD 430). He also explored the earlier creeds and councils, and the works of other luminaries who had gone before him. In this biblical and historical exploration, Luther realized that many of the Roman Catholic Church's doctrines and practices did not match those of the earliest Christians. As such, the Catholic Church's reading of Scripture began to look more and more indefensible. It was Luther's *better* reading of Scripture in light of the most ancient tradition that led him and many others to their revolutionary ideas. It was, in fact, reading Scripture *in light of history*, that sparked the Reformation.

Ironically, today we are often guilty of the same approach to the Bible as the medieval Catholics. We read our Bible outside its original historical and doctrinal context and read into the Bible our own unquestioned presuppositions and beliefs. Today we open our Bibles in readable English translations and imagine that we can follow a few simple rules of observation and come up with sound doctrines. We sit in Bible studies and ante up an equal amount of ignorance, playing dangerous games with the inspired text by sharing with each other what the text "means to me," or debating over our individualistic interpretations. We turn all the passages into convenient practical principles that directly address our personal problems, forgetting that these books were written with a much bigger doctrinal background and meaning than our simplistic list of "dos and don'ts" that constitute our me-centric, application-oriented readings.

In reality, Christians were never meant to understand or apply Scripture completely alone. Scripture must be read in conjunction with three things—*teamwork, teachers,* and *tradition.* The "team" is the church—that is, other believers like you and me, believers committed to submitting themselves to the Word, encouraging each other toward godliness, and depending on insights and wisdom of others as they wrestle not only with what the Bible means but how to live that out. We see this kind of community-oriented devotion in the very first church in the book of Acts: "They devoted themselves to the apostles' teaching and the fellowship, to the breaking of bread and the prayers" (Acts 2:42). And 1 Timothy 4:13 says, "Devote yourself to the public reading of Scripture, to exhortation, to teaching." While we should never neglect devotional reading of the Bible, we must also never forget that many of the books of the Bible—when they are not addressed to pastors like Timothy and Titus—were sent to *churches* and meant to be read, discussed, understood, and obeyed in *community*.

Second, Scripture is supposed to be understood through gifted *teachers*. When the Ethiopian eunuch traveled along the Gaza road reading the prophet Isaiah out loud to himself (Acts 8:26–29), Philip asked, "Do you understand what you are reading?" The man responded, "How can I, unless someone guides me?" (8:30–31). In response, Philip "opened his mouth, and beginning with this Scripture he told him the good news about Jesus" (8:35). Although Christians today have a greater understanding of the Christ-centered meaning of Scripture, Paul says the church has been gifted with evangelists, pastors, and teachers "to equip the saints for the work of ministry" (Eph. 4:12), so that "we may no longer be children, tossed to and fro by the waves and carried about by every wind of doctrine, by human cunning, by craftiness in deceitful schemes" (4:14).

This leads to the third thing that contributes to our proper understanding and application of Scripture—*tradition*. Paul said to the Thessalonians, "Stand firm and hold to the traditions that you were taught by us, either by our spoken word or by our letter" (2 Thess. 2:15). By "tradition" we don't mean a secret teaching outside the Bible and passed down through the centuries. Rather, "tradition" means the history of the church's interpretation and application of Scripture that helps us better understand how to read and live the truths of Scripture. It is, in fact, an attempt to read the Bible responsibly, seeking the biblically, historically, and theologically mature understanding of any doctrinal or practical issue.

Be Taught, Be Stable

So, is the Bible difficult to understand? As we are encouraged to read the Bible for ourselves, to seek answers in its pages, to apply its principles to our daily lives, should we stand in fear, lest we misinterpret its message or misapply its mandates?

Yes and no.

The basic and vital message of the Bible is easy to read, learn, and explain—for those whose eyes have been opened. About AD 185, Irenaeus of Lyons wrote, "The entire Scriptures, the prophets, and the Gospels, can be clearly, unambiguously, and harmoniously understood by all, although all do not believe them."[14] But that famous early pastor assigned this understanding to a particular kind of student who is "devoted to piety and the love of truth," who "will eagerly meditate upon those things which God has placed within the power of mankind, and has subjected to our knowledge, and will make advancement in [acquaintance with] them, rendering the knowledge of them easy to him by means of daily study."[15] The flip side of this is that the impious, the lazy, and those who fail to acknowledge the limitations of their human knowledge will not achieve even the basic level of proficiency in their understanding of the Bible.

Over a hundred years earlier, the apostle Peter gave us a similar warning about understanding Scripture. With reference to Paul's writings, he said, "Some things in them . . . are hard to understand, which the ignorant and unstable twist to their own destruction, as they do the other Scriptures" (2 Pet. 3:16). Who were those people? How do we avoid becoming those Scripture-twisters who are braiding the passages of Scripture into their own hangman's noose? Thankfully, Peter makes this quite clear. And we ought to listen to his warning.

Peter says the "ignorant" and "unstable" twist Paul's writings to their destruction. The Greek word "ignorant" is *amathes*, which is literally the opposite of "discipled." A discipled person was an apprentice who learned a trade or teaching from a mentor or rabbi. One lexicon defines *amathes* as "pertaining to one who has not acquired a formal education."[16] Thus, Peter says that one way to be a Scripture-twister is to be untaught, untrained, and undiscipled. The implication is clear: only those who have been discipled can be expected to read the Scriptures rightly—skillfully weaving them together in a unified whole, centered on Christ, faithfully presenting the fundamental doctrines of the faith, discerning what is crucial for orthodoxy and acknowledging what things are beyond comprehension. Paul calls this skill "rightly handling the word of truth" (2 Tim. 2:15).

Peter also describes Scripture-twisters as "unstable." The word means "unsteady," "weak," "standing on shaky ground." These people are not grounded, not centered. They are "tipsy." Picture the difference between a house trailer standing on cinder blocks and a brick building resting on bedrock. The unstable are like reeds in the wind, waving here and there. They are like butterflies in a field of flowers, fluttering from flower to flower. They are unpredictable, unreliable—unstable.

These untrained and unsteady people distort the Scriptures. They misunderstand the big picture, because they have not submitted themselves to proper teaching. They lacked the patience, the humility, or the endurance to pass from spiritual infancy to adulthood, from the rank of novice to the rank of master. Perhaps they claimed to rest their bad theology and practice on the Bible alone, ignorantly insisting that the sole authority for their views comes from Scripture. Many might have scoffed at authority, rejected tradition, and thrown out the perspectives of others. They may have especially despised believing scholars trained in original languages, history, and theology, calling them "Pharisees" or charging them with focusing on the letter rather than on the Spirit. Scripture-twisters claim the Bible alone as their only source of authority, not realizing that they are simply reading their own ideas into the text.

In light of Peter's warning, we evangelicals—and especially those of us in the free church tradition—need to be particularly cautious about how we present the Protestant notion of *sola Scriptura*. According to Peter, taking the "Bible Only" principle to an unbalanced extreme will breed destructive heretics. In fact, those who have studied the history of the church quickly learn a common formula that repeats itself in every generation:

(Me + the Bible) – Stable Training = Heresy

How, then, do we as individual Christians guarantee that we're reading the Bible rightly and not becoming Scripture-twisters? Peter has already given us the answer: be taught and be stable. How? By the work of the Holy Spirit through his chosen means—gifted teachers. We often appeal to the Holy Spirit's direct, individual, personal work in our hearts to teach us. But this is only half the answer. The New Testament emphasizes over and over that the Spirit not only indwells individuals and makes them responsive to the truth, but he also indwells the church and promotes the faithful teaching of the truth (Eph. 4:11–16).

So as part of your daily regimen of personal spiritual disciplines, continue to read Scripture as the sure source of spiritual fruit. Such personal devotional reading has always had a central place in the Christian faith. Gregory I of Rome (AD 540–604) once wrote regarding the inexhaustible wisdom of Scripture for both the novice and the advanced:

> For as the word of God, by the mysteries which it contains, exercises the understanding of the wise, so usually by what presents itself on the outside, it nurses the simple-minded. It presents in open day that wherewith the little ones may be fed; it keeps in secret that whereby men of a loftier range may be held in suspense of admiration. It is, as it were, a kind of river, if I may so liken it, which is both shallow and deep, wherein both the lamb may find a footing, and the elephant float at large.[17]

The conclusion? Read Scripture. Study it. Memorize it. Meditate on it day and night. But do so with humility, caution, and a healthy accountability to the historical and contemporary community of saints. In short, be taught and be stable.

Renewing the Mind . . . and Matter

A final aspect of our spiritual growth relates to the often neglected realms of the Christian life—those areas that many believe are less spiritual and more fleshly. I'm speaking here of both the physical and spiritual development of the whole person, suggesting that sanctification involves every dimension of our lives, not merely our spirit or soul.

Part of the community aspect of edification and exaltation (described in chapter 9) involves attending to physical needs—food, clothing, and shelter. At the individual level, the physical well-being of a person is directly related to his or her spiritual well-being. Sadly, in their striving after spirituality, too many evangelicals forget that we were created as *embodied* beings. The most ancient church never forgot that humans have both physical and spiritual facets, regarding the balanced Christian life as engaging both of these dimensions of humanity. For example, around AD 110 Ignatius of Antioch wrote this pastoral advice to his colleague, Polycarp of Smyrna: "Do justice to your office with constant care for both physical and spiritual concerns. . . . You are both physical and spiritual in nature for this reason, that you might treat gently whatever appears before you."[18] Thus, Christian ministry concerns itself not merely with spiritual things, but also with physical things.

This embodied or "incarnational" approach to the Christian life is consistent with the Christian doctrine of humanity. When God created Adam, he formed him "from the ground" (the physical aspect) and breathed into that physical form the "breath of life" (the spiritual part). Only *then*, when the material and immaterial parts of the man were united, did Adam become "a living creature" (Gen. 2:7). This is why Christians of every generation have confessed that we will experience the final outcome of our salvation in Christ when we are resurrected in our physical bodies, which will be miraculously raised up, reconstituted, and rendered immortal and glorious (Rom. 8:19–23).

In the second century, Tertullian of Carthage summed up this biblical teaching of the essential embodied nature of humanity:

> Now, neither the soul by itself alone is "man" (it was subsequently implanted in the clay mold to which the name man had been already given), nor is the flesh without the soul "man": for after the exile of the soul from it, it has the title of corpse. Thus the designation man is, in a certain sense, the bond between the two closely united substances, under which designation they cannot but be coherent natures.[19]

In other words, the classic Christian doctrine of human nature can be described as an "integrated dichotomy" or a "psychosomatic unity," in which the whole human person includes both material and immaterial aspects. We are not, as the heretical Gnostics believed, merely spiritual beings dwelling in a temporary shell, as if our God-given bodies are prisons of flesh that must one day be discarded for our true spiritual life to begin. The "real me" is not my internal spirit. Nor are we merely material beings, as much modern science assumes, arguing that everything from love to complex rationality can be reduced to body and brain chemistry. Rather, to be fully and authentically human, we must be both physical and spiritual, flesh and soul, body and mind, material and immaterial. One pastor describes the classic Christian doctrine of human nature in the following way, specifically targeting modern Gnostic tendencies among evangelicals:

> With few exceptions, the Christian church has affirmed, with one voice, that human nature is two-fold. As men and women, we are necessarily a body—the physical element of our nature—and we are also a soul-spirit—an immaterial aspect described in the Bible as either soul or spirit. These two are united together as one person; as a psychosomatic unity.

. . . If the Gnostic impulse is defined as a quest for secret knowledge (gnosis), and a disparaging of matter, including an aversion to things physical and intellectual, coupled to the notion that religion is essentially a quest for a vaguely defined spirituality attained via a mystical ascent into the heavenlies to encounter God apart from means and a mediator, then the notion that humans are essentially spiritual beings rather than a body-soul unity, opens the door to a host of serious theological errors.[20]

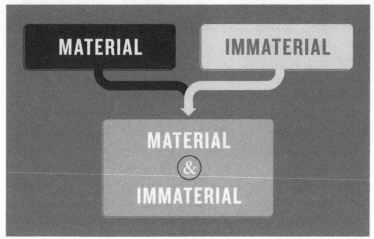

The classic Christian doctrine of human nature can be described as an "integrated dichotomy" or "psychosomatic unity," in which the whole human person includes both material and immaterial facets.

What does this biblical-historical doctrine of human nature mean for our sanctification? It means that God desires us to maintain not only spiritual health, but also physical, emotional, and mental health. He is concerned about the whole physical/spiritual person, not merely about the soul. First Thessalonians 5:23 says, "Now may the God of peace himself sanctify you completely, and may your whole spirit and soul and body be kept blameless at the coming of our Lord Jesus Christ." This not only relates to avoiding sins affecting the body, the mind, and the spirit, but it also relates to cultivating physical health, intellectual development, and spiritual wisdom and insight.

The Christian church has a long history of intellectual development, including serious critical interaction with philosophy, science, culture, politics, and other fields of study beyond the study of Scripture, theology, and practical ministry. This development of the mind acknowledges that valuable truth can be found in God's creation as well as through human reason aided by divine grace (Ps. 19:1–6; Prov. 6:6; Rom. 1:19–20).

In the Patristic period, the "sciences" included primarily philosophy and reason. Even at this early stage, however, Christian interaction with secular philosophy was not without its tensions. The Alexandrian school, characterized by theologians like Clement of Alexandria and his disciple, Origen, freely incorporated the work of philosophical inquiry they believed helped to understand and explain Christian truth. However, a student of Origen, Gregory Thaumaturgus, in a eulogy of that famous teacher, pointed out the limits they applied in the use of secular philosophy:

> For he [Origen] deemed it right for us to study philosophy in such wise, that we should read with utmost diligence all that has been written, both by the philosophers and by the poets of old, rejecting nothing, and repudiating nothing . . . except only the productions of the atheists, who, in their conceits, lapse from the general intelligence of man, and deny that there is either a God or a providence. . . . With respect to these human teachers, indeed, he counseled us to attach ourselves to none of them, not even though they were attested as most wise by all men, but to devote ourselves to God alone, and to the prophets.[21]

At about the same time, on the other side of Africa, Tertullian of Carthage had a much more skeptical view of the dialogue between secular philosophy and Christian theology. He famously wrote:

> Indeed heresies are themselves instigated by philosophy. . . . What indeed has Athens to do with Jerusalem? What concord is there between the Academy and the Church? What between heretics and Christians? . . . . Away with all attempts to produce a mottled Christianity of Stoic, Platonic, and dialectic composition! We want no curious disputation after possessing Christ Jesus, no inquisition after enjoying the gospel! With our faith, we desire no further belief.[22]

This tension between theology and philosophy, or "revelation and reason," resolved itself during the medieval period, when scholastics like Anselm and Aquinas sought to synthesize truth from both general revelation (philosophy, science, and reason) and special revelation (Scripture, theology, and tradition) into an internally consistent, coherent, and comprehensive system of orthodox truth. Thomas Aquinas describes this use of the philosophical sciences in the service of theology in the following way: "This science [theology] can in a sense depend upon the philosophical sciences, not as though it stood in need of them, but only in order to make its teaching clearer."[23]

Now fast-forward to the present day.

In our modern world, the "sciences" include everything from mathematics to philosophy, from history to psychology, and from technology to astronomy. These various fields—to the degree that they represent accurately the truth of God's created world and his unfolding history—all have roles to play in the intellectual growth of the individual believer and of the Christian community. Because Christians believe a right understanding of Scripture corresponds with reality, established truths of science must by necessity correspond to Scripture and to other sources of truth, giving educated believers a better understanding of God's creation.[24]

What does all of this have to do with personal means of sanctification?

Christian spirituality must take into consideration the whole person. Physically, believers must encourage healthy habits of diet, activity, sleep, and other bodily disciplines that promote a healthy mind and spiritual disposition (1 Tim. 4:8; 5:23; 3 John 1:2). Intellectually, believers must acquire knowledge of a variety of subjects and develop skills in critical thinking and communication (1 Kings 4:29–34; Prov. 1:5; Dan. 1:17). They should resist the tendency to dichotomize between faith and reason, Scripture and science.[25] While avoiding the evil and sin of the world system, they must learn to love and serve God with their whole heart, soul, mind, and strength (Mark 12:30).[26]

Conclusion

It is God's will that we be sanctified, that is, that we be set apart for God's service. This process of sanctification—ultimately a work of the Holy Spirit—is accomplished in us through both corporate and individual means. In this chapter we introduced the necessity of individual spiritual disciplines of prayer, Scripture reading, and the cultivation of both the body and the mind.

A classic approach to the Christian life should begin with Bible study and prayer, but it cannot end there. We must also nurture our mental, emotional, physical, and social development in our pursuit of transformation and conformation to the image of Christ.

Where Do We Go from Here?

From Retrospect to Prospects

I hate to admit it, but some of my favorite websites are the various "how to" databases. Just search for "how to ____" and a number of helpful, practical, and virtually idiot-proof options present themselves. "How to tie a bow," "how to make yoghurt," "how to buy a piano"—I've personally consulted sites for everything from fixing a toilet to playing an accordion. Clearly, we're living in an instant "how-to" world. What matters to most people is that seemingly good ideas actually work, and preferably *quickly*.

I don't believe that something is true only if it produces immediate results, or that knowledge is only as important as its practical effects. In fact, I get a little nervous when pastors and teachers so emphasize "practical application" or "relevant teaching" that their exhortations become hollow dos and don'ts or empty platitudes with no real theological or doctrinal core to support them. Biblical, historical, and theological truth must undergird everything we think, say, and do. A change of mind *must* be followed with a change of attitude and change of action.

In this book we explored a lot of theory. We've compared trendy "metrodoxy" and worn-out "petridoxy" with unchanging and ever-relevant orthodoxy. We attempted to navigate the turbulent waters of unity, diversity, primitivism, and progressivism by diagnosing the Benajmin Button Syndrome (extreme primitivism), the Fuddy-Duddy Syndrome (extreme stagnation), and the Émile Coué Syndrome (extreme progressivism), arguing that a balanced biblical, historical, and theological approach to practical Christianity must avoid these extremes. We explored common myths and classic marks of the historical body of Christ, and then we discussed the two pillars of an authentic local church: the essential marks (orthodoxy, order, and ordinances) and the essential works (evangelism, edification, exaltation). We also sought a biblically and historically informed spirituality that neglects neither the individual nor the community and addresses both the physical and spiritual dimensions of a person. Along the way in this introduction to RetroChristianity, we considered a handful of practical ideas on how to implement some of its key concepts. "Going Retro" provided some things that can be done personally and immediately; "Retrofitting" addressed those in church leadership who might have opportunities to make changes in their own ministries.

An underlying assumption behind this book is that evangelicalism in its varied forms has lost its way. It has entered into what we called a period of "midlife crisis," forcing us to think about its identity and to consider how to best move forward. To address this problem, we argued for an adjustment of individuals' and churches' attitudes and actions, retrieving ideas and practices from the Christian past for the present, renewing personal and corporate identity, and thereby providing evangelicalism a positive path toward the future. This was the definition of RetroChristianity presented in chapter 3 and developed throughout this book.

But now what? Let's assume that you've bought the idea that evangelicalism is, in fact, suffering from a midlife crisis and needs to learn from the whole history of Christianity in order to restore its identity. Let's say you're even persuaded by many of the arguments for unity and diversity, for a restoration of a pulpit/altar-centered worship of a covenanted community. Maybe you've checked the facts and have accepted what was presented as the "biblical-historical model" of church order. So, what do you do now?

This is a question I get a lot in my classes at the seminary where I teach. After several lectures on such topics as church order or the sacraments, students raise their hands and ask, "What should I do if my church doesn't do it this way?" or "Can you come to my church and tell my pastor these things?" or "I tried to suggest this at my church and they called a special meeting to figure out what to do with me!" or "If my church doesn't do it this way, should I leave?"

Perhaps similar questions are running through your head right now. In response to these types of questions, I've developed a number of "principles to ponder" and "priorities to pursue." Let's begin with the first.

Principles to Ponder

When it comes to personally "going retro" or corporately "retrofitting," let me recommend three principles. These may go against our "get it done" nature. They will certainly give us an opportunity to exhibit the spiritual fruit of joy, patience, faithfulness, gentleness, and self-control. And they will go a long way toward coming to terms with both the possibilities and limitations of our present ministries.

1. Don't attempt to change a denominational confession or structure. Remember that orthodox evangelicalism accepts unity in the midst of diversity. If your denominational church maintains the essential marks of orthodoxy, order, and ordinances and the essential works of evangelism, edification, and exaltation, you really have no reason to worry too much about your church. You may not agree with your particular church's specific understanding of church order, or your church may not observe baptism and the Lord's Supper exactly the way you think it should be done. But if these are molded and practiced according to an established and unchangeable charter, constitution, or historical confession, you have no authority or opportunity to change them. And if your denomination fits within the realm of orthodox Protestant evangelicalism, you have no real reason to break your covenant commitment to that church by going to another seemingly better, but actually imperfect, church.

So you can't change it and you don't agree with it. Now what? Simple. You endure it. You work with the existing structures, worship within the existing patterns, and minister through the existing methods. No local church is perfect, and no confessional denomination has somehow tapped into a secret source of authoritative interpretation. Remember the canons of RetroOrthodoxy and live within the tension of unity and diversity. Don't forget that RetroChristianity is not just about actions, but attitudes. You can always pursue personal and corporate spirituality described in the previous two chapters and continue to study the faith of the fathers, theologians, Reformers, and pastors of church history to gain knowledge, insight, wisdom, and encouragement.

2. Nudge, don't push; patiently approximate, don't rashly appropriate. If you do happen to be in a position where real adjustments can be made in the way your church is structured or in your ministry and worship function, then take the slow-and-easy approach. Even if your entire congregation or ministry team is fully on board, ride the breaks all the way. Make minor adjustments, establishing priorities and following a plan.

Caution and prudence are especially required if your church just isn't ready for substantial (or even noticeable) changes to structure, governance, worship, and so forth. In situations like this, take the limited opportunities you have to nudge without pushing. If people ask your opinion on certain issues, coax them in a historically informed direction and provide clear rationale. If you're part of a committee, ministry, or leadership team with the chance to give input, encourage others to draw on a full diet of biblical, theological, and historical wisdom, not simply contemporary, sociological, psychological, and practical methodologies. Especially discourage gut feelings, congregational polling, and open mic Fridays where people simply present the results of worldly wisdom. Bible. Theology. History. Ministry experience. These are the sources of *spiritual* wisdom, because through these and in these the Spirit himself has worked and continues to work.

Be satisfied with minor course corrections. If your church has *never* celebrated baptism or the Lord's Supper, then it's a real improvement if it begins to observe them annually. The apostolic model was to weekly celebrate the Eucharist, but if this is simply not an easy sell in your church community, consider that annual observance is better than no observance; quarterly is better than annually; monthly better than quarterly; and weekly Sunday nights is better than monthly Sunday mornings. Every church in every denomination must handle approximations of the ideal. You'll never find a single church that hits the ideal 100 percent of the time.

3. Remember that most issues are not simple, so proceed with humility. Not everything is completely clear in Scripture, in the history of the church, or in the various systems of theological thought. You should expect people in leadership to see things differently. They had different teachers, read different books, and worked in different ministries. Some have a stronger historical and theological grounding than others. And even those who are equipped to interact with questions of historical development may tend toward primitivism or progressivism as a presupposition. In other words, don't become frustrated if decision-makers don't see problems or solutions as clearly as you. They could be wrong. And so could you.

A humble attitude, a team spirit, and a willingness to surrender your own preferences for the sake of unity in the body are to be preferred to a so-called "pure" church that aligns with every view in this or any other book on church renewal. Set aside your personal agenda and seek the Lord's will, his timing, and his purpose in your local body. Strive for agreement among leadership and consensus among the congregation.

Over the years I've learned to appreciate the advice of Cyprian of Carthage regarding making major decisions in the church. Though known for his very high view of the church, in a letter from around AD 250, he wrote:

> In respect of that which our fellow elders, Donatus and Fortunatus, Novatus and Gordius, wrote to me, I have not been able to reply by myself, since, from the first commencement of my position as bishop, I made up my mind to do nothing on my own private opinion, without your advice and without the consent of the people. But as soon as, by the grace of God, I shall have come to you, then we will discuss in common, as our respective dignity requires, those things which either have been or are to be done.[1]

Cyprian clearly saw the wisdom in refusing to simply cast a vision as a dictator and then command specific changes. Rather, Cyprian worked toward the vision through the cooperation of the fellow elders and entire congregation. A pastor with any years of ministry behind him will confirm that this bit of pastoral advice is pure gold. So, arguing from the greater to the lesser, if that preeminent pastor refused to slam his private opinions through without consent and consensus, why would we think we should try to do the same?

Priorities to Pursue

So, where do you start? What would you do if your church handed you a form with three numbered spaces to be filled out and said, "Write down the top three changes you want to make to this ministry and we'll implement them, no questions asked." What would you choose?

Let me list what I believe are some of the most vital changes that most free church or Low Church evangelical congregations need to seriously consider if they are interested in reclaiming the forgotten faith. These are also suggestions for those seeking a church home—or even for missionaries seeking to plant churches at home or abroad.

First, we must move toward a more biblical-historical model of church order. Without forsaking the principles to ponder from the last section, churches ought to seriously consider making some adjustments to their leadership structure. Many of these suggestions were mentioned in chapter 8—abandoning the pastor–elder dichotomy, restoring the "lead" pastor as the head of the team of pastors/elders, revising the political model of term limits, and revisiting the qualifications of elders, especially the notion of less-than-qualified lay elders. Church order is a top priority for RetroChristianity, because without trained and experienced leadership at the helm of our churches, few of the other important changes will be able to be implemented successfully. Why? Because church leaders don't need worldly wisdom, intuitive hunches, business models, sociological theories, or psychological methods. They need biblical, theological, and historical wisdom to apply to ever-changing circumstances.

Second, we must restore a pulpit/altar-centered worship model and the right administration of the sacraments. Our evangelical churches must restore both the pulpit (representing proclamation of the Word) and the altar (representing consecration of the worshiper) to their central place in the gathered community. This means ideally observing the Lord's Supper as frequently as we preach a sermon. It means baptized believers partaking of Communion in response to a call from the pulpit for covenant renewal. This, too, implies a clearer understanding of the sacraments, a greater appreciation for their role in sanctification, and an abandonment of the powerless "symbol only" theology that bears only a slight resemblance to the teaching of the New Testament or early church. All of this also means molding our entire worship experience around the center of the pulpit/altar—including rethinking our music, offering, order of worship, and even our architecture.

Third, we must take steps toward greater intercongregational community. Too many local churches or denominations function like competing shopping centers, vying for customers by offering better or cheaper products. Both independent and denominational churches need to consciously, intentionally, and recognizably take steps to realize and demonstrate interchurch community. This might mean calling regional interdenominational conferences for the purpose of ordination, discipline, or disputation on various issues as the needs arise. It may mean considering appointing leadership from other area churches on your own church's corporate board of directors to increase intercongregational accountability. It may mean praying for other churches by name during your Sunday morning worship service. Whatever it takes, we must overcome our independent spirits and align ourselves with other evangelical churches that share the basic fundamentals of the faith, even though we may never agree on the secondary issues.

Fourth, we must emphasize the fundamentals of orthodoxy rather than our denominational distinctives. Baptists may know their church only immerses believers, but they may not know the difference between Modalism and Arianism. Wesleyans may have learned how the doctrine of entire sanctification sets them apart from other traditions, but they may not know why it's vital that Jesus is both fully God and fully human. And dispensational Bible churches may know that their tradition holds to a pretribulation rapture position, but they may not know what the Christian church has always taught about the resurrection of the flesh and life everlasting.

In other words, every church and denomination must point their people to the essential truths of the Christian faith before they introduce them to their own church's unique perspectives. To confuse uncompromising truth with debatable opinions is to confuse Christianity itself and foster disunity, distrust, and ultimate disaster at a national and global scale.

Fifth, we must encourage both corporate and individual disciplines. We must banish the days in which the key to an abundant, fruitful, and stable Christian life was simply to "read your Bible and pray every day." In this model, joining a Bible-believing church community was almost an afterthought. Thankfully that attitude has been waning over the last several decades, but some have swung the pendulum in the exact opposite direction—forsaking personal devotion for the sake of a fulfilling corporate worship experience.

The Bible emphasizes both of these aspects. Churches ought to embrace a wide range of teaching and training on both individual and corporate spirituality. The Spirit works through both the church and the individual, though the New Testament emphasizes the former.

Conclusion: Boldly Go Where Countless Others Have Gone Before!

Over the years I've heard a number of famous pastors, scholars, evangelists, and missionaries eulogized by their loved ones. The theme is often the same: "So-and-so grew his ministry from humble beginnings to colossal heights. He contributed significantly to his field of study. He stood for progress, development, improvement, and change. He expanded his borders, increased his influence, and established an enduring legacy. He was a creative forward thinker, a dynamic innovator, and a visionary leader. He helped lead the church into the twenty-first century."

This is not the goal of RetroChristianity. Instead of courageously blazing a trail into unknown territory, let's take on a much greater challenge: to boldly go where countless have gone before. When something vital is missing from our church, we need to reclaim that lost treasure from the past and place it in the present. And if our churches have blasted themselves into the postmodern age with little or no biblical, theological, or historical forethought, we need to do the difficult but necessary thing: set the church back hundreds of years.

Many evangelical leaders today seek to renew, reform, and refresh evangelicalism along these same lines—by carefully and critically reflecting on the *whole* history of the church. We reflect not just on what it once was, but what it became, including positive developments to be preserved and negative declines that need to be reversed. We're convinced that great wisdom, insight, and direction can be gained by listening to and learning from the pastors and teachers of the Patristic, medieval, Reformation, and modern eras. This is why evangelicals must stop their erratic search for a new identity and examine their roots. Only then will evangelicalism overcome its midlife crisis.

But the approach of RetroChristianity is costly.

It will mean giving up some of the so-called advances we've made over the last several generations. It will mean restoring some of the things we abandoned. It will also mean breaking new ground as we move forward in an ever-changing world, always unsure of what may come next, but stepping out in confidence because we know who we are.

As a philosophy of ministry rooted in biblical, historical, and theological reflection and dialogue, RetroChristianity is an adjustment of individuals' and churches' attitudes and actions, retrieving ideas and practices from the Christian past for the present, renewing personal and corporate identity, and providing evangelicalism a positive path toward the future.

Are you ready to start this difficult journey?

If so, listen carefully to the words of the prophet and take your first steps:

> Stand by the roads, and look,
>   and ask for the ancient paths,
> where the good way is; and walk in it,
>   and find rest for your souls. (Jer. 6:16)

Suggested Resources

I wrote *RetroChristianity* as an introduction to an ongoing discussion among evangelical laypeople, pastors, teachers, and scholars. As such, I have intentionally left countless topics off the pages and out of the notes, deferring them to an ongoing online forum, www. retrochristianity.com, and for future publications as the needs warrant. I encourage readers to think about the ideas in *RetroChristianity* "out loud," interacting with other readers, practitioners, and scholars from a wide variety of perspectives.

The diversity within the wide world of evangelicalism means that everybody begins the journey of RetroChristianity from different starting points. Perhaps some need much more information, instruction, or interaction before changing direction. Maybe others find themselves (or their churches) mostly in harmony with the attitudes and actions described in this book; all they need is a clearer understanding of the biblical, historical, and theological underpinnings of their tradition. Still others may require help navigating through their particular situations, continuing to draw on the wisdom, insight, education, and experience of others as they take small steps in implementing real change.

For those who want to begin digging deeper, some of the following resources will be helpful.

Websites

The **RetroChristianity** forum (www.retrochristianity.com) promotes ongoing discussion regarding the themes and ideas presented in *Retro-Christianity*. You'll find helpful discussions, useful tools, and additional essays on a variety of related topics, as well as other recommended resources and links to other ministries.

The **Christian Classics Ethereal Library** (www.ccel.org) is an open vault of treasures from every period of church history. I highly recommend this site for those interested in exploring the rich and diverse heritage of evangelicalism by reading the writings of the fathers, theologians, reformers, and pastors themselves.

Credo House Ministries' website (www.reclaimingthemind.org) provides information and resources that resonate with the heart of Retro-Christianity, including The Theology Program and The Discipleship Program.

Books on Historical-Contemporary Dialogue

Though its specific approach may differ from that of others, *Retro-Christianity* stands together with a chorus of voices from different evangelical traditions calling for reform and renewal by reflection on the history of the church. The following are a mere representation of numerous books on this subject.

The Ancient-Future Approach

Hartog, Paul, ed. *The Contemporary Church and the Early Church: Case Studies in* Ressourcement. The Evangelical Theological Society Monograph Series 9. Eugene, OR: Wipf and Stock, 2010. Intermediate.

Husbands, Mark, and Jeffrey P. Greenman, eds. *Ancient Faith for the Church's Future*. Downers Grove, IL: InterVarsity, 2008. Intermediate.

Webber, Robert E. *Common Roots: The Original Call to an Ancient-Future Faith*. Rev. ed. Grand Rapids, MI: Zondervan, 2009. Intermediate.

Williams, D. H. *Retrieving the Tradition and Renewing Evangelicalism: A Primer for Suspicious Protestants*. Grand Rapids, MI: Eerdmans, 1999. Intermediate.

Evangelical Ressourcement: Ancient Sources for the Church's Future Series

Edited by D. H. Williams, the Evangelical *Ressourcement* series seeks "to address the ways in which Christians may draw upon the thought and life of the early church to respond to the challenges of today's church" (series description). Intermediate.

Allert, Craig D. *A High View of Scripture? The Authority of the Bible and the Formation of the New Testament Canon.* Evangelical *Ressourcement.* Grand Rapids, MI: Baker, 2007.

Heine, Ronald E. *Reading the Old Testament with the Ancient Church: Exploring the Formation of Early Christian Thought.* Grand Rapids, MI: Baker, 2007.

Williams, D. H. *Evangelicals and Tradition: The Formative Influence of the Early Church.* Evangelical *Ressourcement.* Grand Rapids, MI: Baker, 2005.

———. *Tradition, Scripture, and Interpretation: A Sourcebook of the Ancient Church.* Evangelical *Ressourcement.* Grand Rapids, MI: Baker, 2006.

The Patristic Period

Hall, Christopher A. *Learning Theology with the Church Fathers.* Downers Grove, IL: InterVarsity, 2002. Intermediate.

Hannah, John D. *The Kregel Pictorial Guide to Church History.* Vol. 2: *The Early Church A.D. 33–500.* Grand Rapids, MI: Kregel, 2005. Beginner.

Haykin, Michael A. G. *Rediscovering the Church Fathers: Who They Were and How They Shaped the Church.* Wheaton, IL: Crossway, 2011. Intermediate.

Litfin, Bryan M. *Getting to Know the Church Fathers: An Evangelical Introduction.* Grand Rapids, MI: Brazos, 2007. Intermediate.

McGuckin, John Anthony. *The Westminster Handbook to Patristic Theology.* Westminster Handbooks to Christian Theology. Louisville: Westminster John Knox, 2004. Beginner.

Oden, Thomas C., gen. ed. *The Ancient Christian Commentary on Scripture,* 28 vols. (Downers Grove, IL: InterVarsity, 2001–2009). Advanced.

Svigel, Michael J. *Heroes and Heretics: Solving the Modern Mystery of the Ancient Church.* Plano: IFL Publishing House, 2006. Beginner.

The Medieval Period

Evans, G. R. *The Medieval Theologians: An Introduction to Theology in the Medieval Period.* The Great Theologians. Oxford, UK: Blackwell, 2001. Advanced.

Ginther, James R. *The Westminster Handbook to Medieval Theology.* Westminster Handbooks to Christian Theology. Louisville: Westminster John Knox, 2009. Beginner.

Hannah, John D. *The Kregel Pictorial Guide to Church History.* Vol. 3: *The Triumph of the Church A.D. 500–1500.* Grand Rapids, MI: Kregel, 2007. Beginner.

Lynch, Joseph H. *The Medieval Church: A Brief History.* 9th ed. Edinburgh: Longman, 1992. Intermediate.

Southern, R. W. *The Making of the Middle Ages.* New Haven: Yale University Press, 1953. Advanced.

The Reformation Period

George, Timothy. *Reading Scripture with the Reformers.* Downers Grove, IL: InterVarsity, 2011. Intermediate.

George, Timothy, gen. ed. *The Reformation Commentary on Scripture.* 28 vols. Downers Grove, IL: InterVarsity, 2011–). Advanced.

George, Timothy. *Theology of the Reformers.* Nashville: Broadman Press, 1988. Beginner.

Hannah, John D. *The Kregel Pictorial Guide to Church History.* Vol. 4: *The Reformation of the Church (The Early Modern Period) A.D. 1500–1650.* Grand Rapids, MI: Kregel, 2009. Beginner.

Holder, R. Ward, ed. *The Westminster Handbook to Theologies of the Reformation.* Westminster Handbooks to Christian Theology. Louisville: Westminster John Knox, 2010. Beginner.

Lindberg, Carter, ed. *The Reformation Theologians: An Introduction to the Early Modern Period.* The Great Theologians. Oxford: Blackwell, 2002. Advanced.

Nichols, Stephen J. *The Reformation: How a Monk and a Mallet Changed the World.* Wheaton, IL: Crossway, 2007. Intermediate.

Payton, James R. Jr. *Getting the Reformation Wrong: Correcting Some Misunderstandings.* Downers Grove, IL: InterVarsity, 2010. Beginner.

The Modern Period

Ford, David F., ed. *The Modern Theologians: An Introduction to Christian Theology Since 1918.* The Great Theologians. Oxford, UK: Blackwell, 2005. Advanced.

Hannah, John D. *The Kregel Pictorial Guide to Church History.* Vol. 5: *The Church in the Late Modern Period A.D. 1650–1900.* Grand Rapids, MI: Kregel, 2010. Beginner.

———. *The Kregel Pictorial Guide to Church History.* Vol. 6: *The Church and Postmodernity A.D. 1900–Present.* Grand Rapids, MI: Kregel, 2011. Beginner.

Lindberg, Carter, ed. *The Pietist Theologians: An Introduction to Theology in the Seventeenth and Eighteenth Centuries.* The Great Theologians. Oxford, UK: Blackwell, 2004. Advanced.

Olson, Roger E. *The Westminster Handbook to Evangelical Theology.* Westminster Handbooks to Christian Theology. Louisville: Westminster John Knox, 2004. Beginner.

Packer, J. I., and Thomas C. Oden. *One Faith: The Evangelical Consensus.* Downers Grove, IL: InterVarsity, 2004. Intermediate.

Sweeney, Douglas A. *The American Evangelical Story: A History of the Movement.* Grand Rapids, MI: Baker, 2005. Intermediate.

Books on Church History

Bettenson, Henry, and Chris Maunder, eds. *Documents of the Christian Church.* 3rd ed. Oxford, UK: Oxford University Press, 1999. Advanced.

Bingham, D. Jeffrey. *Pocket History of the Church.* Downers Grove, IL: InterVarsity, 2002. Beginner.

Catherwood, Christopher. *Church History: A Crash Course for the Curious.* Wheaton, IL: Crossway, 2007. Beginner.

Gonzalez, Justo L. *The Story of Christianity,* Vol. 1: *The Early Church to the Dawn of the Reformation.* 2nd ed. New York: HarperCollins, 2010. Intermediate.

———. *The Story of Christianity,* Vol. 2: *The Reformation to the Present Day.* 2nd ed. New York: HarperCollins, 2010. Intermediate.

Hannah, John D. *Kregel Pictorial Guide to Church History.* Grand Rapids, MI: Kregel, 2001. Beginner.

McDermott, Gerald. *The Great Theologians: A Brief Guide.* Downers Grove, IL: InterVarsity, 2010. Beginner.

Noll, Mark A. *Turning Points: Decisive Moments in the History of Christianity.* 2nd ed. Grand Rapids, MI: Baker, 2001. Intermediate.

Shelley, Bruce. *Church History in Plain Language.* 3rd ed. Nashville: Thomas Nelson, 2008. Beginner.

Books on the Development of Doctrine

Berkhof, Louis. *The History of Christian Doctrines.* Edinburgh, UK: Banner of Truth, 1996. Intermediate.

Hannah, John D. *Our Legacy: The History of Christian Doctrine.* Colorado Springs: NavPress, 2001. Beginner.

Hultgren, Arland J. *The Rise of Normative Christianity.* Eugene, OR: Wipf and Stock, 2004. Advanced.

Kelly, J. N. D. *Early Christian Doctrines.* Rev. ed. New York: HarperOne, 1978. Advanced.

McGrath, Alister E. *Historical Theology: An Introduction to the History of Christian Thought.* Oxford, UK: Blackwell, 1998. Intermediate.

Olson, Roger E. *The Story of Christian Theology: Twenty Centuries of Tradition and Reform.* Downers Grove, IL: InterVarsity, 1999. Intermediate.

Pelikan, Jaroslav. *The Christian Tradition: A History of the Development of Doctrine.* 5 vols. Chicago: University of Chicago Press, 1975–1991. Advanced.

Books on Spirituality

Alexander, Donald L., ed. *Christian Spirituality: Five Views of Sanctification.* Downers Grove, IL: InterVarsity, 1988. Beginner.

Blackaby, Henry, Richard Blackaby, and Claude King. *Fresh Encounter: God's Pattern for Spiritual Awakening.* Rev. and exp. ed. Nashville: B&H, 2009. Beginner.

Collins, Kenneth J., ed. *Exploring Christian Spirituality: An Ecumenical Reader.* Grand Rapids, MI: Baker, 2000. Advanced.

Dieter, Melvin, et al. *Five Views of Sanctification.* Grand Rapids, MI: Zondervan, 1987. Beginner.

Foster, Richard J. *Streams of Living Water: Celebrating the Great Traditions of Christian Faith.* New York: HarperOne, 2001. Intermediate.

McGrath, Alister E. *Christian Spirituality: An Introduction.* Oxford, UK: Blackwell, 1999. Intermediate.

Sittser, Gerald L. *Water from a Deep Well: Christian Spirituality from Early Martyrs to Modern Missionaries.* Downers Grove, IL: InterVarsity, 2007. Beginner.

Theologies with Strong Historical Background

Allison, Gregg R. *Historical Theology: An Introduction to Christian Doctrine.* Grand Rapids, MI: Zondervan, 2011. Advanced.

McGrath, Alister E. *Christian Theology: An Introduction.* 5th ed. Oxford, UK: Blackwell, 2011. Intermediate.

Oden, Thomas C. *Classic Christianity: A Systematic Theology.* New York: HarperOne, 2009. Advanced.

Books on the Church (Ecclesiology)

Bolsinger, Tod E. *It Takes a Church to Raise a Christian: How the Community of God Transforms Lives.* Grand Rapids, MI: Brazos Press, 2004. Intermediate.

Clowney, Edmund. *The Church.* Contours of Christian Theology. Downers Grove, IL: InterVarsity Press, 1995. Advanced.

Cowan, Steven B., ed. *Who Runs the Church? Four Views on Church Government.* Grand Rapids, MI: Zondervan, 2004. Beginner.

Dever, Mark. *Nine Marks of a Healthy Church.* Exp. ed. Wheaton, IL: Crossway, 2004. Beginner.

Stackhouse, John G. Jr., ed. *Evangelical Ecclesiology: Reality or Illusion?* Grand Rapids, MI: Baker, 2003. Advanced.

Webber, Robert E. *The Divine Embrace: Recovering the Passionate Spiritual Life.* Grand Rapids, MI: Baker, 2006. Intermediate.

Willimon, William. *What's Right with the Church?* San Francisco: Harper & Row, 1971. Beginner.

Yancey, Philip. *Church: Why Bother? My Personal Pilgrimage.* Grand Rapids, MI: Zondervan, 1998. Beginner.

Notes

A Note on the Notes

Rather than bogging down the main text with technical discussions on issues debated among scholars, I have chosen to relegate some of the most important issues to endnotes. Therefore, many of the endnotes contain discussions of concern to exegetes, historians, and theologians that may not interest most readers.

However, because *RetroChristianity* is written with the nonexegete, nonhistorian, and nontheologian in view, I have made no attempt at covering all of the scholarly issues in the endnotes that might interest experts in these fields. Nor have I attempted to cover all of the secondary scholarly or popular literature on various subjects. My documentation is representative, illustrative, and therefore selective. This should not be misconstrued as an ignorance, neglect, disdain, or rejection of both scholarly and popular works on the broad range of topics covered in *RetroChristianity*.

Citations of the pastors and teachers from church history are primarily presented in the endnotes. To help facilitate the reader's access to these primary sources, I have used public domain versions when possible, most of which are available online free of charge. Most excerpts or quotations from the Patristic period come from the *Ante-Nicene Fathers* (ANF) or the *Nicene and Post-Nicene Fathers* (NPNF), both of which are available online. I have occasionally modified these older public domain translations after consulting the primary Greek or Latin text, but most of the time I left the quotations "as is."

When citing a classic source, I have tried to keep the nonexpert in mind, using the author's full name and a full English title of the work, even in consecutive citations, though scholarly practice might be to abbreviate and use Greek or Latin titles. Thus, for example, I will cite Ignatius of Antioch's letter to the church in Rome as "Ignatius of Antioch, *Romans*," rather than the scholarly "Ign. *Rom.*" The parenthetical citation after the early Christian writing points to the volume and page number in the *Ante-Nicene Fathers* or *Nicene and Post-Nicene Fathers* series. For example, ANF 3:34 refers to volume 3, page 34 of the *Ante-Nicene Fathers*. The *Nicene and Post-Nicene Fathers* span two separate series. For these I indicate the series in the first number (1 or 2), then the volume within that series, followed by the page within that volume. For example, NPNF 1.3:34 refers to the first series, volume 3, page 34. For quotations of writings that are not part of the ANF or NPNF series, I typically use standard bibliographic form.

I also occasionally cite historical documents from Philip Schaff's three-volume *The Creeds of Christendom*, also available online and in the public domain in various editions. I cite these texts simply as "Schaff, 3:100," where "3" is the volume number and "100" the page number. Unless otherwise indicated, for the writings of the apostolic fathers (*1 Clement, 2 Clement, Ignatius of Antioch, Letter of Polycarp to the Philippians, The Martyrdom of Polycarp*, the *Didache, The Epistle of Barnabas, The Shepherd of Hermas, The Epistle to Diognetus, Fragments of Papias*), I have most frequently used the modern translation of Michael W. Holmes, *The Apostle Fathers: Greek Texts and English Translations*, 3rd ed. (Grand Rapids, MI: Baker, 2007). I will cite this simply as "Holmes, 135," but I also include the page number for the same reference in the *Ante-Nicene Fathers* volume.

Introduction

1. See, for example, Francis J. Beckwith, *Return to Rome: Confessions of an Evangelical Catholic* (Grand Rapids, MI: Brazos, 2009); David B. Currie, *Born Fundamentalist, Born Again Catholic* (San Francisco: Ignatius, 1996); Thomas Howard, *Evangelical Is Not Enough: Worship of God in Liturgy and Sacrament* (San Francisco: Ignatius, 1988).

2. See, for example, Peter E. Gillquist, *Becoming Orthodox: A Journey to the Ancient Christian Faith*, rev. ed. (Ben Lomond, CA: Conciliar, 1992).

3. See, for example, Todd D. Hunter, *The Accidental Anglican: The Surprising Appeal of the Liturgical Church* (Downers Grove, IL: InterVarsity, 2010); Mark Galli, *Beyond Smells and Bells: The Wonder and Power of Christian Liturgy* (Brewster, MA: Paraclete, 2008).

4. Though some might regard these as moves from conservative to liberal traditions, applying the term "liberal" to any church is precarious, as it fails to account for the diversity within various denominations. See discussion of evangelicalism and "liberalism" in chapters 1 and 5.

5. For an example, see Frank Schaeffer, *Dancing Alone: The Quest for Orthodox Faith in the Age of False Religion* (Brookline, MA: Holy Cross Orthodox Press, 1994).

6. See Colleen Carroll Campbell, *The New Faithful: Why Young Adults Are Embracing Christian Orthodoxy* (Chicago: Loyola, 2002); Robert E. Webber, *Evangelicals on the Canterbury Trail: Why Evangelicals Are Attracted to the Liturgical Church* (Harrisburg, PA: Morehouse, 1985).

7. See Paul Hartog's discussion of some of the complexities and tensions related to evangelical engagement with the early church in "The Complexity and Variety of Contemporary Church–Early Church Engagements," in *The Contemporary Church and the Early Church: Case Studies in Ressourcement*, The Evangelical Theological Society Monograph Series, vol. 9 (Eugene, OR: Wipf and Stock, 2010), 1–26.

Part One: The Case for RetroChristianity

1. The term "evangelical" comes from the Greek word for "gospel" (*euangelion*). It was Luther's preferred name for the Protestant churches: "die evangelische Kirche," or "evangelical church." However, this term in German simply meant "Protestant," as opposed to Roman Catholic. By the eighteenth century, the term was used in America to describe conservative Protestantism from a variety of denominational backgrounds, already emphasizing its conservative interdenominational tendency. Though its historical roots can be found in the eighteenth-century "great awakenings," its contemporary expression as a movement developed in the nineteenth and early twentieth centuries.

2. Historian Mark Noll writes, "'Evangelicalism' has always been made up of shifting movements, temporary alliances, and the lengthened shadows of individuals. All discussions of evangelicalism, therefore, are always both descriptions of the way things really are as well as efforts within our own minds to provide some order for a multifaceted, complex set of impulses and organizations" (Mark A. Noll, *The Scandal of the Evangelical Mind* [Grand Rapids, MI: Eerdmans, 1994], 8).

3. Evangelical Manifesto, "The Executive Summary of an Evangelical Manifesto: A Declaration of Evangelical Identity and Public Commitment," http://www.anevangelicalmanifesto.com/docs/ Evangelical_Manifesto_Summary.pdf, 2. Italics in the original.

4. Ibid., 2–3.

5. Cf. Chad Owen Brand, "Defining Evangelicalism," in *Reclaiming the Center: Confronting Evangelical Accommodation in Postmodern Times*, ed. Millard J. Erickson, Paul Kjoss Helseth, and Justin Taylor (Wheaton, IL: Crossway, 2004), 281–304.

Chapter 1: How Did It Come to This?

1. For a detailed—though by no means uncontroversial—perspective on the decline of evangelicalism in America, see Christine Wicker, *The Fall of the Evangelical Nation: The Surprising Crisis Inside the Church* (New York: HarperCollins, 2008).

2. We will explore the marks and works of an authentic local church in part 3.

3. The story of American fundamentalism's apparent traumatic decline, comatose slumber, and gradual reawakening, followed by its dynamic revival as "new evangelicalism," is a common tale told in several histories of twentieth-century American evangelicalism. See especially George M. Marsden, *Fundamentalism and American*

Culture: The Shaping of Twentieth-Century Evangelicalism: 1870–1925 (Oxford, UK: Oxford University Press, 1980); and Joel A. Carpenter, *Revive Us Again: The Reawakening of American Fundamentalism* (Oxford, UK: Oxford University Press, 1999).

4. Gary Dorrien, *The Making of American Liberal Theology: Idealism, Realism, and Modernity 1900–1950* (Louisville: Westminster John Knox, 2003), 1.

5. H. Richard Niebuhr, *The Kingdom of God in America* (New York: Harper & Row, 1937; repr., Middletown, CT: Wesleyan University Press, 1988), 193.

6. The term "fundamentalism" originally described the movement supported by and in support of the publication of *The Fundamentals* (1910–1915), a set of books that drew a line in the sand against the rise of destructive liberalism within mainline denominational churches. However, the term "fundamentalism" has become quite ambiguous over the years. It has been described positively as simply "conservative Christianity" and negatively as "Orthodoxy gone cultic"—and both of these definitions by the same author (Edward J. Carnell, *An Introduction to Christian Apologetics: A Philosophic Defense of the Trinitarian-Theistic Faith* [Grand Rapids, MI: Eerdmans, 1966], 10; and Edward J. Carnell, *The Case for Orthodox Theology* [Philadelphia: Westminster, 1959], 124). Marsden defines fundamentalists as "evangelical Christians, close to the traditions of the dominant American revivalist establishment of the nineteenth century, who in the twentieth century militantly opposed both modernism in theology and the cultural changes that modernism endorsed" (Marsden, *Fundamentalism and American Culture*, 4). Also see Nathan O. Hatch, *The Democratization of American Christianity* (New Haven, CT: Yale University Press, 1989), 214–16.

7. Westminster Theological Seminary and Dallas Theological Seminary represent the two forks in this fundamentalist road. The former was founded to stay true to the Presbyterian Westminster Confession of Faith in reaction to the more liberal Princeton Theological Seminary. At about the same time, Dallas Theological Seminary was founded as a nondenominational training ground for increasingly independent-minded pastors with little or no commitment to traditional creeds or confessions. See John D. Hannah, *An Uncommon Union: Dallas Theological Seminary and American Evangelicalism* (Grand Rapids: Zondervan, 2009).

8. Hatch, *Democratization of American Christianity*, 216.

9. Historian George Marsden traces the formation of twentieth-century evangelicalism from 1870 to 1925, essentially ending at the bludgeoning of fundamentalism at the Scopes Monkey Trial (1925), a media fiasco that unfairly painted fundamentalists as backward, brutish, unsophisticated bigots. Though these caricatures are clearly exaggerated, the early fundamentalist saga is a frustrating tale of fierce conflict against liberal foes that ended in humiliation and marginalization in the public eye (Marsden, *Fundamentalism and American Culture*).

10. Hatch writes, "However differently they defined the essence of 'New Testament' Christianity, the Holiness movement, Fundamentalists, and Pentecostals shared a passion for recovering the 'pure fountain' and were equally dismissive of the church's legacy over twenty centuries" (Hatch, *Democratization of American Christianity*, 215).

11. Marsden, *Fundamentalism and American Culture*.

12. See Carpenter, *Revive Us Again*.

13. We will see in part 4 that the idea of an individual Bible reader, independent of discipleship and training by others, is foreign to the Bible's own concept of biblical reading and interpretation (see 1 Tim. 3:14–15; 2 Pet. 3:16).

14. As we will see in chapter 10, this pulpit-centered worship displaced the classic emphasis on pulpit/altar-centered worship, in which everything circled around both proclamation (sermon) and sacrament (response).

15. Justin Taylor's helpful description of "postconservative evangelicalism" includes the tensions I see manifesting themselves in what I call "postevangelical liberalism" and "quasi-evangelicalism" (Justin Taylor, "An Introduction to Postconservative Evangelicalism and the Rest of This Book," in *Reclaiming the Center: Confronting Evangelical Accommodation in Postmodern Times*, ed. Millard J. Erickson, Paul Kjoss Helseth, and Justin Taylor [Wheaton, IL: Crossway, 2004], 17–26). I believe that in the nearly ten years since the writing of *Reclaiming the Center*, the explicitly higher-critical, progressivist, and liberal tendency has become even more pronounced among evangelical scholars, while the postmodern approach to church and ministry has continued to fragment into various forms of quasi-evangelicalisms.

Chapter 2: Going Retro without Going Wrong

1. C. S. Lewis, *Surprised by Joy: The Shape of My Early Life* (San Diego: Harcourt Brace & Company, 1955), 207–8.

2. Thomas S. Jones Jr., *From Quiet Valleys* (Clinton, NY: George William Browning, 1908), 48.

3. Because the term "catholic" was used frequently in writings from the first few centuries of Christianity in reference to the "whole church," I have decided to reclaim its use in this book. Some have opted for the simple term "Christian" or "universal," but neither of these words conveys the same sense as the term "catholic." This will be described more fully in chapter 4. However, for the time being it is important to know that when I refer to the "catholic church" with a small "c," I refer to the entire orthodox church, of which evangelicals are a major tradition. When I want to refer to the branch of Christendom under the pope or the branches of Christianity in the Eastern Orthodox tradition, I will use "Roman Catholic Church" and "Eastern Orthodox churches," respectively.

4. Baptism as an essential mark of the church will be discussed more fully in chapters 8 and 9.

5. The mark of proper church order will be explored in some detail in chapter 8.

6. This account is a truncated and simplified version of a complex and fascinating period of World War II history. For a well-illustrated overview of the history of the Maginot Line, see William Allcorn, *The Maginot Line 1928–45* (Oxford, UK: Osprey, 2003).

7. Randall Wallace, *Braveheart*, directed by Mel Gibson (USA: Icon Entertainment, 1995).

8. See, for example, Bart D. Ehrman, *Lost Christianities: The Battles for Scripture and the Faiths We Never Knew* (Oxford, UK: Oxford University Press, 2003); Elaine Pagels, *The Gnostic Gospels* (New York: Random House, 1979).

9. "Nescire autem quid antequam natus sis acciderit, id est semper esse puerum" (Cicero, *Orations*, 34.120).

10. *1 Clement*, 5:1–7 (Holmes, 53; cf. ANF, 1:6).

11. The post-Reformation emphasis on principles, rules, and methods of interpretation promised evangelicals more than it was able to deliver. Evangelicals have too often neglected the very important (and somewhat embarrassing) question regarding where their principles of biblical interpretation actually came from (see Kurt Mueller-Vollmer, "Introduction: Language, Mind, and Artifact: An Outline of Hermeneutic Theory since

the Enlightenment," in *The Hermeneutics Reader*, ed. Kurt Mueller-Vollmer [New York: Continuum, 2000], 2–4). The fragmenting of competing interpretations and resulting systems has all but undermined the modernistic, rationalistic, and optimistic understanding of biblical hermeneutics as "the science and art of interpreting the Bible" (Roy B. Zuck, *Basic Bible Interpretation* [Wheaton, IL: Victor, 1991], 10). Nevertheless, defining biblical hermeneutics as the "techniques of biblical interpretation" is common among evangelical Christians (Millard J. Erickson, *Evangelical Interpretation: Perspectives on Hermeneutical Issues* [Grand Rapids, MI: Baker, 1993], 9); cf. Gordon D. Fee, "Issues in Evangelical Hermeneutics: Hermeneutics and the Nature of Scripture," *Crux* 26 [June 1990]: 21; Robert L. Thomas, "Current Hermeneutical Trends: Toward Explanation or Obfuscation?" *JETS* 39 [June 1996]: 242–47).

However, evangelicals who have spent any amount of time engaging in biblical or theological studies quickly realize that the interpretational task is far too subjective and unpredictable even among those who have agreed to play by the same methodological rules. The desperate attempts to validate, defend, or sometimes even explain interpretations seem to set us chasing each other around a circle with "understanding" in the elusive center. Or, if I might push the analogy, these frantic pursuits flush us down that ever-turning but never terminating "hermeneutical spiral" (see Grant R. Osborne, *The Hermeneutical Spiral: A Comprehensive Introduction to Biblical Interpretation* [Downers Grove, IL: InterVarsity, 1991]). Only the naïve or the arrogant would fail to admit that biblical interpretation is a complex task that invites no simple methodological answers. As a science biblical hermeneutics results in no sure findings, only a multiplication of hypotheses. As an art it breeds yawningly unoriginal knockoffs or startlingly innovative heresies.

12. For the history of biblical interpretation, see Alan J. Hauser and Duane F. Watson, eds., *A History of Biblical Interpretation*, vol. 1: *The Ancient Period* (Grand Rapids, MI: Eerdmans, 2003); and Alan J. Hauser and Duane F. Watson, eds., *A History of Biblical Interpretation*, vol. 2: *The Medieval through the Reformation Periods* (Grand Rapids, MI: Eerdmans, 2009). For an excellent resource on ancient Christian interpretation, see Thomas C. Oden, ed., *The Ancient Christian Commentary on Scripture*, 28 vols. (Downers Grove, IL: InterVarsity, 2001–2009).

13. Tertullian, *Against Marcion* 4.5 (ANF, 3:349–50).

14. Irenaeus, *Against Heresies*, 3.4.1 (ANF, 1:417).

15. Such passages seem to suggest at minimum that God's providential care for the church as the "bulwark of the faith" must mean that the church—however corrupt or distracted it became at various points in history and in various regions of the Christianized world—was prevented from absolute apostasy and thus the contributions of its teachers throughout its history ought to be regarded as the Spirit-led expression of this faith. To view any period of church history as a great gap between an absolute apostasy and some glorious restoration of the gospel does not harmonize well with Christ's clear promise to the church that "the gates of hell shall not prevail against it" (Matt. 16:18) (see D. H. Williams, *Retrieving the Tradition and Renewing Evangelicalism: A Primer for Suspicious Protestants* [Grand Rapids, MI: Eerdmans, 1999], 101–31).

16. Christ promised his disciples that when the Spirit of truth comes, "he will guide you into all truth" (John 16:12–13), addressing the community of disciples as a whole. In the Septuagint the verb that is used for guidance of the community is the same verb used in reference to God's leading the nation of Israel from Egypt to the promised land (Ex. 13:17; 15:13; 32:34; Deut. 1:33). This guidance by the Spirit from darkness to greater light, from ignorance to greater understanding, is not

limited in scope merely to the twelve disciples, but to the broader Christian community throughout history. This is suggested by Ephesians 4:11–16, when read in light of Paul's teaching concerning the community and spiritual gifts in 1 Corinthians 12–14. John may also be referring to the outworking of this community guidance of the Spirit when he says of the community (in contrast to the false prophets): "And as for you, the anointing which you received from him abides in you, and you have no need for anyone to teach you; but as his anointing teaches you about all things, and is true and is not a lie, and just as it has taught you, you abide in him" (1 John 2:27). It seems that both Paul and John had a sense of confidence in the Spirit's work in the church by means of community dialogue and mutual accountability (see 1 Cor. 14:29; 1 John 4:1).

17. D. H. Williams's definition of "tradition" is "the core teaching and preaching of the early church which has bequeathed to us the fundamentals of which it is to think and believe Christianly" (*Retrieving the Tradition*, 6).

18. Vincent of Lérins, *The Commonitory*, 2.6 (NPNF, 2.11:132). I find the classic (and oft repeated) critique of the Vincentian Canon, presented quite eloquently by John Henry Newman, to completely miss the point of Vincent's Canon (see John Henry Newman, *An Essay on the Development of Christian Doctrine* [London: James Toovey, 1845], 7–12). Vincent must be read in his own historical context as primarily describing the situation in AD 434. Vincent did not use the principle to fix every detail of doctrine, but to demolish gross heresy and to resist intrusion of mere individual opinions. Newman—and many others who find this approach problematic—appear to be driven by a very modernistic quest for a standard for doctrinal truth that can address every doctrinal question and establish a high degree of certainty and clarity on all issues. True, the Vincentian Canon does not accomplish this. It works only at the macro level, on the *essential truths*, rather than on a micro level. If a doctrine had not been universally established and traceable in an unbroken succession from the first century to the fourth, the Vincentian Canon simply does not address it. The Canon applies to the *preservation* of the core confession of Christianity, resisting the intrusion of opinion and allowing for even radical diversity both prior to and following its articulation. For those, like Newman, who seek a solitary, clear, and consistent Christian voice or representation, the implications of the Vincentian Canon for questions of unity, diversity, continuity, and discontinuity will be disappointing.

19. Augustine, *City of God*, 11.3 (NPNF, 1.1:206).

20. Anselm, *Why God Became Man*, 1.18 (St. Anselm, *Proslogium; Monologium; An Appendix on Behalf of the Fool by Gaunilon; and Cur Deus Homo*, repr. ed., trans. Sidney Norton Deane [La Salle, IL: Open Court, 1926], 220).

Chapter 3: What Is RetroChristianity?

1. RetroChristianity's approach differs from several similar "retro" renewal movements of the twentieth and twenty-first centuries. Though it values the foundational contributions of the early church, it differs from paleo-orthodoxy in that it also values the contributions of every era of church history beyond the Patristic period. Similarly, the ancient-future dialogue tends to overemphasize a specific era of developments (fourth and fifth centuries) without considering the diversity and development leading to this period or the conflict, controversies, developments, and diversification affecting the church in subsequent eras. The trend among some to return to Roman Catholic or Eastern Orthodox traditions finds itself emulating a medieval form of Christianity that institutionalized a number of problematic doctrines and practices not reflected

in the early church and later reformed in the Protestant period. The recent revival of Reformed theology emphasizes another limited sixteenth- to seventeenth-century Reformed and Puritan tradition, neglecting the contributions of the ancient, medieval, and modern eras. Finally, the recent attempts at "reinventing" Christianity typical of postmodern approaches to renewal fail to appreciate the authoritative nature of historical orthodoxy and orthopraxy accumulated throughout the history of Christianity.

2. In chapter 4 I will unpack the actual content of orthodoxy in greater detail based on biblical, historical, and theological reflection.

3. See Peter Fraenkel, *Testimonia Patrum: The Function of Patristic Arguments in the Theology of Philip Melanchthon* (Geneva, Switz.: Droz, 1961); Anthony N. S. Lane, *John Calvin: Student of the Church Fathers* (Edinburgh, UK: T&T Clark, 1999).

4. See, for example, Richard T. Hughes, ed., *The American Quest for the Primitive Church* (Chicago: University of Illinois Press, 1988); and Richard T. Hughes, ed., *The Primitive Church in the Modern World* (Chicago: University of Chicago Press, 1995).

5. The first-century manual of church order called the *Didache* (c. AD 50–100) gives us a glimpse into the actual teaching, worship, and ministry of the churches established by the apostles, yet our modern self-styled New Testament churches bear very little resemblance to this description. See Thomas O'Loughlin, *The Didache: A Window on the Earliest Christians* (Grand Rapids, MI: Baker, 2010). As will be argued later, such primitivism is not desirable anyway, as it neglects centuries of positive doctrinal and practical growth and development.

6. See D. H. Williams, *Retrieving the Tradition and Renewing Evangelicalism: A Primer for Suspicious Protestants* (Grand Rapids, MI: Eerdmans, 1999), 101–31; Robert E. Webber, *Common Roots: The Original Call to an Ancient-Future Faith*, rev. ed. (Grand Rapids, MI: Zondervan, 2009).

7. E.g., Terry L. Johnson, *The Case for Traditional Protestantism: The Solas of The Reformation* (Edinburgh, UK: Banner of Truth, 2004); Collin Hansen, *Young, Restless, Reformed: A Journalist's Journey with the New Calvinists* (Wheaton, IL: Crossway, 2008).

8. In this vein, Longenecker writes, "There has been a progressive illumination throughout the centuries of the church's existence of the meaning and significance of God's definitive activity in Jesus Christ" (Richard N. Longenecker, *Studies in Hermeneutics, Christology, and Discipleship* [Sheffield, UK: Sheffield Phoenix Press, 2004], 25). See Nicholas Lash, "Development, Doctrinal," in *The Westminster Dictionary of Christian Theology*, ed. Alan Richardson and John Bowden (Philadelphia: Westminster, 1983), 155–56.

9. See, for example, John Henry Newman, *An Essay on the Development of Christian Doctrine* (London: James Toovey, 1845). Also compare the moderate "redemptive movement" or "redemptive spirit" hermeneutic of William J. Webb, *Slaves, Women, and Homosexuals: Exploring the Hermeneutics of Cultural Analysis* (Downers Grove, IL: InterVarsity, 2001).

10. See John Shelby Spong, *Why Christianity Must Change or Die: A Bishop Speaks to Believers in Exile* (New York: HarperOne, 1999).

11. See Brian D. McLaren, *A New Kind of Christianity: Ten Questions That Are Transforming the Faith* (New York: HarperOne, 2011); Harvey Cox, *The Future of Faith* (New York: HarperOne, 2010).

Part Two: RetroOrthodoxy: Preserving the Faith for the Future

1. The three canons of RetroOrthodoxy correspond to the two pairs of tensions in the study of historical theology: "continuity vs. discontinuity" and "unity vs. diver-

sity." Much confusion has resulted from a failure to understand the fixed and flexible elements of the Christian tradition (continuity vs. discontinuity), and the failure to consider the concept of the development of doctrine in evangelical circles. Similarly, evangelicals have often been unable to come to terms with the bounds of orthodoxy and the limits of acceptable variety (unity vs. diversity). Some treatments on these subjects include Donald G. Bloesch, *The Future of Evangelical Christianity: A Call for Unity amid Diversity* (New York: Doubleday, 1983); Roger E. Olson, *The Mosaic of Christian Belief: Twenty Centuries of Unity & Diversity* (Downers Grove, IL: InterVarsity, 2002). A constructive description of evangelical consensus can be found in J. I. Packer and Thomas C. Oden, eds., *One Faith: The Evangelical Consensus* (Downers Grove, IL: InterVarsity, 2004).

Chapter 4: The First Canon of RetroOrthodoxy: Some Things Never Change and Never Should

1. This is not an invective against internally consistent theological or doctrinal systems *per se*, but against the attitude with which they are sometimes held. Both dogmatic dispensationalists and dogmatic covenant theologians can err by deeming their theologies as "infallible" and therefore as the only standard of orthodoxy. Whether it's a particular denominational confession (*Westminster, Augsburg,* or *Baptist Faith and Message*) or a particular teacher's writings (Luther's *Catechism,* Calvin's *Institutes,* or Scofield's *Reference Bible*), none can claim to occupy the central place of orthodoxy that must be fully embraced to be truly Christian. However, I will argue that all of these confessions and systems, despite their diversity, are included within the bounds of evangelical Protestant orthodoxy.

2. Vincent of Lérins, *The Commonitory,* 2.6 (NPNF, 2.11:132).

3. Unpublished Records of the First Congregational Church of Dallas, 35.

4. Dallas Theological Seminary, *We Believe: The Doctrinal Statement of Dallas Theological Seminary* (Dallas: Dallas Theological Seminary, 2009), 3.

5. See Ignatius, *Philadelphians,* 8.2 (Holmes, 243; ANF, 1:84).

6. See William R. Schoedel, "Ignatius and the Archives," *Harvard Theological Review* 71 (1978): 97–106.

7. Irenaeus, *Against Heresies,* 4.26.1 (ANF, 1:496).

8. D. H. Williams asserts, "The Rule was not a creed, nor a formula, but an abbreviated body of doctrine wherein the genuine articles of Christianity were articulated" (*Retrieving the Tradition and Renewing Evangelicalism: A Primer for Suspicious Protestants* [Grand Rapids: Eerdmans, 1999], 88). While the rule does not change, the confessions grow and develop. I liken the relationship I am trying to express as one between the thought and the expression, as the latter is always an imperfect version of the former.

9. Irenaeus, *Demonstration of the Apostolic Preaching* 6 (St. Irenaeus, *The Demonstration of the Apostolic Preaching,* trans. J. Armitage Robinson [London: SPCK, 1920], 74–75).

10. Williams, *Retrieving the Tradition,* 172.

11. Timothy George, *Theology of the Reformers* (Nashville: Broadman & Holman, 1988), 314.

12. *Augsburg Confession,* 1 (Schaff, 3:7).

13. *Second Helvetic Confession,* 11 (Schaff, 3:854).

14. Thomas C. Oden, *Systematic Theology,* vol. 1, *The Living God* (New York: HarperCollins, 1987), 130.

15. *Augsburg Confession of Faith,* 1 (Schaff, 3:7).

16. *Brief Statement of the Reformed Faith*, art. 5 (Schaff, 3:922).

17. *The Doctrinal Basis of the Evangelical Alliance*, Second Resolution (Schaff, 3:827).

18. For a thorough (though highly technical) treatment on the history of justification, see Alister E. McGrath, *Iustitia Dei: A History of the Christian Doctrine of Justification*, 3rd ed. (Cambridge, UK: Cambridge University Press, 2005).

19. Adolf Harnack, *The History of Dogma*, 3d. ed., vols. 5–6, trans. (London: Williams and Norgate, 1897; repr., Eugene, OR: Wipf and Stock, 1997); John D. Hannah, *Our Legacy: The History of Christian Doctrine* (Colorado Springs: NavPress, 2001), 216–26; Jaroslav Pelikan, *The Christian Tradition: A History of the Development of Doctrine*, vol. 3, *The Growth of Medieval Theology* (Chicago: University of Chicago Press, 1978), 50–214.

20. McGrath, *Iustitia Dei*, 108.

21. Vincent of Lérins, *The Commonitory*, 3 (NPNF, 2.11:132).

22. The issue dividing the Christian traditions is not whether salvation is received *by grace through faith*, but whether salvation is by grace *alone* through faith *alone* in Christ *alone* (Reformed Protestantism), or by grace through faith received through gracious sacraments (Roman Catholic, Eastern Orthodoxy), or by grace through faith plus responsible cooperation with grace (Roman Catholic, Protestant Arminian), or some other combination of human participation.

23. Gasparo Contarini to an unknown recipient (1537), quoted in Elisabeth G. Gleason, *Gasparo Contarini: Venice, Rome, and Reform* (Berkeley: University of California Press, 1993), 265.

24. See comments in Mark A. Noll, *The Scandal of the Evangelical Mind* (Grand Rapids, MI: Eerdmans, 1994), 243–44.

25. See, e.g., Jack B. Rogers and Donald K. McKim, *The Authority and Interpretation of the Bible: An Historical Approach* (San Francisco: Harper & Row, 1979).

26. This consensus cannot be assigned to the identification of the canon of Scripture—that is, the books of the Old and New Testaments that ought to be regarded as inspired and inerrant Scripture. Nor has there been a complete agreement on how to interpret the Bible. However, that canonical Scripture has the quality of divine inspiration and inerrancy enjoys a long-standing continuity in the Christian faith.

27. Augustine of Hippo, Letter, 82.3 (*To Jerome*) (NPNF, 1.1:350).

28. Erickson notes that "at no point in the history of Christian thought has the doctrine of the church received the direct and complete attention that other doctrines have received. . . . By contrast, Christology and the doctrine of the Trinity had been given special attention in the fourth and fifth centuries, as had the atoning work of Christ in the Middle Ages, and the doctrine of salvation in the sixteenth century" (Millard J. Erickson, *Christian Theology*, 2nd. ed. [Grand Rapids, MI: Baker, 1998], 1037). Unlike the doctrine of salvation, the attention given to the doctrine of the church during the Reformation served to reject Catholic teachings, but not to establish a clear Protestant consensus on the nature of the church itself.

29. Council at Constantinople, *The Constantinopolitan Creed* (381).

30. Euan Cameron, *The European Reformation* (Oxford, UK: Oxford University Press, 1991), 88.

31. For an excellent treatment of this period, see Steven Ozment, *The Age of Reform (1250–1550): An Intellectual and Religious History of Late Medieval and Reformation Europe* (New Haven, CT: Yale University Press, 1980). For a more accessible treatment of this period, see Timothy George, *Theology of the Reformers* (Nashville: Broadman & Holman, 1988).

32. Thomas C. Oden, *Classic Christianity: A Systematic Theology* (New York: HarperOne, 2009), 721.

33. John of Damascus, *An Exact Exposition of the Orthodoxy Faith* 4.27 (NPNF, 2.9: 101).

Chapter 5: The Second Canon of RetroOrthodoxy: Some Things Have Never Been the Same and Never Will Be

1. For a helpful guide on denominations in the United States, see Craig D. Atwood, Frank S. Mead, and Samuel S. Hill, eds., *Handbook of Denominations in the United States*, 13th ed. (Nashville: Abingdon, 2010).

2. *Didache*, 7.1–3 (ANF, 7:379, with minor updates based on the Greek text; cf. Holmes, 355).

3. Skarsaune highlights the similarities between Judaism and early Christianity in both freedom and the order of prayer and worship (Oskar Skarsaune, *In the Shadow of the Temple: Jewish Influences on Early Christianity* [Downers Grove, IL: InterVarsity, 2002], 377–78).

4. Though primarily focusing on the late second-century conflict between Victor of Rome and the Asian bishops (*Church History*, 5.23.2–5.24.10 [NPNF, 2.1:41–42), Eusebius of Caesarea quotes a letter by Irenaeus written around AD 190, which itself provides a window into a similar controversy settled by Anicetus of Rome and Polycarp of Smyrna around 150 to 155 (see Johannes B. Bauer, *Die Polykarpbriefe, übersetzt und erklärt*, Kommentar zu den Apostolischen Vätern, vol. 5 [Göttingen: Vandenhoeck & Ruprecht, 1995], 11).

5. Eusebius of Caesarea, *Church History*, 5.24.16–17 (NPNF, 2.1:243).

6. J. N. D. Kelly, *Early Christian Doctrines*, 5th rev. ed. (New York: HarperOne, 1978), 189.

7. Origen of Alexandria, *First Principles*, preface.10 (ANF, 4:241).

8. I personally see strong historical evidence for the slight historical priority of premillennialism in the late first and early second century (see Adolf Harnack, *The History of Dogma*, vol. 1, trans. Neil Buchanan [London: Williams and Norgate, 1894; repr., Eugene, OR: Wipf and Stock, 1997], 288). However, Charles Hill makes a good (though to me, not compelling) case for the antiquity of both premillennial and amillennial perspectives (Charles E. Hill, *Regnum Caelorum: Patterns of Millennial Thought in Early Christianity*, 2nd ed. [Grand Rapids, MI: Eerdmans, 2001]).

9. Justin Martyr, *Dialogue with Trypho*, 80 (ANF, 1:239).

10. Ibid., 47 (ANF, 1:218, with some updates to the text).

11. Boethius, *On the Catholic Faith* (Boethius, *The Theological Tractates, The Consoluation of Philosophy*, trans. H. F. Stewart and E. K. Rand, The Loeb Classical Library [London: Heinemann, 1918], 71).

12. This was the case of Tertullian, who, although orthodox in the essentials, was rejected as a heretic for following the Montanist movement, an early "charismatic" group that emphasized a rigorous morality and signs and wonders. Tertullian himself insisted that the movement had originally been sanctioned by the Bishop of Rome, and Tertullian's own writings were greatly influential among orthodox teachers for generations to come. However, his unique and divergent views no longer fit with the prevailing consensus in the Roman Catholic Church, and he was increasingly regarded as a schismatic "heretic." On debates regarding Tertullian's Montanist turn, see Eric Osborne, *Tertullian: First Theologian of the West* (Cambridge, UK: Cambridge University Press, 1997), 177.

13. This seems to have been the case with the writings of the second century Father, Papias of Hierapolis, whose literalistic premillennialism attracted scorn by later Fathers (Eusebius, *Church History*, 3.39.12–13 [NPNF, 2.1:171]). It should not surprise us that the medieval scribes simply stopped spending the time, money, and energy copying writings that did not fit later doctrinal opinions.

14. Palémon Glorieux, ed., *Jean Gerson Oeuvres Complètes*, vol. 3 (Paris: Desclée, 1965), 239. See Pelikan, *The Christian Tradition* 4:12.

15. See Heiko A. Oberman, *The Dawn of the Reformation: Essays in Late Medieval and Early Reformation Thought* (Edinburgh: T.&T. Clark, 1986; repr. 1992), 285.

16. *The Doctrinal Basis of the Evangelical Alliance, Adopted at the Organization of the American Branch of the Evangelical Alliance, in January* (1867) (Schaff, 3:827–28).

Chapter 6: The Third Canon of RetroOrthodoxy: Some Things Grow Clear through Trial and Error

1. Vincent of Lérins, *The Commonitory* 25.64 (NPNF, 2.11:150).

2. Ibid., 2.6 (NPNF, 2.11:132)

3. Ibid., 23.54 (NPNF, 2.11:147–48, with clarifying additions).

4. Ibid., 23.56 (NPNF, 2.11:148).

5. Norman Vincent Peale, *The Power of Positive Thinking* (New York: Prentice-Hall, 1952).

6. Émile Coué, *How to Practice Suggestion and Autosuggestion* (New York: American Library Service, 1923), 101.

7. Augustine, *City of God*, 16.2. (NPNF, 1.2:310).

8. Paying close attention to Paul's image of building on the foundation with both valuable and poor materials safeguards against the extremes of some models of doctrinal development that are either overly optimistic or overly pessimistic. Some have argued that Christian theology legitimately evolved and changed over the centuries through external influences and internal conflicts that produced a Christian religion different from—but superior to—its original apostolic spirit, message, and momentum (see Peter C. Hodgson, *The Formation of Historical Theology: A Study of Ferdinand Christian Baur* [Minneapolis: Fortress, 1966]; Shailer Mathews, *The Spiritual Interpretation of History* [Cambridge, MA: Harvard University Press, 1916]). Others have argued the opposite, that Christian theology illegitimately *devolved* over the centuries, capitulating to cultural standards and losing its original apostolic spirit, message, and momentum (see Adolf Harnack, *The History of Dogma*, 7 vols., trans. Neil Buchanan [London: Williams and Norgate, 1894; repr., Eugene, OR: Wipf & Stock, 1997]). As one proponent of this model noted, "The history of Christian dogma, from Justin to Athanasius, is a record of continual progress in the same direction, until the fair body of religion, revealed in almost naked purity by the prophets, is once more hidden under a new accumulation of dogmas and of ritual practices of which the primitive Nazarene knew nothing; and which he would probably have regarded as blasphemous if he could have been made to understand them" (Thomas H. Huxley, "The Evolution of Theology," in *Science and Hebrew Tradition* [London: Macmillan, 1893]: 368). However, both the evolution and devolution models fail to account for Paul's image of building the church through both legitimate and illegitimate development under the sovereign work of God.

9. Individual pastors and teachers need not be wholly bad or wholly good. In fact, it is most reasonable, given the building illustration, that every person in church his-

tory contributes both, and that it takes time to determine what should be kept and what should be rejected.

10. Thus Protestants, though holding to the idea of theological progress, also take seriously the problem of illegitimate development and regression or decay. In this deformation and reformation model, the church as a whole declined through neglect, forgetfulness, sin, and doctrinal deviation. It lost its original purity. However, through a period of reformation and restoration, the purity of the church was regained. Such a model takes seriously the tension between both legitimate and illegitimate development as well as the principle that some things grow clearer through trial and error.

11. See Hans Finzel, *Top Ten Mistakes Leaders Make* (Colorado Springs: David C. Cook, 2007), 75–77.

12. For examples of this growth model, see Maurice Wiles, *The Making of Christian Doctrine: A Study in the Principles of Early Doctrinal Development* (Cambridge, UK: Cambridge University Press, 1967); John Henry Newman, *An Essay on the Development of Christian Doctrine* (London: James Toovey, 1845); Jaroslav Pelikan, *Historical Theology: Continuity and Change in Christian Doctrine* (New York: Corpus, 1975); Jaroslav Pelikan, *The Christian Tradition: A History of the Development of Doctrine*, 5 vols. (Chicago: University of Chicago Press, 1975–1991); Jaroslav Pelikan, *Development of Christian Doctrine: Some Historical Prolegomena* (New Haven, CT: Yale University Press, 1969).

Chapter 7: Church Classic: Four Common Myths and Four Classic Marks

1. Numerous books have been written trying to describe (and predict) the general mentality and typical behavior of modern evangelicals. The "myths" described in this chapter can be substantiated through both anecdotal and statistical evidence. See, for example, George Barna, *Revolution* (Carol Stream, IL: Tyndale House, 2005); Julia Duin, *Quitting Church: Why the Faithful Are Fleeing and What to Do about It* (Grand Rapids, MI: Baker, 2008); Dan Kimball, *They Like Jesus but Not the Church: Insights from Emerging Generations* (Grand Rapids, MI: Zondervan, 2007); David T. Olson, *The American Church in Crisis* (Grand Rapids, MI: Zondervan, 2008); Christine Wicker, *The Fall of the Evangelical Nation: The Surprising Crisis inside the Church* (New York: HarperOne, 2008).

2. This is, in essence, a "docetic" or "gnostic" approach to the church, separating the spiritual from the physical and regarding the spiritual as the real church and the physical as a mere shell that can be disregarded.

3. See Douglas Estes, *SimChurch: Being the Church in the Virtual World* (Grand Rapids, MI: Zondervan, 2009).

4. I am not fundamentally opposed to all "house church" strategies that seek to simplify churches, reduce wasteful overhead, and penetrate neighborhoods. When house churches maintain the authentic marks and works of a local church, they can have quite vibrant and effective ministries. However, some house church leaders have erred by falling into what we called in the last chapter "extreme primitivism." Too often they are plagued by reading the New Testament documents outside their actual historical theological context, thus painting a picture of the "early church" that looked nothing like the full picture of the early church confirmed in other early Christian writings outside the New Testament. Also, they often seek to adopt the first-century pattern of ministry under the apostles and prophets as unalterable norms without recognizing that the apostles themselves left behind a local church order and ministry model somewhat different from the reconstruction of the so-called "New

Testament" church. For examples of this approach, see Steve Atkerson, ed., *House Churches: Simple, Strategic, Scriptural* (Atlanta: New Testament Reformation Fellowship, 2008) and Wolfgang Simson, *The House Church Book: Rediscover the Dynamic, Organic, Relational, Viral Community Jesus Started* (Carol Stream, IL: Tyndale, 2009). Quite simply, such approaches err by failing to understand that the apostolic age itself was the *apostolic* age, an unrepeatable period of the church's infancy to which we cannot return.

5. We will explore the biblical and historical descriptions of these marks and works in the following chapters. It is sufficient here simply to introduce them.

6. The "marks and works" of an authentic local church will be discussed in chapters 8 and 9.

7. A fuller treatment of the individual and corporate aspects of the Christian life and spiritual growth is in part 4.

8. 1 Cor. 3:6–9; 2 Cor. 10:15; Eph. 2:19–22; 4:14–16; Col. 1:3–12; 2:19; 1 Pet. 2:1–5.

9. Some have pointed to the surprising skirmish between Paul and Barnabas in Acts 15:37–40 as an example of separation due to differing ministry strategies. But this incident had nothing to do with leaving a local church—both departed from Antioch with the church's blessing. And besides, this text *described* an unfortunate event; it did not *prescribe* how to handle conflict.

10. For an excellent account of the Cola Wars, see the History Channel's *Cola Wars*, Empires of Industry Series, DVD, A&E Home Video, 2006.

11. *Didache*, 9.4 (Holmes, 359; ANF, 7:380).

12. Boethius, *On the Catholic Faith* (Boethius, *The Theological Tractates, The Consolation of Philosophy*, trans. H. F. Stewart and E. K. Rand, The Loeb Classical Library [London: Heinemann, 1918], 69).

13. John Calvin, *Institutes of the Christian Religion*, 4.1.2 (John Calvin, *Institutes of the Christian Religion*, 2 vols. in 1, trans. Henry Beveridge [Grand Rapids, MI: Eerdmans, 1989], 2:282).

14. *We Believe: The Doctrinal Statement of Dallas Theological Seminary*, article 12.

15. Kelly notes, "The term 'holy', the stock epithet of the Church, expresses the conviction that it is God's chosen people and is indwelt by His Spirit" (J. N. D. Kelly, *Early Christian Doctrines*, 5th rev. ed. [New York: HarperOne, 1978], 189).

16. Irenaeus of Lyons, *Against Heresies*, 1.10.2 (ANF, 1:331).

17. Martin Luther, *The Large Catechism*, article 3.

18. Thomas C. Oden, *Classic Christianity: A Systematic Theology* (New York: HarperOne, 2009), 729.

19. Kelly comments that "catholic" as applied to the church in the second century was used "to underline its universality as opposed to the local character of the individual congregations," though it also became used to refer to "the true Church as distinct from the heretical congregations" (Kelly, *Early Christian Doctrines*, 190).

20. The issue of the leadership structure and offices in the early church will be discussed in the next chapter in some detail under the marks of the church.

21. Ignatius, *Smyrnaeans*, 8.2 (Holmes, 255; ANF, 1:90).

22. The presence of Christ in the believing, worshiping community constituted the visible and local manifestation of the "catholic," or universal, church. Just as the bishop was the head of a local church, Jesus Christ is the head of the entire universal church. What did Ignatius mean by the presence of Christ? *Didache* 4.1 helps us understand this statement: "Wherever the Lord's nature is preached, there the Lord is" (Holmes,

351; ANF, 7:378). The presence of Christ is in his proper proclamation—which, in the early church, took a twofold form—sermon and sacrament.

23. *Martyrdom of Polycarp*, 19.2 (Holmes, 327; ANF, 1:43).

24. Examples of these include the submission to the Roman Pontiff, involvement in a system of seven sacraments, and the satisfaction of the demands of purgatory. Church historians have long demonstrated that these have not, in truth, been believed everywhere, always, and by all. In fact, it can be demonstrated that the church in Rome itself did not always hold such requirements for salvation.

25. *Martyrdom of Polycarp*, 19.2 (Holmes, 327; ANF, 1:43).

26. *Westminster Confession*, 25.1–2 (Schaff, 3:657).

27. Of course, I should remind readers that my understanding of "evangelicalism" includes all orthodox, Protestant, Bible-believing Christians in every denomination, not limited to a specific denomination or to the nondenominational free-church movement. In fact, individual churches in all of these traditions are sometimes more, sometimes less "catholic" as they join with or separate themselves from the whole or slip away toward unwholesome beliefs and practices.

28. Tertullian, *Prescription against Heretics*, 32 (ANF, 3:258).

29. Oden, *Classic Christianity*, 721.

30. Euan Cameron, *The European Reformation* (Oxford, UK: Oxford University Press, 1991), 88.

Chapter 8: The Essential Marks of a Local Church

1. *Augsburg Confession of Faith*, 7 (Schaff, 3:11–12).

2. *Westminster Confession of Faith*, 15.4 (Schaff, 3:658).

3. Today numerous books offer models of healthy churches, some reflecting a biblical, historical model more than others. For a good practical treatment of marks of a healthy church, see Mark Dever, *Nine Marks of a Healthy Church*, exp. ed. (Wheaton, IL: Crossway, 2004). Dever's goal is not to present a full ecclesiology, but to "focus on certain crucial aspects of healthy church life that have grown rare among churches today" (38–39).

4. See 1 Tim. 3:14–15; 2 Tim. 1:13–14; 3:13–4:5.

5. See Eph. 4:11–12; 1 Tim. 3:1–13; 2 Tim. 2:2; Titus 1:5–9; Heb. 13:17; 1 Pet. 5:1–3.

6. The cessation of the offices of apostle and prophet has been the near-unanimous consensus among Christians throughout history. More importantly, however, the earliest generation after the original apostles and prophets referred to the apostles and prophets as a foundation ministry of the church that had ceased. This is why Paul refers to these ministries as first and foundational for the church (1 Cor. 12:28; 15:7–9; Eph. 2:20). See also *1 Clement*, 5.3–4; 42.1–3; Ignatius, *Magnesians*, 13.1; *Romans* 4.3; Polycarp, *Philippians*, 9.1; Tertullian, *Against Marcion*, 4.5. Note especially the wording of the mid-second-century Muratorian Canon regarding the wise rejection of the canonicity of the *Shepherd of Hermas*: "It cannot be read publicly to the people in church either among the Prophets *whose number is complete*, or among the Apostles, *for it is after their time.*" Though some today overgeneralize "apostles" to include missionaries, and "prophets" to include preachers, this is a misrepresentation of the unique, temporary, and foundational ministries of the first-century church.

7. *1 Clement*, 44.1–2 (ANF, 1:17, cf. Holmes, 103).

8. Ignatius, *Trallians*, 3.1 (Holmes, 217; cf. ANF, 1:67).

9. *Augsburg Confession of Faith*, 14 (Schaff, 3:15–16).

10. John Calvin, *Institutes of the Christian Religion*, 4.1.1 (Calvin, *Institutes*, 2:280–81).

11. I am well aware that this threefold order of (1) presiding elder (senior pastor or bishop), (2) elders (presbyters, pastors, or teachers), and (3) deacons (ministers or assistants) challenges popular evangelical reconstructions of church order allegedly drawn from "Scripture alone" (see Gene Getz, *Elders and Leaders* [Chicago: Moody, 2003]; Alexander Strauch, *Biblical Eldership* [Littleton, CO: Lewis and Roth, 1995]; Frank Viola, *Reimagining Church* [Colorado Springs: David C. Cook, 2008]). Although I agree that the office of "presiding elder" (later called the *episkopos*, i.e., "bishop") was not established at the beginning of the apostolic age when most of the New Testament was written, I argue that the biblical and historical evidences from the late first and early second centuries demonstrate that this role of "presiding elder" was established *by the end of the apostolic period*. Therefore, present-day church leadership experts and Bible expositors wrongly insist that a truly "biblical" or "apostolic" church order must include *only* a plurality of elders and deacons with no single pastoral head. Such a view reflects the temporary order that functioned only under the period of the temporary offices of the apostles and prophets until about AD 100; it does not reflect the order intended to be followed after the apostles and prophets departed this world.

12. We first see "elders" mentioned in the Jerusalem church in Acts 11:30, which included the original disciples. When Paul and Barnabas embarked on their first missionary journey among the Gentiles in Asia Minor, they appointed elders in "every church" (Acts 14:23).

13. In the past some have argued that the Greek underlying "pastors and teachers" actually demands a single office of "pastor-teacher," but this view has been set aside in light of more recent research in Greek syntax. See Daniel B. Wallace's monumental work on the Granville Sharp rule as it relates to plural substantives governed by a common article and connected with *kai* (Daniel B. Wallace, *Granville Sharp's Canon and Its Kin* [New York: Peter Lang, 2009], 230).

14. This is in continuity with the pattern of apostles and prophets, along with their delegates, exercising direct authority over the local church leadership of elders and deacons.

15. For a fuller treatment on whether there were deaconesses in the New Testament and early church, visit www.retrochristianity.com.

16. Countless evangelical pastors and teachers have embraced the notion, based on the writings of many church historians in the last hundred years, that the New Testament presents no set ecclesiastical form and that the office of "bishop" or "presiding elder" does not appear in Christian history until the second century (see Adolf Harnack, "On the Origin of the Christian Ministry," *The Expositor*, 3.5 [1881]; Margaret Y. MacDonald, *The Pauline Churches: A Socio-Historical Study of Institutionalization of the Pauline and Deutero-Pauline Writings* [Cambridge, UK: Cambridge University Press, 1988]; Francis A. Sullivan, *From Apostles to Bishops: The Development of the Episcopacy in the Early Church* [New York: Newman, 2001]). However, such evangelical pastors and teachers fail to realize that in order to hold this view, they must also accept the presuppositions that underlie the arguments—that the book of Acts, the pastoral epistles (1 and 2 Timothy and Titus), the letters of Peter, and other writings were not authored by Luke, Paul, and Peter, but were late first or early second-century documents! In short, evangelicals cannot have it both ways. If we date these writings in the early first century, then we cannot accept the late development of the "presiding

elder"; and if we accept the late development of the "presiding elder," we cannot date these New Testament books early.

17. This seems to have been the case in James 5:14, in which a member of the church was encouraged to call several elders to pray.

18. Paul's language in 1 Tim. 5:17 makes it clear that within the broad group of "elders," some, not all, labored at preaching and teaching. Cf. Cyprian of Carthage, *Epistle*, 23 (ANF, 5:301).

19. I must point out that the nonbiblical writings are not themselves inspired or inerrant, but because they were written by those who ministered alongside the first generation of apostles, they help us see what the apostles actually established as the church order they expected the churches to follow. These extrabiblical writings therefore become vital historical sources to help us read the Bible in its actual historical context. They fall under the category of writings I called "early tradition" in chapter 2—those documents that help us better understand the meaning of Scripture.

20. Some scholars date the *Didache* as early as the middle of the first century (Aaron Milavec, *The Didache: Faith, Hope, and Life of the Earliest Christian Communities, 50–70 C.E.* [New York: Newman, 2003]), though most, like me, are more comfortable with the view that the *Didache* is a composite work that brings together various early texts and traditions developed over the course of several decades (Leslie W. Barnard, *Studies in the Apostolic Fathers and Their Background* [Oxford, UK: Blackwell, 1967], 99; Clayton N. Jefford, *The Sayings of Jesus in the Teaching of the Twelve Apostles*, Supplements to Vigiliae Christianae, vol. 11 [Leiden: Brill, 1989], 3–17).

21. *Didache*, 11.3 (Holmes, 363; ANF, 7:380). In fact, the *Didache* explains how these local churches and Christians can tell a true apostle or prophet from false apostles and prophets.

22. *Didache*, 15.1–2 (Holmes, 365–367; cf. ANF, 7:381). The "prophets" and "teachers" most likely indicate prophets and early apostolic delegates such as Timothy, Titus, and others who had been established over local churches to shepherd them in their infancy. Interestingly, this same coupling of offices—prophets and teachers—is found in Acts 13:1, in reference to the leadership at the church in Antioch including Barnabas, Simeon, Lucius, Manaen, and the apostle Paul.

23. *Didache*, 4.1 (Holmes, 349–51; cf. ANF, 7:378). This at least refers to the office of "teacher" in the church (see similar language for the apostles, prophets, and teachers in *Didache*, 11.1–2; 12.4; 13.1–2; 15.1–2). *Didache*, 4.1, however, places special responsibility on the catechumen to show honor "as though he were the Lord," to a particular person, easily identifiable to the reader, who in his proclamation mediates Christ's presence.

24. Burtchaell writes, "The Letters to the Seven Churches in Revelation 2–3 . . . each addressed to 'the angel of the church' there, seem to be messages to a single person responsible for each community. The existence of a presiding office is one strongly plausible implication, but not yet the existence of a commonly accepted title for that office. That would fit well with Clement, written about the same time, which also gives evidence of such an untitled position" (James Tunstead Burtchaell, *From Synagogue to Church: Public Services and Offices in the Earliest Christian Communities* [Cambridge, UK: Cambridge University Press, 1992], 307).

25. It is used of human messengers in the Greek translation of the Old Testament (Gen. 16:7–12; 1 Sam. 19:11–20) and in the New Testament (Matt. 11:10; Luke 7:24, 27; James 2:25).

26. Cf. John F. Walvoord, "Revelation," in *The Bible Knowledge Commentary: New Testament Edition*, ed. John F. Walvoord and Roy B. Zuck (Wheaton, IL: Victor, 1983), 933.

27. It is entirely possible that the general term *angelos* ("messenger") has been misinterpreted and mistranslated several times in the New Testament. If *angelos* is understood as a person in the church functioning in a way similar to that seen in *Didache*, 4.1, then certain other passages might make better sense if the *angelos* is a human leader of the congregation (Gal. 4:14; 1 Cor. 11:10).

28. As in Robert L. Mounce, *The Book of Revelation*, rev. ed., The New International Commentary on the New Testament (Grand Rapids, MI: Eerdmans, 1977), 63. When one examines the entire context of Revelation 1–3, one must conclude that the "messenger" in each church cannot be a personification of the church or a personification of the spiritual temperament of the church. The messengers of the churches are symbolized by the seven stars in Christ's hand, and the text clearly distinguishes these stars from the seven churches, which are symbolized by the seven lampstands (Rev. 1:20; 2:1). Thus, the seven messengers (stars) are not identical to the seven churches (lampstands). Furthermore, in Rev. 2:5 Christ threatens to remove the lampstand (i.e., the "church") from its place if the messenger (still addressed in the second person *singular*) does not repent. This language makes perfect sense if it refers to a human leader called the "messenger" in each church; it makes little sense if it refers to an angelic being, the whole church personified, or as the church's spiritual condition personified.

29. See especially Rev. 3:15, 17, 19. This messenger must be more than merely a person responsible for correspondence, since Christ is holding this individual responsible for the affairs of the local church—either commending or condemning him.

30. The *Shepherd of Hermas*, written in the city of Rome over the course of several decades beginning at about the same time as the book of Revelation, indicates that a man among the leadership of the church in Rome occupies a distinct position of responsibility. The author writes: "Therefore you will write two little books, and you will send one to Clement and one to Grapte. Then Clement will send it to the cities abroad, because that is his job. But Grapte will instruct the widows and orphans. But you yourself will read it to this city, along with the elders [*presbyteroi*] who preside over the church" (*Vision*, 2.4 [Holmes, 469; cf. ANF, 2:12). Clement is singled out as the one responsible for representing the church of Rome to other churches, for he sends and receives messages, similar to the "messenger" of each church in Revelation 2–3.

31. That a leader named Clement wrote *1 Clement* on behalf of the church of Rome is testified to by Irenaeus, *Against Heresies*, 3.3.3 (ANF, 1:416) and in Eusebius, *Church History*, 3.16 (NPNF, 2.1:147). Whether it was a man named Clement or some other man with some other name, it is clear that the letter was written by a single, well-educated person, who was vested with authority to speak on behalf of the entire church in Rome.

32. *1 Clement*, 42 (Holmes, 101; ANF, 1:16).

33. Note that this is consistent with the individual called the "messenger" in the book of Revelation, and the one who is responsible for representing the church in correspondence in *Shepherd of Hermas*, *Vision*, 2.4 (Holmes, 469; ANF, 2:12), which identifies the messenger in the late first century as none other than Clement himself.

34. Burtchaell writes, "The tasks and the political style of each office appear to have been in flux within both [Jewish and Christian] communities. There also seems to have been a fluidity of titles, which eventually yielded to distinct nomenclatures" (*From Synagogue to Church*, xv).

35. Though I describe this as three distinct offices, in reality the early bishop's office was closely associated with the office of elder. In fact, he should be thought of as a presiding elder among the council of elders, a supervisor of the overseers, or a senior pastor among a staff of shepherds. It is therefore to be expected that Polycarp himself would address only elders and deacons in his letter to the Philippians (Polycarp, *Philippians*, 5–6 [Holmes, 287–89; ANF, 1:34]). The presiding elder was himself an elder, so he would have been included in Polycarp's admonition. We must also remember that along with his letter to the Philippians, Polycarp attached copies of Ignatius's letters, which clearly spell out the threefold offices of bishop, elders, and deacons. Polycarp himself endorsed the content of Ignatius's letters when he wrote, "You will be able to receive great benefit from them, for they deal with faith and patient endurance and every kind of spiritual growth that has to do with our Lord" (Polycarp, *Philippians*, 13.2 [Holmes, 297, ANF, 1:36]).

36. Ignatius, *Ephesians*, 1.3 (Holmes, 185; ANF, 1:49).

37. Ignatius, *Magnesians*, 2.1 (Holmes, 203; cf. ANF, 1:59).

38. Ignatius, *To Polycarp*, 6.1 (Holmes, 267; cf. ANF, 1:95).

39. See, for example, Irenaeus, *Against Heresies*, 3.3.4 (ANF, 1:416): "But Polycarp also was not only instructed by apostles, and conversed with many who had seen Christ, but was also, by apostles in Asia, appointed bishop of the Church in Smyrna, whom I also saw in my early youth, for he tarried [on earth] a very long time." Though it has become common for church leadership experts to assert that Ignatius "moved the church toward a three-tier system of leadership" (Gene Getz, *Elders and Leaders: God's Plan for Leading the Church* [Chicago: Moody, 2003], 224), scholars of the early church recognize that these offices were already firmly in place by the time Ignatius wrote his seven letters. Ignatius was strengthening an already-existing church order, not inventing a new one.

40. Early church historian Paul Rorem writes, "For the first two hundred years after Christ, a bishop supervised only one congregation. It was analogous to the modern office of senior pastor of a large church with a staff of clergy" (Paul Rorem, "Mission and Ministry in the Early Church: Bishops, Presbyters and Deacons, but . . ." *Currents in Theology and Missions* 17 [1990]: 18).

41. Louis Berkhof, *The History of Christian Doctrine* (Edinburgh, UK: Banner of Truth, 1969), 232.

42. Rorem, "Mission and Ministry in the Early Church," 18.

43. For varieties of church order, see Edward LeRoy Long Jr., *Patterns of Polity: Varieties of Church Governance* (Cleveland: Pilgrim Press, 2001). Also see Peter Toon, L. Roy Taylor, Paige Patterson, and Samuel E. Waldron, *Who Runs the Church? Four Views on Church Government*, ed. Steven B. Cowan (Grand Rapids, MI: Zondervan, 2004).

44. Robert Reymond sums up the thoughts of many evangelicals this way: "It has become a commonplace in many church circles to say that Scripture requires no particular form of church government. The form a given church employs, it is said, may be determined on an *ad hoc* or pragmatic basis" (*A New Systematic Theology of the Christian Faith*, 2nd. rev. ed. [Nashville: Thomas Nelson, 1998], 896. Also see Millard J. Erickson, *Christian Theology*, 2nd. ed. [Grand Rapids, MI: Baker, 1998], 1084). Part of the reason this idea has been so prevalent for so long is because it allows for unity between denominations and traditions that had at one time fought over questions of church polity and order. Saying the Bible does not prescribe any particular order allows us to live at peace with a plurality of church structures.

45. In fact, no recent books addressing biblical church leadership seriously interact with the earliest historical documents that shed light on how to understand the apostolic order in the New Testament (*Didache, 1 Clement,* Ignatius, and Polycarp). See, for example, Phil A. Newton, *Elders in Congregational Life: Rediscovering the Biblical Model of Church Leadership* (Grand Rapids, MI: Kregel, 2004); Benjamine Merkle, *Why Elders? A Biblical and Practical Guide for Church Members* (Grand Rapids, MI: Kregel, 2009). When they do interact with Patristic sources, they often misinterpret them, likely due to a lack of training and expertise in this tricky field (see, for example, Strauch, *Biblical Eldership*).

46. See discussion on the rise of this historiographical consensus in Burtchaell, *From Synagogue to Church,* 61–100.

47. Burtchaell, *From Synagogue to Church,* 61.

48. Among evangelical Patristic scholars, a constellation of important issues has led to this reconsideration of apostolic church order. First, the acceptance by evangelical scholars of the authenticity and early dating of the Gospels, Acts, and the Pauline and Petrine epistles coupled with the major criticisms leveled against Harnack's model of historical development and the "Bauer Thesis" have led many to return to the sources without a burdensome set of critical presuppositions. Second, the recent trend in dating the *Didache* early in the first century rather than in the late first or early second century, the reassertion of the authenticity and early dating of both the Ignatian letters and the letter of Polycarp to the Philippians, and an openness to dating *Barnabas* and *Shepherd of Hermas* earlier rather than later, have given new motivation to reevaluate old consensuses. Finally, a renewed interest in Greco-Roman and Jewish background along with a suspicion of denominational polemics during the Reformation that tended to distort the biblical data, has led to a more careful attempt at placing the New Testament and early Christian writings in their actual historical contexts.

49. Burtchaell directly challenges the claim of radical discontinuity between the first and second centuries. He writes, "Whatever you wish to make of it, there were the same offices in the church of the first century that we can see there in the second century. Their incumbents, however, were behaving quite differently in those two periods" (*From Synagogue to Church,* xiii).

50. My view is somewhat similar to the ideas expressed in Rothe's work on apostolic origins of the episcopacy, though I see even greater continuity between the church order in the early to latter half of the first century and do not regard the transition from the apostolic to post-apostolic period to have been a desperate move precipitated by a crisis (Richard Rothe, *Die Anfänge der Christlichen Kirche und ihre Verfassung* [Wittenberg: Zimmermann, 1837]). I also have some sympathies with the view of the historical development described by J. B. Lightfoot, though I argue that the office of the presiding elder, or bishop, was not developed by agreement of the presbyters, but by the apostles themselves (J. B. Lightfoot, *The Christian Ministry* [New York: T. Whittaker, 1878]).

51. See, for example, C. Peter Wagner, *Apostles and Prophets: The Foundation of the Church* (Ventura, CA: Regal, 2000); C. Peter Wagner, *Apostles Today: Biblical Government for Biblical Power* (Ventura CA: Regal, 2006). Wagner ignores the historical evidence of the early church's view of apostles and prophets, thus reading the New Testament outside of its actual historical context.

52. See 1 Tim. 5:17–18 for the biblical precedence of compensating elders for their pastoral work.

53. This pastor's view is so far removed from scholarly work on the relationship between the early church's "love feast" and the eucharistic Lord's Supper that I see no reason to waste space here countering it. I will say, though, that the "love feast" held by many in the early church was actually a fellowship meal primarily for the purpose of providing sustenance for the needy members of the congregation (widows, orphans, and the poor). In some places the love feast was supplemented with or supplanted by a monetary offering intended to provide for the poor and needy. On the other hand, the Lord's Supper, or "Thanksgiving (Eucharistic) Meal," was an observance always distinct from the love feast in which bread and wine were ceremonially consumed as a memorial confession of Christ's person and work, a medium of spiritual fellowship with Christ himself, and a means of covenant renewal among the local church community. For an overview of this relationship between the love feast and the Eucharist, see Everett Fergusson, "Lord's Supper and Love Feast," *Christian Studies* 21 (2005–2006): 27–38; and Marcel Metzger, *History of the Liturgy: Three Major Stages*, trans. Madeleine M. Beaumont (Collegeville, MN: Liturgical Press, 1997), 21–22.

Chapter 9: The Essential Works of a Local Church

1. See the account in Justin Martyr, *Dialogue with Trypho*, 1 (ANF, 1:194).

2. See Ibid., 7 (ANF, 1:198, paraphrased).

3. Ibid. (ANF, 1:198).

4. Ibid., 8 (ANF, 1:198).

5. Though Justin's *First Apology* was written about the middle of the second century (c. 150), it reflects Christian practices common throughout the Roman world, indicating that the origin of these practices goes back at least a few decades to the previous generation.

6. Justin Martyr, *First Apology*, 67 (ANF, 1:185–86).

7. Justin Martyr, *Dialogue with Trypho*, 3 (ANF, 1:195).

8. On the early church's concept of "baptismal regeneration," see page 237–38.

9. Justin Martyr, *First Apology*, 61 (ANF, 1:183).

10. Tertullian, *Apology*, 39 (ANF, 3:46, with minor correction).

11. Ibid. (ANF, 3:46).

12. See Mark Dever, *Nine Marks of a Healthy Church*, exp. ed. (Wheaton, IL: Crossway, 2004), 147–165; Joshua Harris, *Stop Dating the Church! Fall in Love with the Family of God* (Sisters, OR: Multnomah, 2004); Charles E. Lawless Jr., *Membership Matters: Insights from Effective Churches on New Member Classes and Assimilation* (Grand Rapids: Zondervan, 2005).

13. Max DePree, *Leadership Is an Art* (New York: Currency Books/Doubleday, 2004), 104.

14. Schaff, 3:676.

15. Justin Martyr, *First Apology*, 67 (ANF, 1:186).

16. In fact, Tertullian's description of Sunday worship even points out that Sunday was the Christians' chosen day of worship because it was also the day that the triune God began the work of the physical creation (Tertullian, *Apology* 39 [ANF, 3:46]).

17. Aristides of Athens, *Apology*, 15, with minor updates in spelling (J. Rendel Harris, ed., *The Apology of Aristides on Behalf of the Christians*, ed. J. Armitage Robinson, 2nd ed., Texts and Studies, vol. 1/1 [Cambridge, UK: Cambridge University Press, 1893], 48–49).

Chapter 10: From "Me" to "We": Growing Together in Christ

1. See Richard Foster, *Streams of Living Water: Essential Practices from the Six Great Traditions of Christian Faith* (San Francisco: HarperSanFrancisco, 1998).

2. Augustine, *Letters*, 194 (cited in Alister E. McGrath, *Iustitia Dei: A History of the Christian Doctrine of Justification*, 3d ed. [Cambridge, UK: Cambridge University Press, 2005], 44).

3. Thomas Aquinas, *Summa Theologica*, 2.1, Q. 14, Art. 5. All references to the *Summa* are from Thomas Aquinas, *The Summa Theologica*, trans. Fathers of the English Dominican Province (New York: Benziger Brothers, 1915).

4. See Thomas Aquinas, *Summa Theologica*, 2.1, Q. 14, Art. 8.

5. McGrath, *Iustitia Dei*, 108.

6. Though it's beyond the scope of this book, for a Reformed evangelical treatment on contemporary challenges to the Protestant understanding of justification, see John Piper, *The Future of Justification: A Response to N. T. Wright* (Wheaton, IL: Crossway, 2007); and Guy Prentiss Waters, *Justification and the New Perspectives on Paul: A Review and Response* (Phillipsburg, NJ: P&R, 2004).

7. Martin Luther, "Commentary on Galatians (1535)," in *Luther's Works*, ed. Jaroslav Pelikan and Helmut T. Lehmann (St. Louis: Concordia, 1955–1976), 26: 232.

8. I prefer the term "means of sanctification" to avoid the misunderstanding that grace itself is some kind of substance transferred from one place to another by mechanical conduits—the image commonly associated with the Roman Catholic view of the sacraments. The essential problem Protestants have with the Roman Catholic form of sacramentalism is not that they view the sacraments as "means of grace," but that by this they mean that *saving grace* or *justifying grace* is transferred to the account of the faithful participant in the sacramental system. Orthodox Protestant evangelicals hold that the only means of justifying grace is the Word of God and faith (Rom. 5:1; 10:17; Gal. 3:2). On the other hand, evangelicals hold that the means of sanctifying grace include activities such as corporate worship, prayer, preaching, spiritual disciplines, Scripture, suffering, etc. So, whereas Protestants have *narrowed* the means of justifying grace, they have *broadened* the means of sanctifying grace.

9. John Wesley, "Sermon 16: The Means of Grace," 2.1.

10. Benjamin B. Warfield, "Sanctification," in *Johnson's Universal Encyclopedia*, new ed., vol. 7 (New York: Appleton, 1895), 287.

11. Dionysius of Alexandria, *Letter to the Alexandrians* (in Eusebius, *Ecclesiastical History*, 7.22 [NPNF, 2.1:307]).

12. Though the New Testament accounts of baptism in the book of Acts do not indicate substantial instruction prior to baptismal initiation, the recipients of baptism were either Jewish believers, Samaritans, or God-fearing Gentiles, all of whom would have already been familiar with the Old Testament promises and the moral lifestyle expected of God's people. For such people, detailed instruction was usually not necessary. However, we do have early biblical and extrabiblical examples of prebaptismal catechesis from the first century that suggests some instruction was occurring in some places during the apostolic period (Heb. 6:1–2; *Didache*, 7.1 [Holmes, 355; ANF, 7:379]).

13. The idea of an "unbaptized Christian" is completely foreign to the Bible and the early church. I know of no credentialed New Testament or Patristic scholar who would suggest that the early church made room for unbaptized Christians. In fact, every example of conversion in the New Testament includes baptism. The burden of proof is on anybody who would admit an unbaptized believer as a covenanted member

of the church. See Oskar Skarsaune, *In the Shadow of the Temple: Jewish Influences on Early Christianity* (Downers Grove, IL: InterVarsity, 2002), 353–75, for the continuity of Christian baptism with Jewish proselyte washing as the rite of conversion to Christianity as well as documentation from biblical and early Christian sources. At no time did the church admit unbaptized believers into fellowship.

14. I do not see infant baptism as a clear New Testament practice, but as an early church development. Because baptism originally marked a person's conversion from a life of unbelief and sin to a life of faith and holiness or from one religion (Judaism/paganism) to another (Christianity), the earliest Christian baptisms would have been for adults. However, as children were born into the Christian life of faith and obedience, it seemed reasonable to apply the sign of initiation to these children. Although I believe infant baptism is a development in early church history, the question of whether this is a *legitimate* or *illegitimate* development is not so easily answered. Depending on one's tendency toward either primitivism or progressivism and one's view of doctrinal development, the baptism of infants may be regarded as either a faulty deviation that must be reformed or a wise development that must be embraced. It is telling that even traditions that baptize infants have added a later step of "confirmation" in which the faith of the baptized member is publically "confirmed."

15. See *Didache*, 9.5 (Holmes, 359; ANF, 7:380); Justin Martyr, *First Apology*, 66 (ANF, 1:185). The Lord's Supper was from the beginning only for members of the new covenant community, and only baptized believers were admitted into the covenant community. Therefore, only baptized believers were admitted to the eucharistic celebration.

16. See *Didache*, 9.1–10.7, 14.1 (Holmes, 357–361, 365; ANF, 7:379–380, 381]; Ignatius, *Smyrnaeans*, 8.1 (Holmes, 255; ANF, 1:89–90); Justin Martyr, *Dialogue with Trypho*, 41 (ANF, 1:215); *First Apology*, 65–67 (ANF, 1:185–86). On the regular worship of the early church on Sunday, not Saturday, see 1 Cor. 16:1–2 and Rev. 1:10, as well as historical background in *Didache*, 14.1 (Holmes, 365; ANF, 7:381); *Barnabas*, 15.8 (Holmes, 429; ANF, 1:147); and Ignatius, *Magnesians*, 9.1 (Holmes, 209; ANF, 1:62).

17. 1 Cor. 10:16; 11:20–32; Ignatius, *Smyrnaeans*, 7.1 (Holmes, 255; ANF, 1:89); Irenaeus, *Against Heresies*, 4.18.5 (ANF, 1:486).

18. This is my English translation from the original Greek text. The second part of this statement has been variously translated as "but an appeal to God for a good conscience" (NASB), "but the answer of a good conscience toward God" (NKJV), and "but the pledge of a good conscience to God" (NET). The Greek text itself is not clear whether baptism is meant to be an act that appeals to God *for* a clean conscience, or that baptism is a response to God because of the conscience that has already been cleansed. It seems to me that the second option best fits the context and the overall teaching of the New Testament. Thus, the emphasis is on baptism itself as a pledge to God to forsake the lifestyle of sinfulness and begin a walk of new life—all as a response to the salvation that has been received by faith.

19. The entry for the word *eperōtēma* in Louw and Nida explains this interpretation: "It is also possible to interpret ἐπερώτημα in 1 Pe 3.21 as meaning 'pledge' or 'promise'. . . . Accordingly, the phrase συνειδήσεως ἀγαθῆς ἐπερώτημα εἰς θεόν may be rendered as 'a promise made to God from a good conscience'" (Johannes E. Louw and Eugene A. Nida, eds., *Greek-English Lexicon of the New Testament Based on Semantic Domains*, vol. 1, 2nd ed. [New York: United Bible Society, 1988], sect. 33.162).

20. Justin Martyr, *First Apology*, 61 (ANF, 1:183).

21. *Didache*, 7.1 (Holmes, 355; ANF, 7:379).

22. Basil of Caesarea, *On the Holy Spirit*, 12.28 (NPNF, 2.8:18).

23. Kelly, *Early Christian Doctrines*, 192.

24. In light of baptism as the mark of repentance and initiation into the church community, the developed practice of baptizing children of church members begins to make historical and practical sense. Because baptism marked a believer's conversion from a lifestyle of sin and death to a lifestyle of righteousness, many in the early church thought infant baptism was reasonable; children of Christians were starting their lives already in the Christian lifestyle. Not surprisingly, the practice of "baby dedication" has developed in many churches that baptize only believers to address the need for some kind of partial admission of the children of believers into the church community with the promise of discipleship toward faith and baptism. In traditions that practice infant baptism, the function is similar, but the order is reversed—water baptism is applied as the mark of initiation, but a rite of confirmation and full admission come later, after confession of faith. Unfortunately, both traditions have historically been reluctant to accept the other's practice as instances of allowable diversity. Doing so, however, would remove several obstacles to evangelical unity.

25. *Barnabas*, 18.1 (Holmes, 433; ANF, 1:148).

26. See Michael J. Svigel and Matthew D. Larsen, "The First Century Two Ways Catechesis as the Background of Hebrews 6.1–6," A paper presented to the Society of Biblical Literature 2010 Annual Meeting (November 21, 2010, Atlanta, GA), 7.

27. Most Protestant theologians use the term "regeneration" in the sense of "salvation" rather than the early church's sense of "change in lifestyle."

28. For traditions practicing infant baptism as the rite of initiation into the covenant community and the beginning of a life of catechesis, a formal and public confirmation that "completes" or "validates" the baptism should precede church membership and participation in the Lord's Supper. Because the "confirmation" ceremony completes the function of baptism, those readers whose traditions practice infant baptism may read "confirmation" in place of "baptism" in these sections, though my personal conviction is that ideally baptism is best observed as a single act of faith, confession, repentance, dedication, and initiation.

29. The views of the presence of Christ in the bread and wine of eucharistic worship are debated among Patristic scholars. Though all would agree that most in the early church taught that Christ was present in the eucharistic worship and that the sharing in bread and wine brought real spiritual benefit to believers, the exact nature of the relationship between Christ's physical body and blood and the bread and wine of the Eucharist is not so clear. Ignatius of Antioch around AD 110 seems to have closely connected the flesh and blood of Christ with the elements (Ignatius, *Smyrnaeans*, 6.2 [Holmes, 255; ANF, 1:89]). However, this is in a context of a confession of faith against docetic heretics who denied the real physical incarnation of Christ, so Ignatius's words may have a more confessional than metaphysical emphasis (see Michael J. Svigel, "The Center of Ignatius of Antioch's Catholic Christianity," *Studia Patristica*, 45 [Leuven: Peeters, 2010], 367–72). Others in the early church referred to the Eucharist as a "bloodless sacrifice" (Athenagoras of Athens, *A Plea for Christians*, 13 [ANF, 2:135]). Others pressed its more symbolic or spiritual nature (Clement of Alexandria, *The Instructor*, 1.5 [ANF, 2:212]). Clement wrote, "The Lord, in the Gospel according to John, brought this out by symbols, when He said: 'Eat ye my flesh, and drink my blood;' describing distinctly by metaphor the drinkable properties of faith and the promise, by means of which the Church, like a human being consisting of many members, is refreshed and grows, is welded together and compacted of

both,—of faith, which is the body, and of hope, which is the soul; as also the Lord of flesh and blood" (Clement of Alexandria, *The Instructor*, 1.6 [ANF, 2:219]). Later Clement explicitly called the wine "the symbol of the sacred blood" (*The Instructor*, 2.2 [ANF, 2:245]). Tertullian, too, described the bread and wine as representing the body and blood of Christ (Tertullian, *Against Marcion*, 1.14 [ANF, 3:418]). Tertullian emphasized the confessional nature of the eucharistic bread and wine when he wrote, "Then, having taken the bread and given it to His disciples, He made it His own body, by saying, 'This is my body,' that is, the figure of my body. A figure, however, there could not have been, unless there were first a veritable body" (*Against Marcion*, 4.40 [ANF, 3:281]). Similarly, Origen of Alexandria wrote that Christians "have a symbol of gratitude to God in the bread which we call the Eucharist" (*Against Celsus*, 8.57 [ANF, 4:662]). However, even when church fathers emphasized the representative nature of the eucharistic elements, they confessed that participation in the Eucharist mediated spiritual blessing and the mysterious active presence of Christ (cf. Tertullian, *On the Resurrection of the Flesh*, 8 [ANF, 3:551]; Cyprian of Carthage, *Epistle*, 53.2 [ANF, 5:337]; cf. 53.4; 55.9; 62.2, 7, 11, 13).

30. Cyprian of Carthage, *Epistle*, 75.6 [ANF, 5: 398].

31. See Acts 9:4–5; Rom. 12:5; 1 Cor. 10:16; 12:12–14; Eph. 4:12–13; 5:23.

32. Some good examples of a perfect balance of doctrine, correction, exhortation, and illustration appear in Christ's Sermon on the Mount in Matthew 5–7 and in the Lord's brief but pointed messages to the seven churches in Revelation 2–3.

33. Augustine, *City of God*, 10.6 (italics added) [NPNF, 1.2: 184].

Chapter 11: From "We" to "Me": Nurturing Personal Christian Identity

1. Clement of Alexandria, *The Miscellanies*, 7.7 [ANF, 2.537].

2. Augustine, *City of God*, 10. 3 (NPNF, 1.2:182).

3. Lactantius, *The Divine Institutes*, 6.25 (ANF, 7:193).

4. Thomas à Kempis, *Thoughts Helpful in the Life of the Soul* 18 (Thomas à Kempis, *The Imitation of Christ* [Milwaukee, WI: Bruce Publishing, 1940], 25). Later, the monk known as Brother Lawrence was famous for his spiritual discipline known as the "practice of the presence of God," and his writings have encouraged Protestants and evangelicals as well as those of other Christian traditions (see Brother Lawrence, *The Practice of the Presence of God with Spiritual Maxims* [Grand Rapids, MI: Revell, 1967]).

5. John Calvin, *Institutes of the Christian Religion*, 3.20.50 (Calvin, *Institutes*, 2:199).

6. *Didache*, 8.3 (Holmes, 357; ANF, 7:379).

7. Martin Luther, *The Large Catechism*, Article 3.

8. Brother Lawrence, "The Spiritual Maxims," in *The Practice of the Presence of God with Spiritual Maxims*, 74–75.

9. An individualistic understanding of the Spirit's work through Scripture is typical of modern evangelicalism. Some Christians emphasize the Spirit's role in the illumination of the individual (see Earl D. Radmacher and Robert D. Preus, eds., *Hermeneutics, Inerrancy, and the Bible* [Grand Rapids, MI: Zondervan, 1984], 449–92; Millard Erickson, *Evangelical Interpretation: Perspectives on Hermeneutical Issues* [Grand Rapids, MI: Baker, 1993], 33–54). Others emphasize the Spirit's role in empowering believers to act upon what is understood (Erickson, *Evangelical Interpretation*, 33–37). However, a more classic concept of Spirit-led interpretation views the church community—both historical and contemporary—as the primary sphere within which individuals must read, study, and apply Scripture.

10. As an evangelical Christian, I do not view Scripture as a merely human document. Rather, I comprehend it as having both a divine and human origin and nature—2 Pet. 1:20–21 (the process) and 2 Tim. 3:16 (the product) (see the discussion in Gordon D. Fee, "Issues in Evangelical Hermeneutics: Hermeneutics and the Nature of Scripture," *Crux* 26 [1990]: 24–26). Thus, Scripture must be distinguished from all other writings, implying a hermeneutic not precisely applicable to any other human composition (Erickson, *Evangelical Interpretation*, 30–31; Fee, "Issues in Hermeneutics," 24; Robert L. Thomas, "Current Hermeneutical Trends: toward Explanation or Obfuscation?" *JETS* 39 [June 1996]: 255).

11. One would be right in generally categorizing my view as "theological interpretation" or a "confessional reading," with some important qualifications. For an overview of theological interpretation, see Daniel J. Treier, *Introducing Theological Interpretation of Scripture: Recovering a Christian Practice* [Grand Rapids, MI: Baker, 2008]).

12. See Timothy George, *Theology of the Reformers* (Nashville: Broadman & Holman, 1988), 314–17.

13. For a helpful correction and a call to return to the original meaning of *Sola Scriptura* among the major Reformers, see Keith A. Mathison, *The Shape of Sola Scriptura* (Moscow, ID: Canon Press, 2001), esp. 19–156. Also see John R. Franke, "Scripture, Tradition, and Authority: Reconstructing the Evangelical Conception of *Sola Scriptura*," in Vincent Bacote, Laura C. Miguélez, and Dennis L. Okholm, eds., *Evangelicals and Scripture: Tradition, Authority, and Hermeneutics* (Downers Grove, IL: InterVarsity, 2004), esp. 192–201.

14. Irenaeus, *Against Heresies*, 2.27.3 (ANF, 1:398).

15. Ibid., 2.27.1 (ANF, 1:398).

16. Johannes E. Louw and Eugene A. Nida, eds., *Greek-English Lexicon of the New Testament Based on Semantic Domains*, vol. 1, 2d ed. [New York: United Bible Society, 1988], sect. 27.24.

17. Gregory the Great, *Morals on the Book of Job*, pref.4 (Gregory the Great, *Morals on the Book of Job*, vol. 1, trans. J. Bliss, [Oxford, UK: John Henry Parker, 1849], 9).

18. Ignatius, *Polycarp*, 1.2; 2.2 (Holmes, 263, 265; cf. ANF, 1:93–94).

19. Tertullian, *On the Resurrection of the Flesh*, 40 (ANF, 3:574, with minor corrections).

20. See Kim Riddlebarger, "Trichotomy: A Beachhead for Gnostic Influences," *Modern Reformation* 4.4 (1995): 22–26. Though it is beyond the scope of my very rudimentary discussion of Christian anthropology, I might point out here that I am advocating a classic "dichotomy" view of the constitution of the human person, rejecting as fallacious and potentially dangerous the "trichotomy" view of human nature. In his article on the essentially Gnostic origins of the trichotomy position, Pastor Riddlebarger rightly notes, "Rejected by virtually all major theologians in all streams of the Christian tradition as a speculative Greek philosophical notion rather than a Biblical conception, trichotomy is very likely the reigning notion of human nature in American Evangelical circles today" (ibid.). Though I do not regard "trichotomy" as heresy *per se*, it certainly falls under the category of "heterodoxy" described in chapters 3 and 5 of this book. Trichotomists produce only one passage, 1 Thessalonians 5:23, as a proof of the threefold nature of humanity, though in the context this passage does not answer the question, "What are the substantial parts of a human being," but, "What aspects of a human person is God sanctifying?" In this case, the terms "body, soul, and spirit" in 1 Thessalonians 5:23 are likely representative aspects of humanity related to the physical, mental, and emotional dimensions of a complete material/

immaterial person. Elsewhere the complexity of the human person is described as "heart and flesh" (Ps. 16:9), "heart, soul, mind, and strength" (Mark 12:30), or "soul, spirit, thoughts, intentions of the heart" (Heb. 4:12). Though many models of sanctification and various pop-theological Christian gimmicks have depended heavily on the trichotomy view, the doctrine has very flimsy biblical, historical, and theological support.

21. Gregory Thaumaturgus, *Oration and Panegyric to Origen*, 13, 15 (ANF, 6:34, 35, with corrections).

22. Tertullian, *Prescription against Heretics*, 7 (ANF, 3:246).

23. Thomas Aquinas, *Summa Theologica*, Part 1, Question 1, Article 5.

24. The conflict between science/reason and Scripture/faith is thus unnecessary. We must always arbitrate between two views of Scripture vs. science (cf. Jeanrond, *Theological Hermeneutics*, 36–37). The first view rejects any scientific assertions that do not align with one's current reading of Scripture: "Whatever (I think) Scripture says, that's what happened" (see, e.g., Henry M. Morris, "A Response to the Trustworthiness of Scripture in Areas Relating to Natural Sciences," in Radmacher and Preus, *Hermeneutics, Inerrancy, and the Bible*, 337–48). The second contorts Scripture to fit with the ever-changing world of scientific theory: "Whatever (I think) happened, that's what Scripture says" (e.g. Keith Ward, "Christianity and Evolution: A Case Study," in Marcel Sarot and Gijsbert van den Brink, eds., *Identity and Change in the Christian Tradition*, Contributions to Philosophical Theology, vol. 2 [Frankfurt: Peter Lang, 1999], 91–104). A *via media* is advocated here, one which acknowledges the tentativeness of both our scriptural interpretation and scientific understandings and desires a harmonization between the two. See Walter L. Bradley and Roger Olsen, "The Trustworthiness of Scripture in Areas Relating to Natural Science," in Radmacher and Preus, *Hermeneutics, Inerrancy, and the Bible*, 285–317, especially their comment, "God has revealed Himself in His Word (the Bible) as well as in his [sic] creation (the world). We believe these revelations are equally valid and essentially complementary" (ibid., 287).

25. See Mark A. Noll's classic critique of evangelical anti-intellectualism, *The Scandal of the Evangelical Mind* (Grand Rapids, MI: Eerdmans, 1994).

26. On the necessity of cultivating the life of the mind as a means of worship, see especially Bradley G. Green, *The Gospel and the Mind: Recovering and Shaping the Intellectual Life* (Wheaton, IL: Crossway, 2010); and John Piper, *Think: The Life of the Mind and the Love of God* (Wheaton, IL: Crossway, 2010).

Chapter 12: Where Do We Go from Here? From Retrospect to Prospects
1. Cyprian of Carthage, *Epistles*, 5.4 (ANF, 5:283, with minor changes).

Index

Printed in the USA
CPSIA information can be obtained
at www.ICGtesting.com
LVHW082247120224
771605LV00018B/46